Dewey Decimal Classification
200
RELIGION
CLASS

Dewey Decimal Classification
200
RELIGION
CLASS

Reprinted from Edition 21 of the
Dewey Decimal Classification

Devised by Melvil Dewey

Edited by

Joan S. Mitchell, Editor
Julianne Beall, Assistant Editor
Winton E. Matthews, Jr., Assistant Editor
Gregory R. New, Assistant Editor
Michael B. Cantlon, Decimal Classification Specialist

With a revised and expanded index,
and Manual notes from Edition 21

FOREST PRESS
A Division of
OCLC Online Computer Library Center, Inc.
ALBANY, NEW YORK
1997

© 1997
OCLC Online Computer Library Center, Inc.

All rights reserved. No part of this publication may be reproduced, stored in a retrieval system, or transmitted, in any form or by any means, electronic, mechanical, photocopying, recording or otherwise, without the prior written permission of the publisher.

DDC, DEWEY, FOREST PRESS, DEWEY DECIMAL CLASSIFICATION, and DEWEY DECIMAL CLASSIFICATION, ADDITIONS, NOTES AND DECISIONS are registered trademarks of OCLC Online Computer Library Center, Inc.

Library of Congress Cataloging-in-Publication Data

Dewey, Melvil, 1851-1931.
    [Dewey decimal classification and relative index. 200 religion class]
    Dewey decimal classification. 200 religion class : reprinted from Edition 21 of the Dewey decimal classification : with a revised and expanded index, and Manual notes from Edition 21 / devised by Melvil Dewey ; edited by Joan S. Mitchell, editor; Julianne Beall, asst. editor; Winton E. Matthews, Jr., asst. editor; Gregory R. New, asst. editor; Michael B. Cantlon, Decimal Classification Specialist.
       p.   cm.
    Includes index.
    ISBN 0-910608-60-1
    1. Classification, Decimal.   2. Classification--Books--Religion.
I. Mitchell, Joan S.   II. Beall, Julianne, 1946-   .   III. Matthews, Winton E.   IV. New, Gregory R.   V. Cantlon, Michael B.   VI. Title.
Z696.D72R455   1997   97-25487
025.4'62--dc21   CIP

The paper used in this publication meets the requirements of ANSI/NISO Z39.48-1992 (Permanence of Paper).

 Recycled paper

Contents

Preface	vii
How to Use This Book	ix
Schedule	1
200 Religion	3
Manual Notes for 200 Religion	165
Appendixes	187
Appendix A: Optional Numbers for Books of Bible as Arranged in Tanakh (Jewish Bible, Hebrew Bible)	189
Appendix B: 170 Ethics	197
Relative Index	205
Use of the Relative Index	206
A-Z	207

Preface

200 Religion Class is a reprint from Edition 21 of the Dewey Decimal Classification (DDC). This work is intended to be used by libraries with in-depth religious collections and small general collections. The latter may be classified using Abridged Edition 13 of the Dewey Decimal Classification.

Michael Cantlon, Decimal Classification specialist, and Julianne Beall, assistant editor, DDC, were the primary revisers of the schedules included in this volume. Mr. Cantlon led revision efforts for 296 Judaism, and religion and philosophy in general. Ms. Beall developed the revision and expansion of 297 Islam. Winton E. Matthews, Jr., and Gregory R. New, assistant editors, DDC, provided invaluable assistance and guidance. David A. Smith, chief of the Library of Congress Decimal Classification Division, and the Decimal Classification Division staff supported the editorial efforts by offering an expert view of emerging topics and areas requiring revision.

We are grateful for the support and encouragement of Peter J. Paulson, executive director of OCLC Forest Press, and the Forest Press staff: Elizabeth Hansen, Judith Kramer-Greene, and Judith Pisarski.

The advice and critical review offered by the members of the Decimal Classification Editorial Policy Committee have enabled us to respond to the needs of our users throughout the world. We value their wise counsel.

Several other groups and individuals have made significant contributions to the development of the 200 Religion schedule. The (British) Library Association Dewey Decimal Committee and subcommittees of the American Library Association Committee on Cataloging: Asian and African Materials reviewed 296 Judaism and 297 Islam. The Cataloging Committee of the Africana Librarians Council, African Studies Association, also provided advice on the revision of 297. We appreciate the criticism and advice offered by all.

> Joan S. Mitchell
> *Editor*
> Dewey Decimal Classification
> OCLC Forest Press

How to Use This Book

Introduction

200 Religion Class is a convenient source of detailed classification numbers for religion. It includes the following information from Edition 21: the schedule for 200 Religion, the Manual notes that discuss numbers in the 200s, and an extended index to religious aspects of topics. Also included are two appendixes: (A) Optional Arrangement for Books of Tanakh, and (B) 170 Ethics.

Since the schedules and Manual notes are reprinted from Edition 21, there may be references to tables and schedules in other areas of the Classification. For aspects of topics that fall outside of religion, *200 Religion Class* must be used in conjunction with Abridged Edition 13 or Edition 21 of the Dewey Decimal Classification.

For example, "marriage" has aspects that fall under several disciplines, including religion. Only the religious aspects of marriage appear in *200 Religion Class*; Abridged Edition 13 or Edition 21 of the DDC must be consulted for aspects of marriage in other disciplines, e.g., sociology of marriage 306.81.

Structure and Notation of the DDC

In the DDC, basic classes are organized by disciplines or fields of study. At the broadest level, the DDC is divided into ten main classes, which together cover the entire world of knowledge. Each main class is further divided into ten divisions and each division into ten sections (not all the numbers for the divisions and sections have been used).

Arabic numerals are used to represent each class in the DDC. A decimal point follows the third digit, after which division by ten continues to the specific degree of classification needed.

Hierarchy in the DDC is expressed through structure and notation. Structural hierarchy means that all topics (aside from the ten main classes) are part of the broader topics above them. Any note regarding the nature of a class holds true for all its subordinate classes, including logically subordinate topics classed at coordinate numbers.

Notational hierarchy is expressed by length of notation. Numbers at any given level are usually subordinate to (i.e., more specific than) a class whose notation is one digit shorter; coordinate with (i.e., equally specific as) a class whose notation has the same number of significant digits; and superordinate to (i.e., less specific than) a class with numbers one or more digits longer.

Sometimes, other devices must be used to express the hierarchy when it is not possible or desirable to do so through the notation. Relationships among topics that violate notational hierarchy are indicated by special types of headings, notes, and entries.

Entries

Entries in the schedules are composed of a DDC number in the number column (the column at the left margin), a heading describing the class that the number represents, and often one or more notes. All entries (numbers, headings, and notes) should be read in the context of the hierarchy.

The first three digits of schedule numbers appear only once in the number column, when first used. They are repeated at the top of each page where their subdivisions continue.

Subordinate numbers appear in the number column, beginning with a decimal point, with the initial three digits understood.

Numbers and notes in parentheses provide options to standard practice. These options enable the Classification to serve needs beyond those represented in the standard English-language edition. An optional arrangement of books of Tanakh is provided in appendix A.

Numbers in square brackets represent topics that have been relocated or discontinued, or are unassigned. Square brackets are also used for standard subdivision concepts that are represented in another location. Numbers in square brackets are not used.

Number Building

Only a fraction of potential DDC numbers are printed in the schedules. The classifier will often find that to arrive at a precise number for a work it is necessary to build (synthesize) a number that is not specifically printed in the schedules. Many synthesized numbers are included in the Relative Index. Since many of these numbers have been constructed using notation from 172-179 Applied ethics, the 170 Ethics schedule has been included in appendix B.

Relative Index

The Relative Index includes the entries for 200 Religion topics from Edition 21, electronic index terms from Dewey for Windows, and some additional index terms. It also includes index terms for notes in the Manual.

In the Relative Index, topics are arranged alphabetically, with the terms identifying the discipline or subdiscipline in which they are treated subarranged alphabetically under them. The first class number displayed in an index entry (opposite the unindented term) is the number for interdisciplinary works.

Manual

The Manual contains notes explaining the classification of selected areas in 200 Religion. It is organized by DDC number. There are references to the notes in the Manual from the 200 Religion schedule and from the Relative Index.

More Information

For more information about the use of the Dewey Decimal Classification, consult the introduction to Abridged Edition 13, or the introduction in volume one of Edition 21 (the unabridged edition of the Classification). *Dewey for Windows*, the electronic version of Edition 21, also includes an introduction to the DDC.

More in-depth discussions of the DDC may be found in *Dewey Decimal Classification: A Practical Guide*, 2nd ed., by Lois Mai Chan, John P. Comaromi, Joan S. Mitchell, and Mohinder P. Satija (Albany, N.Y.: OCLC Forest Press, 1996); and *Abridged 13 Workbook*, by Sydney W. Davis and Gregory R. New (Albany, N.Y., OCLC Forest Press, 1997). Up-to-date information about the Classification, OCLC Forest Press publications, and DDC research projects is posted regularly on the Dewey home page at URL: http://www.oclc.org/fp/.

Schedule
200 Religion

200

200 Religion

Beliefs, attitudes, practices of individuals and groups with respect to the ultimate nature of existences and relationships within the context of revelation, deity, worship

Including public relations for religion [*formerly* 659.292]

Comprehensive works on Christianity relocated to 230

Class comparative religion, works dealing with various religions in 291. Class public relations for a specific religion or aspect of a religion with the religion or aspect, e.g., local Christian church 254.4

> *See also 306.6 for sociology of religion*
>
> *See Manual at 133 vs 200; also at 200 vs. 100*

(Option: To give preferred treatment or shorter numbers to a specific religion other than Christianity, use one of the five options described at 292–299)

SUMMARY

200.1–.9	Standard subdivisions of religion
210	**Philosophy and theory of religion**
.1	Theory of philosophy of religion
211	Concepts of God
212	Existence, knowability, attributes of God
213	Creation
214	Theodicy
215	Science and religion
218	Humankind
220	**Bible**
.01–.09	Standard subdivisions and special topics
.1–.9	Generalities
221	Old Testament (Tanakh)
222	Historical books of Old Testament
223	Poetic books of Old Testament
224	Prophetic books of Old Testament
225	New Testament
226	Gospels and Acts
227	Epistles
228	Revelation (Apocalypse)
229	Apocrypha, pseudepigrapha, intertestamental works

230	Christianity　　Christian theology	
.002–.007	Standard subdivisions of Christianity	
.01–.09	Standard subdivisions and specific types of Christian theology	
.1–.9	Doctrines of specific denominations and sects	
231	God	
232	Jesus Christ and his family　　Christology	
233	Humankind	
234	Salvation (Soteriology) and grace	
235	Spiritual beings	
236	Eschatology	
238	Creeds, confessions of faith, covenants, catechisms	
239	Apologetics and polemics	
240	Christian moral and devotional theology	
241	Moral theology	
242	Devotional literature	
243	Evangelistic writings for individuals and families	
246	Use of art in Christianity	
247	Church furnishings and related articles	
248	Christian experience, practice, life	
249	Christian observances in family life	
250	Local Christian church and Christian religious orders	
.1–.9	Standard subdivisions	
251	Preaching (Homiletics)	
252	Texts of sermons	
253	Pastoral office and work (Pastoral theology)	
254	Parish administration	
255	Religious congregations and orders	
259	Pastoral care of families, of specific kinds of persons	
260	Christian social and ecclesiastical theology	
.9	Historical, geographic, persons treatment	
261	Social theology and interreligious relations and attitudes	
262	Ecclesiology	
263	Days, times, places of religious observance	
264	Public worship	
265	Sacraments, other rites and acts	
266	Missions	
267	Associations for religious work	
268	Religious education	
269	Spiritual renewal	
270	Historical, geographic, persons treatment of Christianity	Church history
.01–.09	Standard subdivisions	
.1–.8	Historical periods	
271	Religious congregations and orders in church history	
272	Persecutions in general church history	
273	Doctrinal controversies and heresies in general church history	
274–279	Treatment by continent, country, locality	

4

	280	Denominations and sects of Christian church
	.01–.09	Standard subdivisions and special topics
	.2–.4	Branches
	281	Early church and Eastern churches
	282	Roman Catholic Church
	283	Anglican churches
	284	Protestant denominations of Continental origin and related bodies
	285	Presbyterian churches, Reformed churches centered in America, Congregational churches
	286	Baptist, Disciples of Christ, Adventist churches
	287	Methodist churches; churches related to Methodism
	289	Other denominations and sects
	290	Comparative religion and religions other than Christianity
	291	Comparative religion
	292	Classical (Greek and Roman) religion
	293	Germanic religion
	294	Religions of Indic origin
	295	Zoroastrianism (Mazdaism, Parseeism)
	296	Judaism
	297	Islam, Babism, Bahai Faith
	299	Other religions

.1 **Systems, value, scientific principles, psychology of religion**

> Philosophy and theory of religion relocated to 210

.11 Systems [*formerly also* 210.11, 291.011]

[.12] Classification

> Relocated to 291.14

.13 Value [*formerly also* 210.13, 291.013]

[.14] Language and communication

> Relocated to 210.14

.15 Scientific principles [*formerly also* 210.15, 291.015]

> Class philosophic treatment of the relation of science and religion in 215

.19 Psychology of religion

> Class here psychological principles [*formerly also* 210.19, 291.019]

.2–.3 **Standard subdivisions** [*formerly also* **291.02–291.03**]

.5 **Serial publications** [*formerly also* **291.05**]

[.6] **Organizations**

> Relocated to 291.65

[.68] Management

> Relocated to 291.6

.7 **Education, research, related topics** [*formerly also* **291.07**]

	.71	Education

> Class here religion as an academic subject
>
> Class religious education for the purpose of encouraging believers in religious life and practice, comprehensive works on religious education in 291.75
>
> > See also 379.28 for place of religion in public schools
> >
> > See Manual at 291.75 vs. 200.71

	.8	**History and description with respect to kinds of persons** [*formerly also* **291.08**]
	.9	**Historical, geographic, persons treatment** [*formerly also* **291.09**]

> See Manual at 200.9 vs. 294, 299.5

	.92	Persons

> See Manual at 200.92 and 291–299

[201] Philosophy and theory of Christianity

Relocated to 230.01

[202–203] Standard subdivisions of Christianity

Relocated to 230.002–230.003

[204] Special topics

Provision discontinued because without meaning in context

[.5] Christian mythology

Relocated to 230

[205] Serial publications of Christianity

Relocated to 230.005

[206] Organizations of Christianity

Relocated to 260

[207] Education, research, related topics of Christianity

Relocated to 230.007

[.1] Education

Relocated to 230.071

[.4–.9] Higher education in specific continents, countries, localities in modern world

Relocated to 230.07114–230.07119

[208]   **Christianity with respect to kinds of persons**
         Relocated to 270.08

[209]   **Historical, geographic, persons treatment of Christianity**
         Relocated to 270

210   **Philosophy and theory of religion [*formerly* 200.1, 291.01]**

Religious beliefs and attitudes attained through observation and interpretation of evidence in nature, through speculation, through reasoning, but not through revelation or appeal to authoritative scriptures

Class here natural theology, philosophical theology

Class a specific topic treated with respect to religions based on revelation or authority with the topic in 291, e.g., concepts of God in world religions 291.211; class a specific topic with respect to a specific religion with the religion, e.g., Christian concepts of God 231

(Option: To give local emphasis and a shorter number to a specific religion other than Christianity, class it in this number, and add to base number 21 the numbers following the base number for that religion in 292–299, e.g., Hinduism 210, Mahabharata 219.23; in that case class philosophy and theory of religion in 200, its subdivisions 211–218 in 201–208, standard subdivisions of religion in 200.01–200.09. Other options are described at 292–299)

.1   **Theory of philosophy of religion**
         Including methodology of the philosophy of religion

[.11]   Systems
         Relocated to 200.11

[.12]   Classification
         Relocated to 291.14

[.13]   Value
         Relocated to 200.13

.14   Language and communication of religion [*formerly also* 200.14, 291.014]

[.15]   Scientific principles
         Relocated to 200.15

[.19]   Psychological principles
         Relocated to 200.19

211   Concepts of God

Including anthropomorphism

Class here comprehensive works on God, on The Holy

For existence, knowability, attributes of God, miracles, see 212

.2	**Pantheism**	
.3	**Theism**	

For pantheism, see 211.2

.32	Polytheism
.33	Dualism
.34	Monotheism
.4	**Rationalism (Free thought)**
.5	**Deism**
.6	**Humanism and secularism**

Standard subdivisions are added for either or both topics in heading

.7   **Agnosticism and skepticism**

Standard subdivisions are added for either or both topics in heading

.8   **Atheism**

212   Existence, knowability, attributes of God

Including miracles

.1   **Existence**

Including proofs

.6   **Knowability**

Class proofs in 212.1

.7   **Attributes**

Including love, omniscience

213   Creation

Including creation of life and human life, evolution versus creation, evolution as method of creation

See Manual at 231.7652 vs. 213, 500, 576.8

214 Theodicy

Vindication of God's justice and goodness in permitting existence of evil and suffering

Class here good and evil [*formerly* 216]

.8 Providence

215 Science and religion

Including technology and religion

Class religion and scientific theories of creation in 213

See also 261.55 for Christianity and science, 291.175 for various religions and science

[.1] Mathematics

Number discontinued; class in 215

.2 Astronomy

Including cosmology

[.24–.25] Life on other worlds and space flight

Numbers discontinued; class in 215

.3 Physics

[.4–.5] Chemistry and geology

Numbers discontinued; class in 215

[.6] Paleontology

Relocated to 215.7

.7 Life sciences

Including paleontology [*formerly* 215.6]

Class evolution versus creation, evolution as method of creation in 213

[.72–.74] Anthropology, ethnology, biology, natural history

Numbers discontinued; class in 215.7

[.8–.9] Archaeology and technology

Numbers discontinued; class in 215

[216] Good and evil

Relocated to 214

[217] [Unassigned]

Most recently used in Edition 18

218 Humankind

Including immortality

For creation of humankind, human evolution, see 213

[219] Unassigned

Most recently used in Edition 19

220 Bible

Holy Scriptures of Judaism and Christianity

Class Christian Biblical theology in 230.041; class Biblical precepts in Christian codes of conduct in 241.52–241.54; class Jewish Biblical theology in 296.3; class Biblical precepts in Jewish codes of conduct in 296.36

See Manual at 220: Biblical theology

(If option A under 292–299 is chosen, class here sources of the specified religion; class Bible in 298)

SUMMARY

220.01–.09	**Standard subdivisions and special topics**
.1–.9	**Generalities**
221	**Old Testament (Tanakh)**
222	**Historical books of Old Testament**
223	**Poetic books of Old Testament**
224	**Prophetic books of Old Testament**
225	**New Testament**
226	**Gospels and Acts**
227	**Epistles**
228	**Revelation (Apocalypse)**
229	**Apocrypha, pseudepigrapha, intertestamental works**

.01–.02	Standard subdivisions
[.03]	Dictionaries, encyclopedias, concordances

> Do not use for dictionaries and encyclopedias; class in 220.3. Do not use for concordances; class in 220.4–220.5

.04	Special topics
.046	Apocalyptic passages

> Class apocalyptic passages in a book or group of books with the book or group of books, plus notation 0046 from add table under 221–229, e.g., apocalyptic passages in the prophets 224.0046, in Book of Daniel 224.50046

For Revelation (Apocalypse), see 228

.05–.08	Standard subdivisions

	.09	Historical, geographic, persons treatment of Bible

Class the canon in 220.12

For geography, history, chronology, persons of Bible lands in Bible times, see 220.9

> **220.1–220.9 Generalities**

Class comprehensive works in 220. Class generalities applied to a specific part of the Bible with the part, plus notation 01–09 from add table under 221–229, e.g., a commentary on Job 223.107

SUMMARY

220.1	Origins and authenticity
.3	Encyclopedias and topical dictionaries
.4	Original texts, early versions, early translations
.5	Modern versions and translations
.6	Interpretation and criticism (Exegesis)
.7	Commentaries
.8	Nonreligious subjects treated in the Bible
.9	Geography, history, chronology, persons of Bible lands in Bible times

.1	**Origins and authenticity**
.12	Canon

Class here selection of the books accepted as Holy Scripture

.13	Inspiration

The Bible as revelation (word of God)

Including authority of Bible

.132	Inerrancy
.15	Biblical prophecy and prophecies

Class Christian messianic prophecies in 232.12; class Christian eschatological prophecies in 236; class Jewish messianic and eschatological prophecies in 296.33

See also 224 for prophetic books of Old Testament

.3	**Encyclopedias and topical dictionaries**

For dictionaries of specific texts, see 220.4–220.5

> **220.4–220.5 Texts, versions, translations**

>> Class here critical appraisal of language and style; concordances, indexes, dictionaries of specific texts; complete texts; selections from more than one part; paraphrases

>> Class texts accompanied by commentaries in 220.77; class comprehensive works in 220.4. Class selections compiled for a specific purpose with the purpose, e.g., selections for daily meditations 242.2

.4 Original texts, early versions, early translations

Class here original texts accompanied by modern translations, comprehensive works on texts and versions

For modern versions and translations, see 220.5

.404   Textual criticism and word studies

.404 6   Textual (Lower) criticism

   Use of scientific means to ascertain the actual original texts

.404 7   Theological studies of words or phrases

> **220.42–220.49 Texts in specific languages**

>> Add to each subdivision identified by † the numbers following 220.404 in 220.4046–220.4047, regardless of specific version, e.g., textual criticism of Bible in Latin, of Vulgate 220.476, of Old Testament in Greek, of Septuagint 221.486

>> Class comprehensive works in 220.4

.42   †Aramaic versions

.43   †Syriac versions

.44   †Hebrew version

.45   †Samaritan versions

.46   Other Semitic language versions

   Including Arabic, Ethiopic

.47   †Latin versions

.48   †Greek versions

.49   Other early versions

   Including Armenian, Coptic

.5 Modern versions and translations

---

†Add as instructed under 220.42–220.49

	.51	Polyglot
	.52	Versions in English and Anglo-Saxon

>Standard subdivisions are added for versions in English and Anglo-Saxon, for English alone

Works containing translations in English and one other modern language are classed with the other language in 220.53–220.59

.520 01–.520 09 Standard subdivisions

> 220.520 1–220.520 9 English

Add to each subdivision identified by * as follows:
```
01–02    Standard subdivisions
[03]     Dictionaries, encyclopedias, concordances
            Do not use; class in 3
05–08    Standard subdivisions
09       Geographic and persons treatment
            Do not use for historical treatment of the translation; class in 8
2        Standard editions
3        Concordances, indexes, dictionaries
4        Special editions
            Including annotated editions, study editions, editions notable for
              illustrations
6        Selections
7        Paraphrases
8        History, criticism, explanation of the translation
```

Class comprehensive works in 220.52

.520 1 English versions before 1582

>Including Coverdale, Tyndale, Wycliffe versions

.520 2 *Douay version

>Class here Rheims-Douay, Rheims-Douay-Challoner versions

>*See also 220.5205 for Confraternity-Douay-Challoner version*

.520 3 *Authorized (King James) version

.520 4 Revised version

>Including English Revised (1881–1885), American Revised (American Standard) (1901) versions

.520 42 *Revised Standard version (1946–1957)

.520 43 *New Revised Standard version (1990)

---

*Add as instructed under 220.5201–220.5209

13

.520 5		*Confraternity Bible and New American Bible

.520 5   *Confraternity Bible and New American Bible

                 Class here Confraternity-Douay-Challoner version

                 Subdivisions are added for either or both topics in heading

                 See also 220.5202 for Rheims-Douay, Rheims-Douay-Challoner versions

.520 6   *New English Bible and Revised English Bible

                 Subdivisions are added for either or both topics in heading

.520 7   *Jerusalem Bible and New Jerusalem Bible

                 Subdivisions are added for either or both topics in heading

.520 8   Other English translations since 1582

                 Including New King James, New Century versions

                 For translations by individuals, see 220.5209

.520 81   *New International Version

.520 82   *Today's English Bible (Good News Bible)

.520 83   *Living Bible

.520 9   Translations by individuals

                 Including Goodspeed, Knox, Moffatt, Phillips

.529   Anglo-Saxon

.53–.59   Versions in other languages

                 Add to base number 220.5 notation 3–9 from Table 6, e.g., the Bible in German 220.531

                 Works containing translations in two modern languages other than English are classed with the language coming later in Table 6; in more than two modern languages in 220.51

.6   **Interpretation and criticism (Exegesis)**

                 Class Christian meditations based on Biblical passages and intended for devotional use in 242.5; class material about the Bible intended for use in preparing Christian sermons in 251; class Christian sermons based on Biblical passages in 252; class material about the Bible for preparation of Jewish sermons and texts of Jewish sermons in 296.47; class Jewish meditations based on Biblical passages and intended for devotional use in 296.72

                 For textual (lower) criticism, see 220.4046; for commentaries, see 220.7

.601   Philosophy and theory

                 Class here hermeneutics

.61   General introductions to the Bible

                 Including isagogics (introductory studies prior to actual exegesis)

---

*Add as instructed under 220.5201–220.5209

.64		Symbolism and typology
		Standard subdivisions are added for either or both topics in heading
		Class here interpretation of specific symbols
.65		Harmonies
.66		Literary criticism
		Literary examination of the text in order to reach conclusions about its meaning, structure, authorship, date
		Class here higher criticism, internal criticism, redaction criticism
		Class language and style of specific texts in 220.4–220.5
		See also 809.93522 for the Bible as literature
.663		Form criticism
		Analysis of preliterary or oral forms and traditions in Biblical text
.67		Historical criticism
		Interpretation of texts in light of the cultural, historical, religious, social milieu in which written
		Class form criticism in 220.663
.68		Mythological, allegorical, numerical, astronomical interpretations
		Including mythology in the Bible, demythologizing
.7		**Commentaries**
		Criticism and interpretation arranged in textual order
.77		Commentaries with text
.8		**Nonreligious subjects treated in Bible**
		Class a religious subject treated in Bible with the specific religion and topic, e.g., Christian theology 230, Jewish theology 296.3
.800 01–.800 09		Standard subdivisions
.800 1–.899 9		Specific nonreligious subjects
		Add to base number 220.8 notation 001–999, e.g., natural sciences in Bible 220.85; however, for geography, history, chronology, persons of Bible lands in Bible times, see 220.9
.9		**Geography, history, chronology, persons of Bible lands in Bible times**
		Class general history of Bible lands in ancient world in 930
.91		Geography
		Class here description and civilization
		Class civilization treated separately from geography in 220.95

.92	Collected persons

> Class an individual person with the part of the Bible in which the person is chiefly considered, e.g., Abraham 222.11092
>
> See Manual at at 220.92; also at 230–280: Biography

.93	Archaeology (Material remains)
.95	History

> Including civilization treated separately from geography
>
> Class geographic description and civilization treated together in 220.91

.950 01–.950 09	Standard subdivisions
.950 5	Bible stories retold

> Including picture books

> ## 221–229 Specific parts of Bible, Apocrypha, pseudepigrapha, intertestamental works

Add to each subdivision identified by * as follows (subdivisions from this table may be added for a part of any work that has its own number):
001–08   Standard subdivisions and generalities
              Add to 0 the numbers following 220 in 220.01–220.8, e.g., interpretation of the work or of a part of the work 06
09   Geography, history, chronology, persons
              Add to 09 the numbers following 221.9 in 221.91–221.95, e.g., biography 092

Class comprehensive works in 220

221 Old Testament (Tanakh)

Holy Scriptures of Judaism, Old Testament of Christianity

Class Jewish Biblical theology in 296.3; class Biblical precepts in Jewish codes of conduct in 296.36

For historical books, see 222; for Torah, see 222.1; for poetic books, Ketuvim, see 223; for prophetic books, Nevi'im, see 224

See Manual at 220: Biblical theology; also at 221: Optional numbers for books of Tanakh

(Option: To arrange the books of the Old Testament (Tanakh) as found in Jewish Bibles, use one of the following:
(Option A: Use the optional arrangement of 222–224 given in appendix A
(Option B: Class in 296.11

(A table giving the three numbers for each book is given in the Manual at 221)

[.03]	Dictionaries, encyclopedias, concordances
	Do not use for dictionaries and encyclopedias; class in 221.3. Do not use for concordances; class in 221.4–221.5
.04	Special topics
[.042]	Ketuvim (Hagiographa, Writings)
	Relocated to 223
.044	Megillot (Five scrolls)
	For a specific book of Megillot, see the book, e.g., Ruth 222.35
.046	Apocalyptic passages
	Class apocalyptic passages in a book or group of books with the book or group of books, plus notation 0046 from add table under 221–229, e.g., apocalyptic passages in the prophets 224.0046, in Book of Daniel 224.50046
.09	Historical, geographic, persons treatment of Old Testament
	Class the canon in 221.12
	For geography, history, chronology, persons of Old Testament lands in Old Testament times, see 221.9
.1–.8	**Generalities**
	Add to base number 221 the numbers following 220 in 220.1–220.8, e.g., Targums 221.42, commentaries 221.7
.9	**Geography, history, chronology, persons of Old Testament lands in Old Testament times**
	Class general history of ancient areas in 930
.91	Geography
	Class here description and civilization
	Class civilization treated separately from geography in 221.95
.92	Persons
	See Manual at 220.92; also at 230–280: Biography
.922	Collected treatment
.93	Archaeology (Material remains)
.95	History
	Including civilization treated separately from geography
	Class geographic description and civilization treated together in 221.91
.950 01–.950 09	Standard subdivisions

	.950 5	Old Testament stories retold
		Including picture books

222 *Historical books of Old Testament

.1   *Pentateuch (Torah)

        Class here Hexateuch

        For Joshua, see 222.2

    .11   *Genesis

    .12   *Exodus

        For Ten Commandments, see 222.16

    .13   *Leviticus

    .14   *Numbers

    .15   *Deuteronomy

        For Ten Commandments, see 222.16

    .16   *Ten Commandments (Decalogue)

        Class Ten Commandments as code of conduct in Christianity in 241.52; class Ten Commandments as code of conduct in Judaism in 296.36

.2   *Joshua (Josue)

.3   *Judges and Ruth

    .32   *Judges

    .35   *Ruth

.4   *Samuel

    .43   *Samuel 1

        Variant name: Kings 1

    .44   *Samuel 2

        Variant name: Kings 2

.5   *Kings

    .53   *Kings 1

        Variant name: Kings 3

    .54   *Kings 2

        Variant name: Kings 4

.6   *Chronicles (Paralipomena)

---

*Add as instructed under 221–229

	.63	*Chronicles 1 (Paralipomenon 1)
	.64	*Chronicles 2 (Paralipomenon 2)
	.7	***Ezra (Esdras 1)**

> See also 229.1 for Esdras 1 (also called Esdras 3) of the Apocrypha

	.8	***Nehemiah (Esdras 2, Nehemias)**

> See also 229.1 for Esdras 2 (also called Esdras 4) of the Apocrypha

	(.86)	*Tobit (Tobias)

> (Optional number; prefer 229.22)

	(.88)	*Judith

> (Optional number; prefer 229.24)

	.9	*Esther

> (Option: Class here deuterocanonical part of Esther; prefer 229.27)

223   ***Poetic books of Old Testament***

Class here Ketuvim (Hagiographa, Writings) [*formerly* 221.042], wisdom literature

> *For Apocryphal wisdom literature, see 229.3. For a specific book of Ketuvim not provided for here, see the book, e.g., Ruth 222.35*

	.1	***Job**
	.2	***Psalms**
	.7	***Proverbs**
	.8	***Ecclesiastes (Qohelet)**
	.9	***Song of Solomon (Canticle of Canticles, Song of Songs)**
	(.96)	*Wisdom of Solomon (Wisdom)

> (Optional number; prefer 229.3)

	(.98)	*Ecclesiasticus (Sirach)

> (Optional number; prefer 229.4)

224   ***Prophetic books of Old Testament***

Class here Major Prophets, Nevi'im

> *For a specific book of Nevi'im not provided for here, see the book, e.g., Joshua 222.2*

	.1	***Isaiah (Isaias)**
	.2	***Jeremiah (Jeremias)**

*Add as instructed under 221–229

.3	*Lamentations	
(.37)	*Baruch	

> (Optional number; prefer 229.5)

.4	*Ezekiel (Ezechiel)
.5	*Daniel

> (Option: Class here Song of the Three Children, Susanna, Bel and the Dragon; prefer 229.6)

.6	*Hosea (Osee)
.7	*Joel
.8	*Amos
.9	*Minor Prophets

> For Hosea, see 224.6; for Joel, see 224.7; for Amos, see 224.8

.91	*Obadiah (Abdias)
.92	*Jonah (Jonas)
.93	*Micah (Micheas)
.94	*Nahum
.95	*Habakkuk (Habacuc)
.96	*Zephaniah (Sophonias)
.97	*Haggai (Aggeus)
.98	*Zechariah (Zacharias)
.99	*Malachi (Malachias)
(.997)	*Maccabees 1 and 2 (Machabees 1 and 2)

> (Optional number; prefer 229.73)

225 New Testament

> For Gospels and Acts, see 226; for Epistles, see 227; for Revelation, see 228

[.03]	Dictionaries, encyclopedias, concordances

> Do not use for dictionaries and encyclopedias; class in 225.3. Do not use for concordances; class in 225.4–225.5

.04	Special topics

---

*Add as instructed under 221–229

	.046	Apocalyptic passages

.046 — Apocalyptic passages

Class apocalyptic passages in a book or group of books with the book or group of books, plus notation 0046 from add table under 221–229, e.g., apocalyptic passages in Gospels 226.0046, in Gospel of Mark 226.30046

For Revelation (Apocalypse), see 228

.09 — Historical, geographic, persons treatment of New Testament

Class the canon in 225.12

For geography, history, chronology, persons of New Testament lands in New Testament times, see 225.9

.1–.8 Generalities

Add to base number 225 the numbers following 220 in 220.1–220.8, e.g., Authorized Version 225.5203

.9 Geography, history, chronology, persons of New Testament lands in New Testament times

Add to base number 225.9 the numbers following 221.9 in 221.91–221.95, e.g., individual persons 225.92; however, for Jesus Christ, Mary, Joseph, Joachim, Anne, John the Baptist, see 232

See Manual at 220.92; also at 230–280: Biography

226 *Gospels and Acts

Class here synoptic Gospels

Subdivisions are added for Gospels and Acts together, for Gospels alone

See Manual at 230–280: Biography

.095 05 — Gospel stories retold

Number built according to instructions under 221–229

Class Jesus as a historical figure, biography and specific events in life of Jesus in 232.9

.1 Harmonies of Gospels

> **226.2–226.5 Specific Gospels**

Class comprehensive works in 226

For miracles, see 226.7; for parables, see 226.8

.2 *Matthew

Class Golden Rule as code of conduct in 241.54

For Sermon on the Mount, see 226.9

---

*Add as instructed under 221–229

	.3	*Mark
	.4	*Luke

        Class Golden Rule as code of conduct in 241.54

          For Sermon on the Mount, see 226.9

	.5	*John

        Class here comprehensive works on Johannine literature

          For Epistles of John, see 227.94; for Revelation (Apocalypse), see 228

	.6	*Acts of the Apostles
	.7	*Miracles

        Class miracles in context of Jesus' life in 232.955

	.8	*Parables

        Class parables in context of Jesus' life in 232.954

	.9	*Sermon on the Mount

        Class Sermon on the Mount as code of conduct in 241.53

	.93	*Beatitudes
	.96	*Lord's Prayer
227		***Epistles**

        Class here comprehensive works on Pauline epistles

	.1	*Romans
	.2	*Corinthians 1

        Class here comprehensive works on Epistles to Corinthians

          For Corinthians 2, see 227.3

	.3	*Corinthians 2
	.4	*Galatians
	.5	*Ephesians
	.6	*Philippians
	.7	*Colossians
	.8	*Other Pauline epistles
	.81	*Thessalonians 1

        Class here comprehensive works on Epistles to Thessalonians

          For Thessalonians 2, see 227.82

*Add as instructed under 221–229

	.82	*Thessalonians 2
	.83	*Timothy 1

> Class here comprehensive works on Epistles to Timothy, on Pastoral Epistles
>
> *For Timothy 2, see 227.84; for Titus, see 227.85*

	.84	*Timothy 2
	.85	*Titus
	.86	*Philemon
	.87	*Hebrews
	.9	***Catholic epistles**
	.91	*James
	.92	*Peter 1

> Class here comprehensive works on Epistles of Peter
>
> *For Peter 2, see 227.93*

	.93	*Peter 2
	.94	*John 1

> Class here comprehensive works on Epistles of John
>
> *For John 2, see 227.95; for John 3, see 227.96*

	.95	*John 2
	.96	*John 3
	.97	*Jude
228		***Revelation (Apocalypse)**
229		***Apocrypha, pseudepigrapha, intertestamental works**

> Apocrypha: works accepted as deuterocanonical in some Bibles
>
> Pseudepigrapha, intertestamental works: works from intertestamental times connected with the Bible but not accepted as canonical
>
> Subdivisions are added for Apocrypha, pseudepigrapha, intertestamental works together; for Apocrypha alone

> \> **229.1–229.7 Specific books and works of Apocrypha**
>
> Class comprehensive works in 229

*Add as instructed under 221–229

.1	***Esdras 1 and 2**

> Variant names: Esdras 3 and 4
>
> *See also 222.7 for Ezra, 222.8 for Nehemiah*

.2	***Tobit, Judith, deuterocanonical part of Esther**
.22	*Tobit (Tobias)

> (Option: Class in 222.86)

.24	*Judith

> (Option: Class in 222.88)

.27	*Deuterocanonical part of Esther

> (Option: Class in 222.9)

.3	***Wisdom of Solomon (Wisdom)**

> Class here Apocryphal wisdom literature
>
> *For Ecclesiasticus, see 229.4*
>
> (Option: Class in 223.96)

.4	***Ecclesiasticus (Sirach)**

> (Option: Class in 223.98)

.5	***Baruch and Epistle of Jeremiah**

> Song of the Three Children relocated to 229.6
>
> (Option: Class Baruch in 224.37)

.6	***Song of the Three Children [*formerly* 229.5], Susanna, Bel and the Dragon, Prayer of Manasseh**

> (Option: Class Song of the Three Children, Susanna, Bel and the Dragon in 224.5)

.7	***Maccabees (Machabees)**
.73	*Maccabees 1 and 2 (Machabees 1 and 2)

> (Option: Class in 224.997)

.75	*Maccabees 3 and 4 (Machabees 3 and 4)

>	**229.8–229.9 Pseudepigrapha, intertestamental works**

> Class comprehensive works in 229.9
>
> *For Maccabees 3 and 4, see 229.75*

---

*Add as instructed under 221–229

.8	*Pseudo gospels
	Including agrapha (Jesus' words not appearing in canonical Gospels), Gospel of Thomas
	Class comprehensive works on New Testament pseudepigrapha in 229.92
.9	**Pseudepigrapha**
	For pseudo gospels, see 229.8
.91	*Old Testament
	For Maccabees 3 and 4, see 229.75
.911	*Historical books
.912	*Poetic books
	Including Odes of Solomon
.913	*Prophetic books
	Including Apocalypse of Elijah, Ascension of Isaiah, Assumption of Moses, Books of Enoch, Jewish apocalypses
.914	*Testaments
	Including Testament of the Twelve Patriarchs
.92	*New Testament
	For pseudo gospels, see 229.8; for Epistles, see 229.93; for Apocalypses, see 229.94
.925	*Acts of the Apostles
.93	*Epistles
.94	*Apocalypses

*Add as instructed under 221–229

> ## 230–280 Christianity

Unless other instructions are given, observe the following table of preference for the history of Christianity and the Christian church (except for biography, explained in Manual at 230–280: Biography), e.g., Jesuit missions in India 266.254 (*not* 271.53054); persecution of Jesuits by Elizabeth I 272.7 (*not* 271.53042, 274.206, or 282.42):

Specific topics	220–260
Persecutions in general church history	272
Doctrinal controversies and heresies in general church history	273
Religious congregations and orders in church history	271
Denominations and sects of Christian church	280
Treatment of Christianity and Christian church by continent, country, locality	274–279
General historical, geographic, persons treatment of Christianity and Christian church (*except* 271–279)	270

Class comprehensive works in 230

For Bible, see 220

See Manual at 230–280: Biography; also at 280: Biography

(Option: To give local emphasis and shorter numbers to a specific religion other than Christianity, e.g., Buddhism, class it in these numbers, its sources in 220, comprehensive works in 230; in that case class the Bible and Christianity in 298. Other options are described at 292–299)

> ## 230–270 Specific elements of Christianity

Class here specific elements of specific denominations and sects
    (Option: Class specific elements of specific denominations and sects in 280)

Class comprehensive works in 230

230 Christianity [*formerly* 200]   Christian theology

Including Christian mythology [*formerly* 204.5]

Class here contextual theology

Class doctrinal controversies in general church history in 273

> *For Christian moral and devotional theology, see 240; for local Christian church and Christian religious orders, see 250; for Christian social and ecclesiastical theology, see 260; for historical, geographic, persons treatment of Christianity and Christian church, see 270; for denominations and sects of Christian church, see 280*

See Manual at 230: Contextual theology

Christianity   Christian theology

SUMMARY

230.002–.007		**Standard subdivisions of Christianity**
.01–.09		**Standard subdivisions and specific types of Christian theology**
.1–.9		**Doctrines of specific denominations and sects**
231		**God**
232		**Jesus Christ and his family Christology**
233		**Humankind**
234		**Salvation (Soteriology) and grace**
235		**Spiritual beings**
236		**Eschatology**
238		**Creeds, confessions of faith, covenants, catechisms**
239		**Apologetics and polemics**

[.001]   Philosophy and theory of Christianity

> Do not use; class in 230.01

.002–.003   Standard subdivisions of Christianity [*formerly* 202–203]

.005   Serial publications of Christianity [*formerly* 205]

[.006]   Organizations and management of Christianity

> Do not use; class in 260

.007   Education, research, related topics of Christianity [*formerly* 207]

[.007 1]   Education

> Do not use; class in 230.071

[.008]   Christianity with respect to kinds of persons

> Do not use; class in 270.08

[.009]   Historical, geographic, persons treatment of Christianity

> Do not use; class in 270

.01   Philosophy and theory of Christianity [*formerly* 201], of Christian theology

.02–.03   Standard subdivisions of Christian theology

.04   Specific types of Christian theology

> Class theology of specific denominations and sects in 230.1–230.9

> *See Manual at 230.04 vs. 230.092, 230.1–230.9*

[.040 1–.040 9]   Standard subdivisions

> Do not use; class in 230.01–230.09

27

.041		Biblical theology

Class theology of a specific part of Old or New Testament with the part, e.g., theology of Pauline epistles 227.06; class biblical theology of a specific topic with the topic in 231–260, e.g., New Testament writers' view of war and peace 261.87309015

See Manual at 220: Biblical theology

.041 1		Christian theology of Old Testament
.041 5		Christian theology of New Testament
.042		Theology of Eastern and Roman Catholic churches

Class specific schools and systems of theology in 230.046

.044		Protestant theology

Class specific schools of Protestant theology in 230.046

.046		Specific schools and systems of theology

Including dominion, existentialist, liberal, neo-orthodox, process theologies

See Manual at 230: Contextual theology

[.046 01–.046 09]		Standard subdivisions

Do not use; class in 230.01–230.09

.046 2		Evangelical and fundamentalist theology
.046 24		Evangelical theology
.046 26		Fundamentalist theology
.046 3		Dispensationalist theology
.046 4		Liberation theology
.05–.06		Standard subdivisions of Christian theology
.07		Education, research, related topics of Christian theology
.071		Education in Christianity [*formerly* 207.1], in Christian theology

Class here Christianity as an academic subject

Class comprehensive works on Christian religious education, religious education to inculcate Christian faith and practice, catechetics in 268

See Manual at 268 vs. 230.071

	.071 1	Higher education in Christianity, in Christian theology

> Class here Bible colleges, divinity schools, theological seminaries, graduate and undergraduate faculties of theology; education of ministers, pastors, priests, theologians
>
> Class training for clergy in a specialized subject with the subject, e.g., education in pastoral counseling 253.5071
>
> *For higher education for specific denominations and sects, see 230.073*
>
> *See Manual at 268 vs. 230.071*

	.071 14–.071 19	Higher education in specific continents, countries, localities [*formerly* 207.4–207.9]

> Class here nondenominational and interdenominational schools and courses

	.073	Higher education for specific denominations and sects

> Add to base number 230.073 the numbers following 28 in 281–289, e.g., Roman Catholic seminaries 230.0732, a Roman Catholic seminary in Dublin 230.073241835

	.08–.09	Standard subdivisions of Christian theology

> *See Manual at 230: Contextual theology; also at 230.04 vs. 230.092, 230.1–230.9*

	.1–.9	**Doctrines of specific denominations and sects**

> Add to base number 230 the numbers following 28 in 281–289, e.g., Methodist doctrines 230.7
>
> *See Manual at 230.04 vs. 230.092, 230.1–230.9; also at 230.15–230.2*
>
> (Option: Class here specific doctrines of specific denominations and sects; prefer 231–236. If option is chosen, add as above, then add 0* and to the result add the numbers following 23 in 231–236, e.g., Methodist doctrines on salvation 230.704)

>	**231–239 Christian doctrinal theology**

> Class specific types of Christian doctrinal theology in 230.042–230.046; class comprehensive works on doctrines of specific denominations and sects in 230.1–230.9; class comprehensive works in 230
>
> *See Manual at 261.5 vs. 231–239*

---

*Add 00 for standard subdivisions; see instructions at beginning of Table 1

> **231–236 Specific topics in Christian doctrinal theology**

> Class here specific doctrines of specific denominations and sects
> (Option: Class specific doctrines of specific denominations and sects in 230.1–230.9)
>
> Class comprehensive works in 230

231 God

- .04   Special topics
- .042   Ways of knowing God

   Including faith, reason, tradition

   Class proofs of existence of God based on reason alone in 212.1; class revelation in 231.74

- .044   General concepts of God

   Including non-Trinitarian concepts

   Class here comprehensive works on Holy Trinity

> **231.1–231.3 Holy Trinity**

> Class comprehensive works in 231.044

- .1   **God the Father**
- .2   **God the Son**

   For Jesus Christ, see 232

- .3   **God the Holy Spirit**

   For gifts of the Holy Spirit, baptism in the Holy Spirit, see 234.13

- .4   **Attributes**

   Including omnipotence, omnipresence, omniscience, transcendence

   For love and wisdom, see 231.6; for sovereignty, see 231.7; for justice and goodness, see 231.8

- .5   **Providence**
- .6   **Love and wisdom**

.7	**Relation to the world**	

> Including relation to nature, sovereignty
>
> Class here God's relation to individual believers
>
> Class redemption in 234.3; class divine law in 241.2; class believers' experience of God in 248.2; class God's relation to the church in 262.7
>
>> *For Providence, see 231.5*

.72	Kingdom of God	

> Class Kingdom of God to come in 236

.73	Miracles	

> Class here miracles associated with saints, comprehensive works on miracles
>
>> *For miracles associated with Mary, see 232.917; for miracles of Jesus, see 232.955; for stigmata, see 248.29*

.74	Revelation	

> *For private visions, see 248.29*

.745	Prophecy	

>> *For Biblical prophecy and prophecies, see 220.15; for messianic prophecies, see 232.12; for eschatological prophecies, see 236*

.76	Relation to and action in history	

> Including covenant relationship, relationship to the Jewish people

.765	Creation	

> *For creation of humankind, see 233.11*

.765 2	Relation of scientific and Christian viewpoints of origin of universe	

> Class here creationism, creation science, evolution versus creation, reconciliation of evolution and creation
>
> *See also 379.28 for teaching creationism in public schools*
>
> *See Manual at 231.7652 vs. 213, 500, 576.8*

.8	**Justice and goodness**	

> Including good and evil
>
> Class here theodicy (vindication of God's justice and goodness in permitting existence of evil and suffering)
>
> *For providence, see 231.5; for moral theology, see 241*

232   Jesus Christ and his family   Christology

> *See Manual at 232*

> **232.1–232.8 Christology**

    Class life of Jesus in 232.9; class comprehensive works in 232

.1 **Incarnation and messiahship of Christ**

    Including typology

.12   Messianic prophecies

.2 **Christ as Logos (Word of God)**

.3 **Christ as Redeemer**

    Including atonement

    Class comprehensive works on the doctrine of redemption in 234.3

    For sacrifice of Christ, see 232.4

.4 **Sacrifice of Christ**

.5 **Resurrection of Christ**

.8 **Divinity and humanity of Christ**

    Including Person; offices as Prophet, Priest, King; intercession

    Class here hypostatic union

    Class non-Trinitarian concepts of Jesus in 232.9

    For incarnation, see 232.1; for Christ as Logos, see 232.2; for Christ as Redeemer, see 232.3

.9 **Family and life of Jesus**

    Class here non-Trinitarian concepts of Jesus, rationalistic interpretations of Jesus

    For Islamic doctrines about Jesus, see 297.2465

    See Manual at 230–280: Biography

.900 1–.900 9   Standard subdivisions

.901   Life of Jesus

    For birth, infancy, childhood of Jesus, see 232.92; for adulthood of Jesus, see 232.95–232.97

.903   Character and personality of Jesus

.904   Jesus as teacher and exemplar

    Including influence

    Class teachings in 232.954

.906   Jewish interpretations of Jesus

.908		Historicity of Jesus
.91		Mary, mother of Jesus

> Class here Mariology
>
> Class Mary's husband and parents in 232.93

.911		Immaculate Conception
.912		Annunciation
.913		Virginity
.914		Assumption (Ascent to heaven)
[.915–.916]		Sanctity and virtues, spiritual powers

> Numbers discontinued; class in 232.91

.917		Miracles and apparitions
.92		Birth, infancy, childhood of Jesus

> Including Holy Family, circumcision, massacre of innocents, flight into Egypt
>
> Class here Christmas story
>
> *For Mary, see 232.91; for Joseph, see 232.932*

.921		Virgin birth
.922		Adoration of shepherds
.923		Wise men (Magi)
[.924–.926]		Circumcision, massacre of innocents, flight into Egypt

> Numbers discontinued; class in 232.92

.927		Childhood of Jesus

> *For presentation in temple, see 232.928; for Jesus among doctors in temple, see 232.929*

.928		Presentation in temple
.929		Jesus among doctors in temple
.93		Mary's husband and parents
.932		Joseph
.933		Joachim and Anne
.94		John the Baptist
.95		Public life of Jesus

> Including baptism, temptation, calling of apostles

.954		Teachings

> Class texts and interpretations of New Testament passages narrating parables in 226.8

.955		Miracles

> Class texts and interpretations of New Testament passages narrating miracles in 226.7

.956		Transfiguration
.957		Last Supper
.958		Last words to disciples
.96		Passion and death of Jesus
.961		Betrayal by Judas
.962		Trial and condemnation
.963		Crucifixion and death
.963 5		Seven last words on cross
.964		Burial
.966		Relics of Passion
.967		Descent into hell
.97		Resurrection, appearances, ascension of Jesus

233 Humankind

> Class salvation in 234

.1	**Creation and fall**
.11	Creation

> Including relation of human creation and human evolution
>
> Class comprehensive works on creation in 231.765

.14	Original sin and fall

> Class sins in 241.3

.4	**Accountability**

> Including guilt

.5	**Nature**	

Including body, soul, spirit, sexuality; humankind as image and likeness of God, as child of God

Class free will in 233.7

> *For original sin, see 233.14; for death, see 236.1; for immortality, see 236.22*

.7	**Freedom of choice between good and evil**	

Class predestination and free will in relation to salvation in 234.9

> *For accountability, see 233.4*

234 Salvation (Soteriology) and grace

Including election, innate virtues, merit, universal priesthood

.1	**Kinds and means of grace**	

Including actual and sanctifying grace

[.12]	Gifts of and baptism in the Holy Spirit	

Relocated to 234.13

.13	Spiritual gifts	

Including interpretation of tongues, prophecy, working of miracles, helps, governments, apostleship, teaching, exhortation, speaking words of wisdom and knowledge

Class here gifts of and baptism in the Holy Spirit [*both formerly* 234.12]

> *For faith, see 234.2*

.131	Healing	

Spiritual, emotional, or physical

> *For discussion of whether cures are miracles, see 231.73*
>
> *See Manual at 615.852 vs. 234.131, 291.31*

.132	Speaking in tongues (Glossolalia) [*formerly also* 248.29]	
.16	Sacraments	

Class liturgy and ritual of sacraments in 265

.161	Baptism	
.161 2		Infant baptism
.161 3		Adult baptism
.162	Confirmation	
.163	Eucharist (Holy Communion, Lord's Supper)	

	.164	Holy Orders
	.165	Matrimony
	.166	Penance

                      Including confession

	.167	Anointing of the sick
	.2	**Faith and hope**

                      See also 236 for eschatology, 241.4 for virtues

	.23	Faith
	.25	Hope
	.3	**Redemption**
	.4	**Regeneration**
	.5	**Repentance and forgiveness**

                      Including atonement, reconciliation

	.6	**Obedience**
	.7	**Justification**
	.8	**Sanctification and holiness**
	.9	**Predestination and free will**
235		**Spiritual beings**

                      For Mariology, see 232.91

	.2	**Saints**

                      Class miracles associated with saints in 231.73

                          For Joseph, see 232.932; for Joachim and Anne, see 232.933; for John the Baptist, see 232.94

                    See Manual at 230–280: Biography

	.24	Beatification and canonization
>		**235.3–235.4 Pure spirits**

                    Class comprehensive works in 235

                      For God, see 231

	.3	**Angels**

                    Including archangels, celestial hierarchy, cherubim, seraphim

.4		**Devils (Demons)**
.47		Satan (Lucifer)
236		**Eschatology**

> Including Antichrist
>
> Class here Kingdom of God to come

.1	**Death**
.2	**Future state (Life after death)**

> Class resurrection of the dead in 236.8
>
> *For intermediate state, see 236.4*

.21	Eternity
.22	Immortality

> *For conditional immortality, see 236.23*

.23	Conditional immortality (Annihilationism)
.24	Heaven
.25	Hell
.4	**Intermediate state**

> Probation after death
>
> Including limbo of fathers (limbus patrum) [*formerly* 236.6], limbo of infants (limbus infantium) [*formerly* 236.7]
>
> *For purgatory, see 236.5*

.5	**Purgatory**
[.6]	**Limbo of fathers (Limbus patrum)**

> Relocated to 236.4

[.7]	**Limbo of infants (Limbus infantium)**

> Relocated to 236.4

.8	**Resurrection of the dead**
.9	**Last Judgment and related events**

> Including Armageddon, Day of the Lord, end of the world, Judgment of Christ, millennium, rapture, Second Coming of Christ, tribulation
>
> Class interdisciplinary works on end of the world in 001.9

[237]	**[Unassigned]**

> Most recently used in Edition 16

238   Creeds, confessions of faith, covenants, catechisms

Class catechetics in 268. Class creeds and catechisms on a specific doctrine with the doctrine, e.g., attributes of God 231.4

.1	**Early and Eastern creeds**
.11	Apostles' Creed
.14	Nicene and post-Nicene creeds of Western Church

        Including Constantinopolitan Creed

.142	Nicene Creed
.144	Athanasian Creed
.19	Eastern Church
.2–.9	**Other denominations**

        Add to base number 238 the numbers following 28 in 282–289, e.g., Lutheran catechisms 238.41

239   Apologetics and polemics

Apologetics: systematic argumentation in defense of the divine origin and authority of Christianity

Standard subdivisions are added for either or both topics in heading

Class apologetics of specific denominations in 230.1–230.9. Class apologetics and polemics on a specific doctrine with the doctrine, e.g., on doctrine of Holy Trinity 231.044

See also 273 for doctrinal controversies and heresies in general church history

[.001–.009]	Standard subdivisions

        Relocated to 239.01–239.09

.01–.09	Standard subdivisions [*formerly* 239.001–239.009]
.1	**Apologetics and polemics in apostolic times**

        For polemics against doctrines of specific groups in apostolic times, see 239.2–239.4

>   **239.2–239.4 Polemics against doctrines of specific groups in apostolic times**

        Class comprehensive works in 239.1

.2	**Polemics against Jews in apostolic times**
.3	**Polemics against pagans and heathens in apostolic times**
.4	**Polemics against Neoplatonists in apostolic times**

| | Christianity | Christian theology | |

[.5] **Polemics against deists**

Relocated to 239.7

[.6] **Polemics against encyclopedists**

Relocated to 239.7

.7 **Polemics against rationalists, agnostics, apostates, atheists in postapostolic times**

Including polemics against deists [*formerly* 239.5], against encyclopedists [*formerly* 239.6], against scientists and materialists [*both formerly* 239.8], against secular humanists [*formerly* 239.9]

[.8] **Polemics against scientists and materialists**

Relocated to 239.7

.9 **Polemics against other groups in postapostolic times**

Polemics against secular humanists relocated to 239.7

Class comprehensive postapostolic defenses of and attacks on doctrines of specific denominations or sects in 230.1–230.9. Class attacks on doctrines of a specific religion with the religion, e.g., doctrines of Judaism 296.3

.93 Polemics against new age groups and doctrines

240 Christian moral and devotional theology

SUMMARY

241 Moral theology
242 Devotional literature
243 Evangelistic writings for individuals and families
246 Use of art in Christianity
247 Church furnishings and related articles
248 Christian experience, practice, life
249 Christian observances in family life

241 Moral theology

See Manual at 241 vs. 261.8

.04 Specific denominations and sects

Add to base number 241.04 the numbers following 28 in 280.2–289.9, e.g., Protestant moral theology 241.0404

.1 **Conscience**

.2 **Laws and bases of morality**

Including divine law, natural law

Class here relation of law and gospel

For codes of conduct, see 241.5

.3	**Sin and vices**	

> Standard subdivisions are added for either or both topics in heading
>
> Including specific vices
>
> Class original sin in 233.14
>
> > *For specific moral issues, see 241.6*
> >
> > *See Manual at 241.3–241.4 vs. 241.6*

.31	Mortal and venial sin
[.32]	Sins against the Holy Spirit

> Number discontinued; class in 241.3

.4	**Virtues**

> Including specific virtues
>
> Class faith and hope as means of salvation in 234.2
>
> > *For specific moral issues, see 241.6*
> >
> > *See Manual at 241.3–241.4 vs. 241.6*

.5	**Codes of conduct**

> *For specific moral issues, see 241.6*

.52	Ten Commandments
.53	Sermon on the Mount
.54	Golden Rule
[.57]	Precepts of the church

> Number discontinued; class in 241.5

.6	**Specific moral issues**

> Add to base number 241.6 the numbers following 17 in 172–179, e.g., morality of warfare 241.6242, of abortion 241.6976; however, for specific vices, see 241.3; for specific virtues, see 241.4
>
> *See Manual at 241.3–241.4 vs. 241.6*

242 Devotional literature

Class here texts of meditations, contemplations, prayers for individuals and families, religious poetry intended for devotional use

Unless other instructions are given, observe the following table of preference, e.g., prayers and meditations for daily use based on passages from the Bible 242.2 (*not* 242.5):

Prayers and meditations for use in times of illness, trouble, bereavement	242.4
Prayers and meditations for specific classes of persons	242.6
Prayers and meditations for daily use	242.2
Prayers and meditations for church year, other Christian feast and fast days	242.3
Prayers and meditations based on passages from the Bible	242.5
Specific prayers and groups of prayers	242.7
Collections of prayers	242.8

Class devotional literature on a specific subject with the subject, e.g., meditations on passion and death of Jesus 232.96

For evangelistic writings, see 243; for hymns, see 264.23

.08 History and description with respect to kinds of persons

Do not use for devotional literature for specific classes of persons; class in 242.6

.2 **Prayers and meditations for daily use**

Not limited to saints' days or specific parts of the church year

Including meditations and prayers for Sunday, Sabbath

Prayers and meditations for daily use for specific classes of persons relocated to 242.6

.3 **Prayers and meditations for church year, other Christian feast and fast days**

Prayers and meditations for church year, other Christian feast and fast days for specific classes of persons relocated to 242.6

\> 242.33–242.36 Church year

Class comprehensive works in 242.3

For Pentecost and time after Pentecost (Ordinary time), see 242.38

.33 Advent and Christmas

.332 Advent

.335	Christmas season
	Class here Christmas day
.34	Lent
	For Holy Week, see 242.35
.35	Holy Week
.36	Easter season
	Including Ascension Day [*formerly* 242.37]
	Class here Easter Sunday
.37	Other Christian feast and fast days
	Including saints' days
	Ascension Day relocated to 242.36
.38	Pentecost and time after Pentecost (Ordinary time)
.4	**Prayers and meditations for use in times of illness, trouble, bereavement**
.5	**Prayers and meditations based on passages from the Bible**
	Class interpretation and criticism of Bible passages for other than devotional use in 220.6; class Bible prayers in 242.722
.6	**Prayers and meditations for specific classes of persons**
	Class here prayers and meditations for daily use for specific classes of persons [*formerly* 242.2], prayers and meditations for church year, other Christian feast and fast days for specific classes of persons [*formerly* 242.3]
	Add to base number 242.6 the numbers following 248.8 in 248.82–248.89, e.g., prayers and meditations for college students 242.634; however, for prayers and meditations for use in times of illness, trouble, bereavement, see 242.4
	Class collections of prayers for specific classes of persons in 242.82–242.89
.7	**Specific prayers and groups of prayers**
.72	Specific types of prayers
	Including doxologies
	Class here prayers to Father, Son, Holy Spirit
[.721]	Doxologies (Prayers of praise)
	Number discontinued; class in 242.72
.722	Bible prayers
[.723–.726]	Prayers of faith, thanksgiving, penitence, petition
	Numbers discontinued; class in 242.72

>		242.74–242.76 Prayers addressed to spiritual beings other than God
		Class comprehensive works in 242.7
	.74	Prayers to Mary
		Including Ave Maria (Hail Mary), Rosary
	.75	Prayers to Joseph, Joachim, Anne
	.76	Prayers to saints and angels
		For Joseph, Joachim, Anne, see 242.75
	.8	**Collections of prayers**
		Class here prayer books
		For specific prayers and groups of prayers, see 242.7
	.800 1–.800 7	Standard subdivisions
	.800 8	History and description with respect to kinds of persons
		Do not use for collections of prayers for specific classes of persons; class in 242.82–242.89
	.800 9	Historical, geographic, persons treatment
	.801–.809	Collections of prayers by adherents of specific denominations and sects
		Add to base number 242.80 the numbers following 28 in 281–289, e.g., collections of private prayers by Methodists 242.807
	.82–.89	Collections of prayers for specific classes of persons
		Add to base number 242.8 the numbers following 248.8 in 248.82–248.89, e.g., collections of private prayers for college students 242.834
		For collections of prayers by adherents of specific denominations and sects, see 242.801–242.809

243 Evangelistic writings for individuals and families

Works designed to convert readers, promote repentance

Class evangelistic sermons in 252.3

[244] [Unassigned]

Most recently used in Edition 15

[245] Texts of hymns for devotional use of individuals and families

Relocated to 264.23

246   **Use of art in Christianity**

Religious meaning, significance, purpose

Class attitude of Christianity and Christian church toward secular art, the arts in 261.57; class creation, description, critical appraisal as art in 700

For church furnishings and related articles, see 247

> **246.1–246.4 Schools and styles**
>
> Class specific elements by school and style in 246.5–246.9; class comprehensive works in 246; class interdisciplinary works on schools and styles of Christian art in 709.015–709.05

.1   **Byzantine and Gothic art**

.2   **Early Christian and Romanesque art**

.4   **Renaissance and modern art**

     Including Protestant art

> **246.5–246.9 Specific elements**
>
> Class comprehensive works in 246

.5   **Icons, symbols, insignia**

.53   Icons

.55   Symbols

     Including banners, emblems, incense, votive offerings

     Class here Christian symbolism

     For colors and lights, see 246.6

.558   Crosses and crucifixes

     Standard subdivisions are added for either or both topics in heading

.56   Insignia

     Including insignia of rank

.6   **Colors and lights**

.7   **Dramatic, musical, rhythmic arts**

     Including dance, liturgical dance

.72   Dramatic arts

.723   Passion plays

	.725	Puppetry
	.75	Music

        Class here comprehensive works on music in Christianity

        Class attitude of Christianity and Christian church toward secular music in 261.578; class interdisciplinary works on Christian sacred music in 781.71

       For music in public worship, see 264.2

	.9	**Architecture**

        Add to base number 246.9 the numbers following 726 in 726.4–726.9, e.g., cathedral church buildings 246.96; however, for church furnishings, see 247

247 Church furnishings and related articles

        Including paintings, plastic arts, sculpture, structural decoration, textiles

	.1	**Furniture**

248 Christian experience, practice, life

        Class here spirituality

       See Manual at 230–280: Biography

SUMMARY

248.06	**Organizations and management**
.2	**Religious experience**
.3	**Worship**
.4	**Christian life and practice**
.5	**Witness bearing**
.6	**Stewardship**
.8	**Guides to Christian life for specific classes of persons**

	.06	Organizations and management

        Pious societies, sodalities, confraternities relocated to 267

	.2	**Religious experience**
	.22	Mysticism
	.24	Conversion

       For moral renewal and commitment, see 248.25

>   248.242–248.246 Conversion from one system of belief to another

        Class comprehensive works in 248.24

        For conversion of Christians to another religion, see the religion, e.g., conversion of Christians to Judaism 296.714

	.242	Conversion from Protestantism to Roman Catholicism

	.244	Conversion from Roman Catholicism to Protestantism
	.246	Conversion from non-Christianity to Christianity
	.25	Moral renewal and commitment
	.29	Other religious experiences

        Including stigmata, private visions

        Speaking in tongues (glossolalia) relocated to 234.132

        Class spiritual gifts in 234.13

.3   **Worship**

        Class here comprehensive works on worship

        Class texts of prayers and devotions in 242

        For observances in family life, see 249; for public worship, see 264

    .32   Prayer

    .34   Meditation and contemplation

        Standard subdivisions are added for either or both topics in heading

.4   **Christian life and practice**

        Class here Christian marriage and family

        Class guides to Christian life for specific classes of persons in 248.8

        For moral theology, see 241; for worship, see 248.3; for witness bearing, see 248.5; for stewardship, see 248.6; for Christian observances in family life, see 249

    .408   History and description with respect to kinds of persons

        Do not use for guides to Christian life for specific classes of persons; class in 248.8

    .46   Individual observances

        Including ceremonial and ritual observances, observance of restrictions and limitations

        For asceticism, see 248.47

    [.463]   Pilgrimages

        Relocated to 263.041

	.47	Asceticism

> Attitudes and practices aside from and beyond normal moral duties adopted as aids to moral and spiritual development
>
> Including practice of celibacy, fasting and abstinence, poverty, solitude, other physical austerities, e.g., flagellation
>
> *For clerical celibacy, see 253.25; for practices of religious congregations and orders, see 255*

.48   Guides to Christian life by or for adherents of specific denominations and sects

> Add to base number 248.48 the numbers following 28 in 280.2–289.9, e.g., guides for Roman Catholics 248.482
>
> Class guides to Christian life for specific classes of persons who are adherents of specific denominations and sects in 248.8

.5   **Witness bearing**

.6   **Stewardship**

.8   **Guides to Christian life for specific classes of persons**

> Class here guides to Christian life for specific classes of persons who are adherents of specific denominations and sects
>
> Class guides to a specific aspect of Christian life with the aspect, e.g., prayer 248.32

\>   248.82–248.85 Guides to Christian life for specific age groups

> Class persons of specific ages in specific occupational groups or experiencing illness, trouble, bereavement in 248.86–248.89; class comprehensive works in 248.8

.82   Children

> Through age eleven

.83   Adolescents and college students

> Standard subdivisions are added for adolescents and college students together, for adolescents alone

.832   Male adolescents

.833   Female adolescents

.834   College students

> Male and female

.84   Adults

> *For persons in late adulthood, see 248.85*

.842		Men
.842 1		Fathers
		Regardless of marital status
.842 2–.842 9		Men by marital status

Add to base number 248.842 the numbers following —0865 in notation 08652–08659 from Table 1, e.g., guides for husbands 248.8425

Class fathers in 248.8421

.843		Women
.843 1		Mothers
		Regardless of marital status
.843 2–.843 9		Women by marital status

Add to base number 248.843 the numbers following —0865 in notation 08652–08659 from Table 1, e.g., guides for wives 248.8435

Class mothers in 248.8431

.844		Married couples

Class husbands in 248.8425; class wives in 248.8435

.845		Parents

Class here Christian child rearing, Christian religious training of children in the home

For fathers, see 248.8421; for mothers, see 248.8431

.846		Separated and divorced persons

For separated and divorced men, see 248.8423; for separated and divorced women, see 248.8433

.85		Persons in late adulthood

> 248.86–248.89 Guides to Christian life for occupational classes; persons experiencing illness, trouble, bereavement

Class comprehensive works in 248.8

.86		Persons experiencing illness, trouble, bereavement
.861–.864		Persons experiencing illness, disability

Add to base number 248.86 the numbers following 362 in 362.1–362.4, e.g., persons experiencing addiction 248.8629

See Manual at 616.86 vs. 158.1, 248.8629, 291.442, 362.29

.866		Persons experiencing bereavement
.88		Occupational classes

> For religious groups, see 248.89

.89		Religious groups
.892		Clergy

> For persons in religious orders, see 248.894

.894		Persons in religious orders
.894 2		Men
.894 22		Vocation
.894 25		Selection and novitiate
.894 3		Women
.894 32		Vocation
.894 35		Selection and novitiate

249 Christian observances in family life

Class here family prayer; family observance of religious restrictions, rites, ceremonies

> ## 250–280 Christian church

Class comprehensive works in 260

250 Local Christian church and Christian religious orders

Standard subdivisions are added for local Christian church and Christian religious orders together, for local Christian church alone

Class public worship in 264; class missions in 266; class religious education in 268

SUMMARY

250.1–.9	Standard subdivisions
251	Preaching (Homiletics)
252	Texts of sermons
253	Pastoral office and work (Pastoral theology)
254	Parish administration
255	Religious congregations and orders
259	Pastoral care of families, of specific kinds of persons

[.68] Management

Do not use for management of local church; class in 254

.9	**Historical, geographic, persons treatment**
	Class general historical treatment of local church in specific continents, countries, localities in 274–279; class historical, geographic, persons treatment of specific denominations in 280

> **251–254 Local church**

Class here basic Christian communities

Class the local church in overall church organization in 262.2; class comprehensive works in 250

For pastoral care of families, of specific kinds of persons, see 259

See Manual at 260 vs. 251–254, 259

251 Preaching (Homiletics)

Class texts of sermons in 252; class pastoral methods in 253.7

.001–.009	Standard subdivisions
.01	Preparation
.02	Sermon outlines
.03	Delivery
	Class here voice, expression, gesture
.07	Radio and television preaching
	Class specific aspects of radio and television preaching in 251.01–251.03
.08	Homiletic illustrations
.1–.9	**Material for preparation of sermons for specific occasions, for specific classes of persons**
	Add to base number 251 the numbers following 252 in 252.1–252.9, e.g., material for preparation of sermons arranged for the church year 251.6

252 Texts of sermons

Class sermons on a specific subject with the subject, e.g., God's Providence 231.5

.001–.009	Standard subdivisions
.01–.09	Texts of sermons by specific denominations and sects
	Add to base number 252.0 the numbers following 28 in 281–289, e.g., Anglican sermons 252.03
.1	**Texts of sermons for baptisms, confirmations, funerals, weddings**
	Class sermons for memorial occasions in 252.9

	.3	**Texts of sermons for evangelistic meetings**
	.5	**Texts of sermons for specific classes of persons**
	.53	Children

> Through age eleven

	.55	Adolescents and young adults

> Junior-high-school, high-school, college students
>
> Including academic, chapel, convocation, commencement sermons

	.56	Persons in late adulthood, and persons experiencing illness, trouble, bereavement
	.58	Occupational classes

> *For religious groups, see 252.59*

	.59	Religious groups
	.592	Clergy

> *For persons in religious orders, see 252.594*

	.594	Persons in religious orders
	.6	**Texts of sermons for church year and public occasions**

> Standard subdivisions are added for texts of sermons for church year and public occasions together, for church year alone

---

> 252.61–252.64 Church year

> Class comprehensive works in 252.6

	.61	Advent and Christmas
	.612	Advent
	.615	Christmas season

> Class here Christmas day

	.62	Lent
	.625	Holy Week
	.63	Easter season

> Including Ascension Day [*formerly* 252.67]
>
> Class here Easter Sunday

	.64	Pentecost and time after Pentecost (Ordinary time)

	.67	Other feast and fast days

.67 Other feast and fast days

> Including saints' days
>
> Ascension Day relocated to 252.63

.68 Secular occasions

> Including elections, holidays, thanksgivings

.7 **Texts of sermons for consecrations, ordinations, installations**

.9 **Texts of sermons for memorial occasions**

253 Pastoral office and work (Pastoral theology)

Class here the work of priests, ministers, pastors, rectors, vicars, curates, chaplains, elders, deacons, assistants, laity in relation to the work of the church at the local level

Class local clergy and laity in relation to the government, organization and nature of the church as a whole in 262.1; class the ordination of women in 262.14; class the role of clergy in religious education in 268

.08 History and description with respect to kinds of persons

> Do not use for pastoral care of specific kinds of persons; class in 259
>
> Class here pastoral care performed by kinds of persons

.09 Historical, geographic, persons treatment

.092 Persons treatment

> Do not use for biography of clergy in the period prior to 1054; class in 270.1–270.3. Do not use for biography of clergy in the period subsequent to 1054; class in 280
>
> *See Manual at 230–280: Biography*

.2 **Life and person**

> Including professional and personal qualifications
>
> Class education of clergy in 230.0711; class guides to Christian life for clergy in 248.892

.22 Families of clergy

.25 Clerical celibacy

> Add to base number 253.25 the numbers following 28 in 281–289, e.g., clerical celibacy in Roman Catholic church 253.252, in Roman Catholic church in United States 253.25273

Local Christian church and religious orders

> **253.5–253.7 Pastoral duties and responsibilities**

Class methods for services to families, to specific kinds of persons in 259; class comprehensive works in 253

For preaching, see 251; for parish administration, see 254

.5   Counseling and spiritual direction

Class pastoral counseling, spiritual direction of specific kinds of persons in 259; class premarital, marriage, family counseling in 259.12–259.14

.52   Pastoral psychology

.53   Spiritual direction

.7   Pastoral methods

Including specific types of activity [*formerly* 259.8], group work, telephone work

[.73]   Outdoor pastoral methods

Number discontinued; class in 253.7

.76   Pastoral methods in homes

.78   Use of radio and television

254   Parish administration

.001–.009   Standard subdivisions

.01–.09   Parish administration by specific denominations and sects

Add to base number 254.0 the numbers following 28 in 281–289, e.g., administration of Roman Catholic parishes 254.02

.1   Initiation of new churches

.2   Parish administration in specific kinds of communities

Class a specific activity in a specific kind of community with the activity, e.g., membership promotion 254.5

.22   Urban communities

.23   Suburban communities

.24   Rural communities

.3   Use of communications media

Including use of audiovisual materials

.4   Public relations and publicity

For use of communications media, see 254.3

.5	**Membership**	

Promotion and growth

.6	**Programs**	

Planning and execution

.7	**Buildings, equipment, grounds**	
.8	**Finance**	

Including budget, expenditures, income, methods of raising money

255 Religious congregations and orders

Class here monasticism, comprehensive works on Christian religious congregations and orders

When adding from 271 to indicate kinds of orders or specific orders, add only the notation for the kind or order. Do not use the footnote instruction to add as instructed under 271, but add notation from the table under 255.1–255.7 if it applies, or add notation 01–09 from Table 1. For example, the correct number for contemplative orders in the United Kingdom is 255.010941 (*not* 255.01041); for Benedictines in the United Kingdom 255.100941 (*not* 255.1041)

> *For guides to Christian life for persons in religious orders, see 248.894; for religious congregations and orders in church organization, see 262.24; for religious congregations and orders, monasticism in church history, see 271. For specific types of activity of religious congregations and orders, see the activity, e.g., pastoral counseling 253.5, missionary work 266*

.001–.009   Standard subdivisions

.01–.09   Specific kinds

> Add to base number 255.0 the numbers following 271.0 in 271.01–271.09 for the kind only, e.g., contemplative orders 255.01; then, for each kind having its own number, add notation 01–09 from Table 1 (*not* as instructed under 271), e.g., contemplative orders in the United Kingdom 255.010941

.1–.7   Roman Catholic orders of men

> Add to base number 255 the numbers following 271 in 271.1–271.7 for the order only, e.g., Benedictines 255.1; then, for each order having its own number, add further as follows (*not* as instructed at 271), e.g., Benedictines in the United Kingdom 255.100941, the rule of St. Benedict 255.106:
>
> 001–009   Standard subdivisions
> 02   Constitutions
> 04   Statutes, ordinances, customs
> 06   Rule

.8   Non-Roman Catholic orders of men

.81   Monasticism of Eastern churches

> Add to base number 255.81 the numbers following 281 in 281.5–281.9, e.g., Eastern Orthodox monasticism 255.819

.83		Anglican orders of men
.9		**Congregations and orders of women**
.900 1–.900 9		Standard subdivisions
.901–.909		Specific kinds

> Add to base number 255.90 the numbers following 271.0 in 271.01–271.09 for the kind only, e.g., contemplative orders 255.901; then, for each kind having its own number, add notation 01–09 from Table 1 (*not* as instructed under 271), e.g., contemplative orders in the United Kingdom 255.9010941

.91–.97	Roman Catholic orders of women

> Add to base number 255.9 the numbers following 271.9 in 271.91–271.97 for the order only, e.g., Dominican sisters 255.972; then, for each order having its own number, add further as instructed under 255.1–255.7 (*not* as instructed at 271), e.g., Dominicans in the United Kingdom 255.97200941, the rule of the Dominicans 255.97206

.98	Non-Roman Catholic orders of women
.981	Monasticism of women of Eastern churches

> Add to base number 255.981 the numbers following 281 in 281.5–281.9, e.g., Eastern Orthodox monasticism of women 255.9819

.983	Anglican orders of women

[256–257] [Unassigned]

Most recently used in Edition 14

[258]   [Unassigned]

Most recently used in Edition 17

259 Pastoral care of families, of specific kinds of persons

Former heading: Activities of the local church

Performed by clergy or laity

Class here pastoral counseling of specific kinds of persons

Unless other instructions are given, observe the following table of preference, e.g., pastoral care of bereaved young people 259.6 (*not* 259.2):

Pastoral care of the bereaved	259.6
Pastoral care of delinquents and criminals	259.5
Pastoral care of persons with disabilities, with physical or mental illnesses	259.4
Pastoral care of families	259.1
Pastoral care of young people	259.2
Pastoral care of persons in late adulthood	259.3

Class comprehensive works on pastoral care of more than one kind of person in 253

See also 253.08 for pastoral care performed by kinds of persons, 361.75 for works limited to social welfare work by religious organizations

See Manual at 260 vs. 251–254, 259

[.01–.07] Standard subdivisions

Do not use; class in 253.01–253.07

.08 History and description with respect to kinds of persons

Do not use for bereaved persons; class in 259.6

[.083] Young people

Do not use; class in 259.2

.084 Persons in specific stages of adulthood

[.084 2] Young adults

Do not use; class in 259.25

[.084 6] Persons in late adulthood

Do not use; class in 259.3

.086 Persons by miscellaneous social characteristics

[.086 92] Antisocial and asocial persons

Do not use; class in 259.5

.087 Gifted persons

Do not use for persons with disabilities and illnesses; class in 259.4

.088 Occupational and religious groups

[.088 375]		Students
		Do not use; class in 259.2
[.09]		Historical, geographic, persons treatment
		Do not use; class in 253.09

.1   **Pastoral care of families**

.12   Family counseling

> *For premarital counseling, see 259.13; for marriage counseling, see 259.14*

.13   Premarital counseling

.14   Marriage counseling

.2   **Pastoral care of young people**

.22   Pastoral care of children

> Through age eleven

.23   Pastoral care of adolescents

> Ages twelve through seventeen; junior-high-school and high-school students
>
> Class here comprehensive works on pastoral care of adolescents and young adults
>
> *For pastoral care of young adults eighteen and older, see 259.25*

.24   Pastoral care of college students

> Class here campus ministry

.25   Pastoral care of young adults

> Aged eighteen and above
>
> *For pastoral care of college students, see 259.24*

.3   **Pastoral care of persons in late adulthood**

.4   **Pastoral care of persons with disabilities, with physical or mental illnesses**

> Class here programs for visiting the sick
>
> Add to base number 259.4 the numbers following 362 in 362.1–362.4, e.g., pastoral care of those who have attempted suicide 259.428

.5   **Pastoral care of delinquents and criminals**

> Class here prison chaplaincy, pastoral care of antisocial and asocial persons

.6   **Pastoral care of the bereaved**

| [.8] | Specific types of activity |

Relocated to 253.7

260 Christian social and ecclesiastical theology

Institutions, services, observances, disciplines, work of Christianity and Christian church

Class here organizations of Christianity [*formerly* 206], comprehensive works on Christian church

For local church and religious orders, see 250; for denominations and sects, see 280

See Manual at 260 vs. 251–254, 259

SUMMARY

260.9	Historical, geographic, persons treatment
261	Social theology and interreligious relations and attitudes
262	Ecclesiology
263	Days, times, places of religious observance
264	Public worship
265	Sacraments, other rites and acts
266	Missions
267	Associations for religious work
268	Religious education
269	Spiritual renewal

| .9 | Historical, geographic, persons treatment |

Do not use for historical, geographic, persons treatment of Christian church; class in 270

261 Social theology and interreligious relations and attitudes

Attitude of Christianity and Christian church toward and influence on secular matters, attitude toward other religions, interreligious relations

Class here Christianity and culture

Class sociology of religion in 306.6

| .1 | Role of Christian church in society |

Class specific socioeconomic problems in 261.8

| .2 | Christianity and other systems of belief |
| .21 | Christianity and irreligion |

Including Christianity and communism, Christianity and the apostate and indifferent

| .22–.29 | Christianity and other religions |

Add to base number 261.2 the numbers following 29 in 292–299, e.g., Christianity and Islam 261.27

.5		**Christianity and secular disciplines**
		See Manual at 261.5; also at 261.5 vs. 231–239
.51		Philosophy, logic, related disciplines
.513		Paranormal, occult phenomena and arts
.515		Psychology
.52		Communications media
		Class here comprehensive works on attitude toward and use of communications media
		For a specific use of communications media by the church, see the use, e.g., use in parish administration 254.3
.55		Science
		Class the relation of scientific and Christian views on creation in 231.765
.56		Technology
.561		Medicine
.57		The arts
.578		Music
.58		Literature
.7		**Christianity and political affairs**
		Including civil war and revolution
		Class here Christianity and civil rights
		For Christianity and international affairs, see 261.87
		See Manual at 322.1 vs. 261.7, 291.177
.72		Religious freedom
.73		Theocracy
		Supremacy of church over civil government
.8		**Christianity and socioeconomic problems**
		Class here comprehensive works on the Christian view of socioeconomic and political affairs
		For Christianity and political affairs, see 261.7
		See also 361.75 for welfare services of religious organizations
		See Manual at 241 vs. 261.8
.83		Social problems

.832		Social welfare problems and services
.832 1–.832 5		Problems of and services to persons with illnesses and disabilities, the poor
		Add to base number 261.832 the numbers following 362 in 362.1–362.5, e.g., Christian attitude toward alcoholism 261.832292, toward the poor 261.8325
.832 6		Hunger
.832 7		Abuse within the family
.832 71		Child abuse and neglect
		For sexual abuse, see 261.83272
.832 72		Sexual abuse
.832 73		Adults who were victims of abuse as children
.832 8		Refugees and victims of political oppression
.833		Crime
		Add to base number 261.833 the numbers following 364 in 364.1–364.8, e.g., Christian attitude toward treason 261.833131, toward capital punishment 261.83366
.834		Relations of age groups, the sexes, social classes, language groups, ethnic groups
		Add to base number 261.834 the numbers following 305 in 305.2–305.8, e.g., Christian attitude toward women 261.8344; however, for Christianity in relation to other religions, see 261.22–261.29; for attitude toward the poor, see 261.8325
.835		Sexual relations, marriage, divorce, family
		Add to base number 261.835 the numbers following 306 in 306.7–306.8, e.g., Christian attitude toward homosexuality 261.835766
		Class abuse within the family in 261.8327
.836		Ecology and population
		Add to base number 261.836 the numbers following 304 in 304.2–304.8, e.g., Christian attitude toward ecology 261.8362
.85		The economic order
		Including management of business enterprises
.87		International affairs
.873		War and peace
		For civil war and revolution, see 261.7
.873 2		Nuclear weapons and nuclear war

262 Ecclesiology

Church government, organization, nature

See Manual at 260 vs. 251–254, 259

SUMMARY

262.001–.009		Standard subdivisions
.01–.09		Government and organization, ecclesiology of specific denominations and sects
	.1	Governing leaders of churches
	.2	Local church and religious congregations and orders in church organization
	.3	Government and organization of systems governed by papacy and episcopacy
	.4	Government and organization of systems governed by election
	.5	General councils
	.7	Nature of the church
	.8	Church and ministerial authority and its denial
	.9	Church law and discipline

.001   Philosophy and theory

.001 1   Ecumenism

> Do not use for systems; class in 262.001
>
> *See Manual at 280.042 vs. 262.0011*

.001 109   Historical, geographic, persons treatment

> Do not use for history of the ecumenical movement; class in 280.042

.001 7   Church renewal

.002–.005   Standard subdivisions

.006   Organizations and particular aspects of administration

.006 8   Particular aspects of administration

> Notation 068 from Table 1 is not used by itself in 262; however, add notation 0681–0688 as appropriate for particular aspects of administration, e.g., financial administration of United Methodist Church 262.0760681

.007–.009   Standard subdivisions

.01–.09   Government and organization, ecclesiology of specific denominations and sects

> Add to base number 262.0 the numbers following 28 in 281–289, e.g., government and organization of the United Methodist Church 262.076

.1 Governing leaders of churches

Authority, function, role

	[.109 2]	Persons treatment

> Do not use for biography of church leaders; class in 270. Do not use for biography of leaders of specific denominations; class in 280
>
> *See Manual at 230–280: Biography*

	.11	Apostolic succession

> **262.12–262.15 Governing leaders by rank**
>
> Class comprehensive works in 262.1

	.12	Episcopacy

Class here bishops, archbishops, national conferences of bishops

Add to base number 262.12 the numbers following 28 in 281–289, e.g., episcopacy of Anglican churches 262.123, of Church of England 262.12342

For papacy and patriarchate, see 262.13

	.13	Papacy and patriarchate

Standard subdivisions are added for papacy and patriarchate together, for Roman Catholic papacy alone

> **262.131–262.136 Specific aspects of Roman Catholic papacy**
>
> Class comprehensive works in 262.13

	.131	Papal infallibility
	.132	Temporal power of the pope
	.135	College of Cardinals
	.136	Administration

Including congregations, offices of Curia Romana, Synod of Bishops, tribunals

For national conferences of bishops, see 262.12; for College of Cardinals, see 262.135

	.14	Local clergy

Class here ordination of women

Add to base number 262.14 the numbers following 28 in 281–289, e.g., local Methodist clergy 262.147

Class works that treat the ordination of women only in relation to its effect on the local church in 253

	.15	Laity

Body of church members

Add to base number 262.15 the numbers following 28 in 281–289, e.g., laity of Lutheran church 262.1541, in United States 262.154173

> **262.17–262.19 Governing leaders by system of government**

Class leaders by rank in a specific system of government in 262.12–262.15; class comprehensive works in 262.1

.17 Governing leaders in papal and episcopal systems

.18 Governing leaders in presbyterian systems

.19 Governing leaders in congregational systems

.2 Local church and religious congregations and orders in church organization

For administration of parishes, see 254; for government and administration of religious congregations and orders, see 255

See Manual at 260 vs. 251–254, 259

.22 Parishes

.24 Religious congregations and orders

.26 Small groups

Including basic Christian communities

> **262.3–262.4 Specific forms of church organization**

Class comprehensive works on government and organization of specific denominations and sects regardless of form of organization in 262.01–262.09; class comprehensive works in 262. Class a specific aspect of government and organization with the aspect, e.g., role of bishops in a system governed by episcopacy 262.12 (*not* 262.3)

.3 Government and organization of systems governed by papacy and episcopacy

Including sees, dioceses, cathedral systems

.4 Government and organization of systems governed by election

Including congregational systems, presbyteries, synods

.5	**General councils**	

  Add to base number 262.5 the numbers following 28 in 281–289, e.g., ecumenical councils of Roman Catholic Church 262.52

  Class legal acts of general councils in 262.9. Class nonlegal decrees on a specific subject with the subject, e.g., statements on original sin 233.14

.7 **Nature of the church**

  Including God's relation to the church

.72 Attributes, marks, notes

  Including apostolicity, catholicity, credibility, holiness, infallibility, necessity, unity, visibility and invisibility

.73 Communion of saints

.77 Mystical body of Christ

.8 **Church and ministerial authority and its denial**

  Including heresy, schism

.9 **Church law and discipline**

  Class here canon (ecclesiastical) law

  Class civil law relating to church or religious matters in 340

  See also 364.188 for offenses against religion as defined and penalized by the state

---

> 262.91–262.94 Roman Catholic law

  Class comprehensive works in 262.9

.91 Acts of the Holy See

  Including apostolic letters, briefs, encyclicals, papal bulls and decrees

  Class acts on a specific subject with the subject, e.g., on the nature of the church 262.7

.92 Early Roman Catholic codes

.922   Early codes to Gratian, ca. 1140

.923   Corpus iuris canonici

.924   Quinque compilationes antiquae

.93 Codex iuris canonici (1917)

.931   General principles (Canons 1–86)

.932   Persons (Canons 87–725)

   Clergy, religious, laity

	.933	Things (Canons 726–1551)
		Including benefices, sacraments, sacred times and places, teaching office, temporal goods, worship
	.934	Procedure (Canons 1552–2194)
		Including trials, cases of beatification and canonization
	.935	Crimes and penalties (Canons 2195–2414)
	.94	Codex iuris canonici (1983)
	.98	Branches and other denominations
		Add to base number 262.98 the numbers following 28 in 280.2–289.9, e.g., Anglican ecclesiastical law 262.983

263 Days, times, places of religious observance

.04	Special topics
.041	Pilgrimages [*formerly* 248.463]
[.041 093–.041 099]	Specific continents, countries, localities
	Do not use; class in 263.0423–263.0429
.042	Holy places
	Class here pilgrimages to holy places in specific continents, countries, localities
	For works treating miracles and shrines associated with them, see 231.73; for miracles associated with Mary and shrines associated with them, see 232.917; for miracles of Jesus and shrines associated with them, see 232.955
[.042 093–.042 099]	Specific continents, countries, localities
	Do not use; class in 263.0423–263.0429
.042 3–.042 9	Specific continents, countries, localities
	Add to base number 263.042 notation 3–9 from Table 2, e.g., Santiago de Compostela 263.0424611

> **263.1–263.3 Sabbath and Sunday**

Class comprehensive works in 263.3

.1 **Biblical Sabbath**

.2 **Observance of the seventh day**

.3 Sunday

Class here Sunday observance [*formerly* 263.4], comprehensive works on Sabbath and Sunday

For Biblical Sabbath, see 263.1; for observance of the seventh day, see 263.2

[.4] Sunday observance

Relocated to 263.3

.9 Church year and other days and times

Standard subdivisions are added for church year and other days and times together, for church year alone

See Manual at 263.9, 291.36 vs. 394.265–394.267

> 263.91–263.94 Church year

Class comprehensive works in 263.9

.91		Advent and Christmas
.912		Advent
.915		Christmas season

Class here Christmas day

.92 Lent

.925 Holy Week

.93 Easter season

Including Ascension Day [*formerly* 263.97]

Class here Easter Sunday

.94 Pentecost and time after Pentecost (Ordinary time)

.97 Other feast and fast days

Ascension Day relocated to 263.93

For saints' days, see 263.98

.98 Saints' days

Standard subdivisions are added for individual saint's days

264 Public worship

Ceremonies, rites, services (liturgy and ritual)

Class works not limited by denomination or sect about sacraments, other rites and acts in 265; class Sunday school services in 268.7; class comprehensive works on worship in 248.3

264 Christian social and ecclesiastical theology

SUMMARY

264.001–.009	**Standard subdivisions**
.01–.09	**Public worship by denominations and sects**
.1	**Prayer**
.2	**Music**
.3	**Scripture readings and communion sacrament**
.4	**Responsive readings**
.7	**Prayer meetings, Holy Hours, novenas**
.9	**Sacramentals**

.001   Philosophy and theory

> Class here liturgical renewal

.002–.009   Standard subdivisions

> 264.01–264.09   Public worship by denominations and sects

Class here works limited by denomination or sect about sacraments, other rites and acts

Class comprehensive works in 264; class comprehensive works on sacraments, other rites and acts in 265

.01   Early and Eastern churches

> Add to base number 264.01 the numbers following 281 in 281.1–281.9, e.g., liturgy and ritual of Eastern Orthodox churches 264.019; then add further as instructed under 264.04–264.09, e.g., Eastern Orthodox Mass 264.019036

.02   Roman Catholic Church

.020 01–.020 09   Standard subdivisions

.020 1–.020 9   History, meaning, place of liturgy, ritual, prayers in public worship

> Add to base number 264.02 notation 01–09 from the table under 264.04–264.09, e.g., the Mass 264.02036; however, for texts, see 264.021–264.029

> 264.021–264.029   Texts of liturgy, ritual, prayers

Class comprehensive works in 264.02

.021   Texts of calendars and ordos

.022   Texts of ceremonials

> Ceremonials: canonization of saints, election and coronation of popes, creation of cardinals, other papal functions and services; instructions for bishops

.023		Texts of missals

> Class here sacramentaries
>
> *For lectionary, see 264.029*

.024		Texts of breviaries

> *For psalters, see 264.028*

.025		Texts of ritual

> Class here Pontificale Romanum, Rituale Romanum
>
> Add to base number 264.025 the numbers following 265 in 265.1–265.7, e.g., text of baptism 264.0251

.027		Texts of special books
.027 2		Texts for special times of year

> Including Holy Week

.027 4		Texts for special liturgical services

> Including funeral services outside the Mass, litanies, novenas, stations of the cross

.028		Texts of psalters
.029		Texts of lectionary
.03		Anglican churches

> Including rubrics
>
> Class here Book of Common Prayer

.030 01–.030 09		Standard subdivisions
.030 1–.030 9		History, meaning, place of liturgy, ritual, prayers in public worship

> Add to base number 264.03 notation 01–09 from the table under 264.04–264.09, e.g., prayer 264.0301; however, for texts, see 264.031–264.038

> **264.031–264.038 Texts of liturgy, ritual, prayers**
>
> Class comprehensive works in 264.03

.031		Texts of calendars, festivals, fasts
.032		Texts of lectionary

> Including texts of epistles, Gospels [*formerly also* 264.036]
>
> Use of this number for rubrics discontinued; class in 264.03

.033		Texts of morning prayer and litany

.034		Texts of evening prayer and vespers
.035		Texts of sacraments, ordinances, services

       Add to base number 264.035 the numbers following 265 in 265.1–265.7, e.g., text of baptism 264.0351

       Class texts of morning prayer and litany in 264.033; class texts of evening prayer and vespers in 264.034

.036		Texts of collects

       Texts of epistles, Gospels relocated to 264.032

[.037]		Texts of ordinal, articles, creeds

       Number discontinued; class in 264.03

.038		Texts of psalters
.04–.09		Other specific denominations and sects

       Add to base number 264.0 the numbers following 28 in 284–289, e.g., United Methodist services 264.076; then add further as follows:

       001–009   Standard subdivisions
       01–07   Specific elements
                    History, meaning, place in public worship, texts
                    Add to 0 the numbers following 264 in 264.1–264.7, e.g., the Lord's Supper 036, the Lord's Supper in the United Methodist Church 264.076036
       08   Sacraments
                    History, meaning, place in public worship, texts
                    Add to 08 the numbers following 265 in 265.1–265.7, e.g., the ceremony of baptism 081, the ceremony of baptism in the United Methodist Church 264.076081; however, for Holy Communion (Eucharist, Lord's Supper, Mass), see 036
       09   Sacramentals, other rites and acts
                    History, meaning, place in public worship, texts
       091   Sacramentals
       098–099 Other rites and acts
                    Add to 09 the numbers following 265 in 265.8–265.9, e.g., funeral services 0985, United Methodist funerals 264.0760985

> **264.1–264.9 Specific elements**

    History, meaning, place in public worship, texts

    Class specific elements in public worship of specific denominations and sects in 264.01–264.09; class use of the arts (except music), of color in public worship in 246; class liturgical year in 263.9; class comprehensive works in 264

    Specific elements as part of the Mass are classed in 264.36, e.g., Eucharistic prayers (*not* 264.1)

.1	**Prayer**

Class prayers for a specific ceremony with the ceremony, e.g., prayers for funerals 265.85

.13	Texts of prayers

Including litanies

Class comprehensive collections of public and private prayers in 242.8

.15	Liturgy of the hours (Divine office)

Including psalters

Class here breviaries

.2	**Music**

Class comprehensive works on music in Christianity in 246.75; class interdisciplinary works on Christian sacred music in 781.71; class interdisciplinary works on sacred vocal music in 782.22

.23	Hymns

Class here texts of hymns for devotional use of individuals and families [*formerly* 245]

Class hymnals containing both text and music, interdisciplinary works on hymns in 782.27

.3	**Scripture readings and communion sacrament**
.34	Scripture readings

Class here common lectionary

.36	Holy Communion (Eucharist, Lord's Supper, Mass)

Including specific elements when part of the Mass

For viaticum, see 265.7

.4	**Responsive readings**
[.5–.6]	**Creeds, confessions of faith, sermons, exhortations, instructions**

Numbers discontinued; class in 264

.7	**Prayer meetings, Holy Hours, novenas**
.9	**Sacramentals**

For consecrations and dedications, see 265.92

265 Sacraments, other rites and acts

Standard subdivisions are added for sacraments and other rites and acts together, for sacraments alone

Not limited by denomination or sect

Class works limited by denomination or sect about sacraments, other rites and acts in 264.01–264.09

> **265.1–265.7 Sacraments**

Class comprehensive works in 265

For Holy Communion (Eucharist, Lord's Supper, Mass), see 264.36

.1	**Baptism**
.12	Infant baptism
.13	Adult baptism

Class here Christian initiation (baptism and confirmation) of adults, catechumenate

For confirmation, see 265.2; for religious education for catechumens, see 268.434

.2	**Confirmation**
.4	**Holy Orders**
.5	**Matrimony**
.6	**Penance**
.61	Contrition

Examination of conscience, prayers preparatory to confession

.62	Confession
.63	Satisfaction

Penitential prayers and acts for the remission of sin

.64	Absolution
.66	Indulgences
.7	**Viaticum and anointing of the sick**
.8	**Rites in illness and death**
.82	Religious ceremonies for the afflicted

For viaticum and anointing of the sick, see 265.7

	.85	Religious ceremonies for the dead

                 Class here funeral services

                 For requiem Mass, see 264.36

.9   **Other acts**

                 Including ceremonies of joining a church, foot washing, laying on of hands, love feasts (agapes)

.92   Consecrations and dedications

.94   Exorcism

266   Missions

                 Class here missionary societies, religious aspects of medical missions

                 Class medical services of medical missions in 362.1

                 For mission schools, see 371.071

.001–.008   Standard subdivisions

.009   Historical, geographic, persons treatment

                 Do not use for foreign missions originating in specific continents, countries, localities; class in 266.023. Do not use for historical, geographic, persons treatment of missions of specific denominations and sects; class in 266.1–266.9

                 Class here joint and interdenominational missions; foreign missions by continent, country, locality served

.02   Kinds of missions

.022   Home missions

.023   Foreign missions

[.023 091–.023 099]   Geographic and persons treatment

                 Do not use for foreign missions characterized only by place served; class in 266.009. Do not use for foreign missions originating in specific areas; class in 266.0231–266.0239

.023 1–.023 9   Persons treatment and foreign missions originating in specific areas

                 Add to base number 266.023 notation 1–9 from Table 2, e.g., missions originating in France 266.02344; then add 0* and again add notation 1–9 from Table 2 for place served, e.g., French missions to Africa 266.0234406

.1–.9   **Missions of specific denominations and sects**

                 Add to base number 266 the numbers following 28 in 281–289, e.g., Anglican missions 266.3; Anglican missions serving Africa 266.36

---

*Add 00 for standard subdivisions; see instructions at beginning of Table 1

267 Associations for religious work

Class here pious societies, sodalities, confraternities [*all formerly* 248.06]

For religious congregations and orders, see 255; for missionary societies, see 266

See Manual at 230–280: Biography

.1	**Associations for religious work for both men and women**
.13	Interdenominational and nondenominational associations
	For Moral Rearmament, see 267.16
.16	Moral Rearmament
.18	Specific branches, denominations, and sects
	Add to base number 267.18 the numbers following 28 in 280.2–289.9, e.g., Baptist Adult Union 267.186132
.2	**Men's associations**
.23	Interdenominational and nondenominational associations
	For Young Men's Christian Associations, see 267.3
.24	Specific branches, denominations, and sects
	Add to base number 267.24 the numbers following 28 in 280.2–289.9, e.g., Baptist societies 267.246
.3	**Young Men's Christian Associations**
.306	Organizations and management [*formerly also* 267.33]
[.309]	Historical, geographic, persons treatment
	Do not use; class in 267.39
[.31–.32]	Program and objectives, buildings and equipment
	Numbers discontinued; class in 267.3
[.33]	Organization and management
	Relocated to 267.306
[.34–.35]	Staff and departments
	Numbers discontinued; class in 267.3
.39	Historical, geographic, persons treatment
	Add to base number 267.39 notation 01–9 from Table 2, e.g., Young Men's Christian Association in New York City 267.397471
.4	**Women's associations**

.43		Interdenominational and nondenominational associations

.43   Interdenominational and nondenominational associations

For Young Women's Christian Associations, see 267.5

.44   Specific branches, denominations, and sects

Add to base number 267.44 the numbers following 28 in 280.2–289.9, e.g., Baptist societies 267.446

.5   **Young Women's Christian Associations**

.506   Organizations and management [*formerly also* 267.53]

[.509]   Historical, geographic, persons treatment

Do not use; class in 267.59

[.51–.52]   Program and objectives, buildings and equipment

Numbers discontinued; class in 267.5

[.53]   Organization and management

Relocated to 267.506

[.54–.55]   Staff and departments

Numbers discontinued; class in 267.5

.59   Historical, geographic, persons treatment

Add to base number 267.59 notation 01–9 from Table 2, e.g., Young Women's Christian Association in New York City 267.597471

.6   **Young adults' associations**

.61   Interdenominational and nondenominational associations

For Young Men's Christian Associations, see 267.3; for Young Women's Christian Associations, see 267.5

[.613]   Young People's Society of Christian Endeavor

Number discontinued; class in 267.61

.62   Specific branches, denominations, and sects

Add to base number 267.62 the numbers following 28 in 280.2–289.9, e.g., Baptist Young People's Union 267.626132

.7   **Boys' associations**

For Young Men's Christian Associations, see 267.3

.8   **Girls' associations**

For Young Women's Christian Associations, see 267.5

268 Religious education

Class here catechetics (the science or art devoted to organizing the principles of religious teaching), curricula, comprehensive works on Christian religious education

Class Christian religious schools providing general education in 371.071; class place of religion in public schools in 379.28. Class textbooks on a specific subject with the subject, e.g., textbooks on missions 266

For religious education at the university level, see 230.0711; for study of Christianity in secular secondary schools, see 230.0712

See Manual at 268 vs. 230.071

[.068]	Management

Do not use; class in 268.1

.08 History and description with respect to kinds of persons

Do not use for education of specific groups; class in 268.4

Class here education, teaching performed by kinds of persons

[.088 2] History and descriptions with respect to religious groups

Do not use; class in 268.8

[.088 375] Students

Do not use; class in 268.4

.1 Administration

For plant management, see 268.2; for personnel management, see 268.3

.2 Buildings and equipment

.3 Personnel

Class here preparation, role, training, personnel management

See Manual at 230–280: Biography

.4 Religious education of specific groups

Class here curricula, records and rules, teaching methods, services for specific groups

.43 Specific age groups

.432 Children

Through age eleven

See also 372.84 for religion courses in secular elementary schools

(.432 04) Special topics

(.432 045)		Textbooks
		(Option: Class here religious education textbooks; prefer the specific subject, e.g., textbooks on Christianity 230, textbooks on missions 266)
.433		Adolescents
(.433 04)		Special topics
(.433 045)		Textbooks
		(Option: Class here religious education textbooks; prefer the specific subject, e.g., textbooks on Christianity 230, textbooks on missions 266)
.434		Adults
(.434 04)		Special topics
(.434 045)		Textbooks
		(Option: Class here religious education textbooks; prefer the specific subject, e.g., textbooks on Christianity 230, textbooks on missions 266)
.5	**Records and rules**	
	Including attendance, decorations, honor rolls, prizes, promotion	
	Class records and rules for specific groups in 268.4	
.6	**Methods of instruction and study**	
	Class methods for a specific group with the group, e.g., methods for instruction of children 268.432071	
[.61–.62]	Value and use of textbooks, textbook method	
	Numbers discontinued; class in 268.6	
.63	Lecture and audiovisual methods	
.632		Lecture method
.635		Audiovisual methods
.67	Dramatic method	
	Class use of dramatic arts for religious purposes not limited to religious education in 246.72	
[.68]	Laboratory methods	
	Number discontinued; class in 268.6	
.7	**Services**	
	Including anniversaries, festivals, music, rallies, special days	
	Class services for specific groups in 268.4	

.8	**Specific branches, denominations, and sects**

Add to base number 268.8 the numbers following 28 in 280.2–289.9, e.g., Presbyterian religious education 268.85

Class a specific element in religious education by specific denominations and sects with the element in 268.1–268.7, e.g., religious education of children in Baptist churches 268.432088261

269 Spiritual renewal

Class history of the pentecostal movement in 270.82

.2	**Evangelism**

See also 243 for evangelistic writings for individuals and families, 248.5 for witness bearing by individual lay Christians, 252.3 for texts of evangelistic sermons, 266 for missionary evangelization

.24	Revival and camp meetings
.26	Evangelism by radio and television
[.4]	**Pentecostalism**

Number discontinued; class in 269

.6	**Retreats**

Add to base number 269.6 the numbers following 248.8 in 248.82–248.89, e.g., retreats for men 269.642

> ## 270–280 Historical, geographic, persons treatment of Christianity; Church history; Christian denominations and sects

Unless other instructions are given, observe the following table of preference for the history of Christianity and the Christian church (except for biography, explained in Manual at 230–280: Biography), e.g., persecution of Jesuits by Elizabeth I 272.7 (*not* 271.53042, 274.206, or 282.42):

Persecutions in general church history	272
Doctrinal controversies and heresies in general church history	273
Religious congregations and orders in church history	271
Denominations and sects of Christian church	280
Treatment of Christianity and Christian church by continent, country, locality	274–279
General historical, geographic, persons treatment of Christianity and Christian church (*except* 271–279)	270

Class comprehensive works in 270

See Manual at 230–280: Biography; also at 280: Biography

270 Historical, geographic, persons treatment of Christianity [*formerly* 209]   Church history

Class here collected writings of apostolic and church fathers (patristics)

Observe table of preference under 230–280

For historical, geographic, persons treatment of specific denominations and sects, see 280

See Manual at 230–280: Biography

SUMMARY

270.01–.09	Standard subdivisions
.1–.8	Historical periods
271	Religious congregations and orders in church history
272	Persecutions in general church history
273	Doctrinal controversies and heresies in general church history
274–279	Treatment by continent, country, locality

.01–.07   Standard subdivisions

.08   Christianity with respect to kinds of persons [*formerly* 208], church history with respect to kinds of persons

See Manual at 230: Contextual theology

.09	Areas, regions, places in general, persons
[.093–.099]	Treatment by continent, country, locality
	Do not use; class in 274–279

> **270.1–270.8 Historical periods**

Class historical periods in specific continents, countries, localities in 274–279; class comprehensive works in 270

See Manual at 281.1–281.4

.1	**Apostolic period to 325**
.2	**Period of ecumenical councils, 325–787**
.3	**787–1054**

Class here comprehensive works on Middle Ages

For a specific part of Middle Ages, see the part, e.g., late Middle Ages 270.5

.38	Great schism, 1054
.4	**1054–1200**
.5	**Late Middle Ages through Renaissance, 1200–1517**
.6	**Period of Reformation and Counter-Reformation, 1517–1648**

Including 17th century

For 1648–1699, see 270.7

.7	**Period from Peace of Westphalia to French Revolution, 1648–1789**
.8	**Modern period, 1789–**
.81	1789–1900

.82 1900–1999

Class here comprehensive works on evangelicalism, fundamentalism, pentecostalism, charismatic movement

Add to base number 270.82 the numbers following —0904 in notation 09041–09049 from Table 1, e.g., 1960–1969 in church history 270.826

Ecumenical movement relocated to 280.042

Class pentecostal churches that are independent denominations in 289.94; class evangelical churches, fundamentalist churches that are independent denominations in 289.95

For evangelicalism, fundamentalism, pentecostalism, charismatic movement in the period 2000– , see 270.83. For evangelicalism, fundamentalism, pentecostalism, charismatic movement in a specific branch or denomination, see the branch or denomination, e.g., Protestant fundamentalism 280.4

.83 2000–

> **271–273 Special topics of church history**

Class comprehensive works in 270

271 Religious congregations and orders in church history

Class here history of monasticism, history of specific monasteries and convents even if not connected with a specific order

Add to each subdivision identified by * as follows:
001–008   Standard subdivisions
[009]   Historical treatment
          Do not use; class in base number without further addition
[0091–0099] Geographic and persons treatment
          Do not use; class in 01–09
01–09   Geographic and persons treatment
          Add to base number 0 notation 1–9 from Table 2, e.g., collected biography 022, collected biography of Benedictines 271.1022, Benedictines in the United Kingdom 271.1041

Class persecutions involving religious congregations and orders in 272; class doctrinal controversies and heresies involving congregations and orders in 273

History of Christianity

SUMMARY

	271.001–.009	Standard subdivisions
	.01–.09	Specific kinds
	.1	Benedictines
	.2	Dominicans (Friars Preachers, Black Friars)
	.3	Franciscans (Gray Friars)
	.4	Augustinians
	.5	Regular clerics
	.6	Passionists and Redemptorists
	.7	Roman Catholic orders of men not otherwise provided for
	.8	Non-Roman Catholic orders of men
	.9	Congregations and orders of women

.001–.009   Standard subdivisions

> 271.01–271.09   Specific kinds

Class comprehensive works in 271

.01   *Contemplative religious orders

.02   *Eremitical religious orders

.03   *Teaching orders

.04   *Preaching orders

[.05]   Military orders

         Relocated to 271.791

.06   *Mendicant religious orders

.07   *Nursing orders

.08   *Canons regular

.09   Other specific kinds

.092   *Brothers

See also 271.093 for lay brothers

.093   *Lay brothers

.094   *Third orders

         Secular and regular

.095   *Secular institutes

> **271.1–271.8   Specific orders of men**

Class comprehensive works in 271

---

*Add as instructed under 271

> **271.1–271.7 Roman Catholic orders of men**

Class comprehensive works in 271

.1 ***Benedictines**

.11 *Confederated Benedictines

For Olivetans, see 271.13

.12 *Cistercians (Bernardines)

.125 *Trappists

.13 *Olivetans

.14 *Cluniacs

Including Camaldolese, Silvestrians, Monks of Saint Paul the Hermit

For Carthusians, see 271.71

.16 *Celestines

.17 Mechitarists and Basilians

.18 Antonines (Antonians), Maronites, Chaldeans, Syrians

.19 *Canons

Including Crosier Fathers, Crosiers of the Red Star, Premonstratensians

Class Augustinians in 271.4

.2 ***Dominicans (Friars Preachers, Black Friars)**

.3 ***Franciscans (Gray Friars)**

Including Alcantarines, Observants, Recollects

See also 271.4 for Augustinian Recollects

.36 *Capuchins

.37 *Conventuals

.38 *Third Order Regular

.4 ***Augustinians**

Including Augustinian Recollects

.42 *Trinitarians

.45 *Mercedarians

.47 *Servites

---

*Add as instructed under 271

.49		Other Augustinians

> Including Brothers Hospitallers of St. John of God, Minims

.5		***Regular clerics**
.51		*Theatines
.52		*Barnabites
.53		*Jesuits (Society of Jesus)
.54		*Somaschi
.55		*Camillians
.56		*Minor Clerks Regular (Caracciolini)
.57		*Clerks Regular of the Mother of God
.58		*Piarists
.6		***Passionists and Redemptorists**
.62		*Passionists
.64		*Redemptorists
.7		**Roman Catholic orders of men not otherwise provided for**
.71		*Carthusians
.73		*Carmelites (White Friars)
.75		*Sulpicians
.76		*Oblates
.77		*Lazarists (Vincentians)
.78		*Christian Brothers (Brothers of the Christian Schools)
.79		Other Roman Catholic orders of men
.791		*Orders of knighthood

> Class here military orders [*formerly* 271.05]

.791 2		*Knights of Malta (Knights Hospitalers of St. John of Jerusalem)
.791 3		*Knights Templars
.791 4		*Teutonic Knights
.8		**Non-Roman Catholic orders of men**
.81		Monasteries of Eastern churches

> Add to base number 271.81 the numbers following 281 in 281.5–281.9, e.g., Eastern Orthodox monasteries 271.819, on Mount Athos 271.81949565

---

*Add as instructed under 271

	.83	Anglican orders of men
	.9	**Congregations and orders of women**
	.900 01–.900 08	Standard subdivisions
	.900 09	Historical treatment
	[.900 091–.900 099]	Geographic and persons treatment
		Do not use; class in 271.9001–271.9009
	.900 1–.900 9	Geographic and persons treatment
		Add to base number 271.900 notation 1–9 from Table 2, e.g., collected biography of women religious 271.90022, congregations and orders of women in France 271.90044
	.901–.909	Specific kinds
		Add to base number 271.90 the numbers following 271.0 in 271.01–271.09, e.g., contemplative orders 271.901

> 271.91–271.98 Specific orders of women

Class comprehensive works in 271.9

> 271.91–271.97 Roman Catholic orders of women

Class comprehensive works in 271.9

.91	*Sisters of Charity orders
.92	*Sisters of Mercy orders
.93	*Sacred Heart orders
.94	*Sisters of Bon Secours
.95	*Little Sisters of the Poor
.97	Other Roman Catholic orders of women
.971	*Carmelites
.972	*Dominicans
.973	*Franciscan orders
	Class here Poor Clares
.974	*Ursulines
.975	*Visitation orders
.976	*Saint Joseph orders

*Add as instructed under 271

	.977	*Presentation orders
	.98	Non-Roman Catholic orders of women
	.981	Women's convents of Eastern churches

> Add to base number 271.981 the numbers following 281 in 281.5–281.9, e.g., Eastern Orthodox convents of women 271.9819

	.983	Anglican orders of women

272 Persecutions in general church history

Regardless of denomination

Class here martyrs

Class relation of state to church in 322.1

> See also 364.188 for offenses against religion as defined and penalized by the state

.1	Persecutions of Apostolic Church by imperial Rome
.2	Persecutions by Inquisition
.3	Persecutions of Waldenses and Albigenses
.4	Persecutions of Huguenots
.5	Persecutions of Molinists and Quietists
.6	Persecutions of Anglican reformers by Mary I
.7	Persecutions of Roman Church by Elizabeth I and Anglicans
.8	Persecutions of Quakers, Baptists, witches by Puritans and others of Puritan times
.9	Modern persecutions and martyrs

273 Doctrinal controversies and heresies in general church history

Class persecutions resulting from controversies and heresies in 272; class churches founded on specific doctrines in 280

> See also 239 for apologetics and polemics

.1 1st–2nd centuries

Class here Christian Gnosticism

Class comprehensive works and non-Christian Gnosticism in 299.932

> For Gnosticism of 3rd century, see 273.2

---

*Add as instructed under 271

.2		**3rd century**

Including Christian Manicheism

Class comprehensive works and non-Christian Manicheism in 299.932

For Sabellianism, see 273.3

.3	**Sabellianism**
.4	**4th century**

Including Arianism, Donatism

.5	**5th century**

Including Pelagianism

.6	**6th–16th centuries**

Including Albigensianism, Catharism, Waldensianism

Class here antinomianism

For later antinomianism, see 273.7–273.9; for Albigensian, Catharist, Waldensian churches, see 284.4

.7	**17th century**

Including Molinism, Pietism, comprehensive works on Jansenism

For Jansenist churches, see 284.84

.8	**18th century**
.9	**19th century and later centuries**

Including modernism

274–279 Treatment by continent, country, locality

Add to base number 27 notation 4–9 from Table 2, e.g., Christianity, Christian church in Europe 274, in France 274.4; then to the result add the numbers following 27 in 270.01–270.8, e.g., Christian church in France during the Reformation 274.406

Class geographic treatment of a specific subject with the subject, plus notation 09 from Table 1, e.g., persecutions in France 272.0944

280 Denominations and sects of Christian church

Including nondenominational and interdenominational churches

Class here general historical and geographic treatment of, comprehensive works on specific denominations and sects and their individual local churches

Class persecution of or by specific churches in 272

> *See also* 273 for doctrines of specific churches considered as heresies
>
> *See Manual at* 230–280: Biography; *also at* 280: Biography; *also at at* 291: Denominations and sects

(Option: Class here specific elements of specific denominations and sects; prefer 230–270. If option is chosen, add to the number for each specific denomination, sect, group as follows:

001–008	Standard subdivisions
[009]	Historical, geographic, persons treatment Do not use; class in 07
02	Basic textual sources Class Bible in 220
03–06	Doctrinal, moral, devotional, social, ecclesiastical theology Add to 0 the numbers following 2 in 230–260, e.g., the denomination and international affairs 06187
07	Historical, geographic, persons treatment Add to 07 the numbers following 27 in 270.1–279, e.g., 20th century 07082)

SUMMARY

280.01–.09	Standard subdivisions and special topics
.2–.4	Branches
281	Early church and Eastern churches
282	Roman Catholic Church
283	Anglican churches
284	Protestant denominations of Continental origin and related bodies
285	Presbyterian churches, Reformed churches centered in America, Congregational churches, Puritanism
286	Baptist, Disciples of Christ, Adventist churches
287	Methodist churches; churches related to Methodism
289	Other denominations and sects

.01–.03 Standard subdivisions

.04 Special topics

.042 Relations between denominations

> Class here ecumenical movement [*formerly* 270.82]
>
> *See Manual at* 280.042 vs. 262.0011

.05–.09 Standard subdivisions

> **280.2–280.4 Branches**

Class specific denominations and sects in 281–289; class comprehensive works in 280

.2 **Eastern and Roman Catholic churches**

Class comprehensive works on Roman Catholic Church and Eastern churches in communion with Rome in 282

For specific denominations and sects, see 281–282

.4 **Protestant churches and Protestantism**

Standard subdivisions are added for either or both topics in heading

Class here dissenters, free churches, nonconformists (British context); works on Protestant evangelicalism, fundamentalism, pentecostalism, charismatic movement

Class comprehensive works on evangelicalism, fundamentalism, pentecostalism, charismatic movement in general church history in 270.82

For specific Protestant denominations, see 283–289

> **281–289 Specific denomination**

Class comprehensive works in 280

(Option: Class a specific denomination or sect requiring local emphasis in 289.2)

281 Early church and Eastern churches

> **281.1–281.4 Early church**

Use these subdivisions only for building other numbers in 230–260, e.g., theology in the Ante-Nicene church 230.13; never use these subdivisions by themselves. When building numbers in 230–260 using these subdivisions, use 281.1 for comprehensive works

Class collected writings of apostolic and church fathers (patristics) in 270; class all works on early church in 270.1–270.3. Class a specific work of an apostolic or church father on a specific subject with the subject, e.g., philosophy 189.2

See Manual at 281.1–281.4

.1 **Apostolic Church to the time of the great schism, 1054**

For Apostolic Church to 100, see 281.2; for Ante-Nicene church, see 281.3; for Post-Nicene church, see 281.4

.2	**Apostolic Church to 100**	
.3	**Ante-Nicene church, 100–325**	
.4	**Post-Nicene church, 325–1054**	
.5	**Eastern churches**	

>Including Catholics of Eastern rites (Eastern rite churches in communion with Rome), St. Thomas (Mar Thoma, Syro-Malabar) Christians
>
>*For Monophysite churches, see 281.6; for Coptic and Ethiopian churches, see 281.7; for Nestorian churches, see 281.8; for Eastern Orthodox churches, see 281.9*
>
>See Manual at 281.1–281.4

.6	**Monophysite churches**	

>Including Eutychian Church
>
>*For Coptic and Ethiopian churches, see 281.7*

.62	Armenian Church	
.63	Jacobite Church	

>Class here Syrian Orthodox Church, Jacobite Patriarchate of Antioch
>
>*See also 281.95691 for Eastern Orthodox Church in Syria*

.7	**Coptic and Ethiopian churches**	
.72	Coptic (Coptic Orthodox) church	
.75	Ethiopian (Ethiopian Orthodox) church	
.8	**Nestorian churches**	
.9	**Eastern Orthodox churches**	
.909	Historical, geographic, persons treatment	

>See Manual at 281.1–281.4

[.909 3]	Geographic treatment in the ancient world	

>Do not use; class early church in 270

[.909 4–.909 9]	Treatment by specific continents, countries, localities in the modern world	

>Do not use; class in 281.94–281.99

.94–.99	Treatment by continent, country, locality	

>Add to base number 281.9 notation 4–9 from Table 2, e.g., Russian Orthodox Church 281.947, Orthodox Church in America 281.97

282 Roman Catholic Church

Class here the Catholic traditionalist movement, comprehensive works on Roman Catholic Church and Eastern rite churches in communion with Rome

Class modern schisms in Roman Catholic Church in 284.8

For Eastern rite churches in communion with Rome, see 281.5–281.8

.09   Historical, geographic, persons treatment

See Manual at 281.1–281.4

[.093]   Geographic treatment in the ancient world

Do not use; class early church in 270

[.094–.099]   Treatment by specific continents, countries, localities in the modern world

Do not use; class in 282.4–282.9

.4–.9   **Treatment by continent, country, locality**

Add to base number 282 notation 4–9 from Table 2, e.g., Roman Catholic Church in Latin America 282.8

> ## 283–289 Protestant and other denominations

Class comprehensive works on Protestant churches in 280.4; class comprehensive works on Protestant and other denominations in 280

See Manual at 283–289

283 Anglican churches

[.094–.099]   Treatment by specific continents, countries, localities in the modern world

Do not use; class in 283.4–283.9

.3   **Branches not in communion with the See of Canterbury**

Including Reformed Episcopal Church and its affiliates

See Manual at 280: Biography; also at 283–289

.4–.9   **Treatment by continent, country, locality**

Class here national churches in communion with the See of Canterbury

Add to base number 283 notation 4–9 from Table 2, e.g., Church of England 283.42, Episcopal Diocese of Long Island 283.74721

284 Protestant denominations of Continental origin and related bodies

> For Protestant denominations of Continental origin not provided for here, see the denomination, e.g., Baptists 286

.1 Lutheran churches

[.109 4–.109 9]	Treatment by specific continents, countries, localities in the modern world
	Do not use; class in 284.14–284.19
(.12)	(Permanently unassigned)
	(Optional number used to provide local emphasis or a shorter number for Lutheran church in a specific country other than the United States; prefer 284.14–284.19)
.13	Specific denominations, branches, synods centered in the United States
	See Manual at 280: Biography; also at 283–289
[.130 1–.130 9]	Standard subdivisions
	Do not use; class in 284.101–284.109
.131	*The American Lutheran Church
.131 2	*The Evangelical Lutheran Church
.131 3	*United Evangelical Lutheran Church
.131 4	*The Lutheran Free Church
.132	*The Evangelical Lutheran Synodical Conference of North America
	For Wisconsin Evangelical Lutheran Synod, see 284.134
.132 2	*The Lutheran Church—Missouri Synod
	For Synod of Evangelical Lutheran Churches, see 284.1323
.132 3	*Synod of Evangelical Lutheran Churches (Slovak)
.133	*The Lutheran Church in America
.133 2	*American Evangelical Lutheran Church
.133 3	*Augustana Evangelical Lutheran Church
.133 4	*Finnish Evangelical Lutheran Church
.133 5	*The United Lutheran Church in America
.134	*Wisconsin Evangelical Lutheran Synod
.135	*Evangelical Lutheran Church in America

---

*Do not use notation 094–099 from Table 1; class in 284.14–284.19

.14–.19   Treatment by continent, country, locality

> Add to base number 284.1 notation 4–9 from Table 2, e.g., Lutheran Church of Sweden 284.1485, Memorial Evangelical Lutheran Church of Washington, D.C. 284.1753
>
> *See Manual at 284.143*
>
> (Option: Class Lutheran churches in a specific country other than the United States in 284.12)

.2   **Calvinistic and Reformed churches of European origin**

> Standard subdivisions are added for either or both topics in heading
>
> Class here comprehensive works on Calvinistic churches, on Reformed churches
>
> *For Huguenot churches, see 284.5; for Presbyterian churches, see 285; for Reformed churches centered in America, see 285.7*
>
> *See also 285.9 for Puritanism*

[.209 4–.209 9]   Treatment by specific continents, countries, localities in the modern world

> Do not use; class in 284.24–284.29

.24–.29   Treatment by continent, country, locality

> Add to base number 284.2 notation 4–9 from Table 2, e.g., Reformed churches in Holland 284.2492, in South Africa 284.268

.3   **Hussite and Anabaptist churches**

> Including Lollards, Wycliffites
>
> *See also 289.7 for Mennonite churches*

.4   **Albigensian, Catharist, Waldensian churches**

.5   **Huguenot churches**

.6   **Moravian churches**

> *For Hussite churches, see 284.3*

[.609 4–.609 9]   Treatment by specific continents, countries, localities in the modern world

> Do not use; class in 284.64–284.69

.64–.69   Treatment by continent, country, locality

> Add to base number 284.6 notation 4–9 from Table 2, e.g., Moravian churches in Germany 284.643

.8   **Modern schisms in Roman Catholic Church**

> Including Constitutional Church, Gallican schismatic churches, Liberal Catholic Church, Little Church of France, Old Catholic churches, Philippine Independent Church

| | | Denominations and sects of Christian church | |

.84	Jansenist churches
.9	**Arminian and Remonstrant churches**

285 Presbyterian churches, Reformed churches centered in America, Congregational churches, Puritanism

Standard subdivisions are added for Presbyterian churches, Reformed churches centered in America, Congregational churches together; for Presbyterian churches alone

> **285.1–285.2 Presbyterian churches of United States, of British Commonwealth origin**
>
> Class comprehensive works on Presbyterian churches, Presbyterian churches of other origin in 285
>
> (If option under 280 is followed, use 285.001–285.008 for standard subdivisions, 285.02–285.07 for specific elements of Presbyterian churches)

.1	**Presbyterian churches of United States origin**
[.109 4–.109 9]	Treatment by specific continents, countries, localities in the modern world
	Do not use; class in 285.14–285.19
.13	Specific denominations
	See Manual at 280: Biography; also at 283–289
[.130 1–.130 9]	Standard subdivisions
	Do not use; class in 285.101–285.109
.131	*United Presbyterian Church in the U.S.A.
.132	*Presbyterian Church in the United States of America
.133	*Presbyterian Church in the United States
.134	*United Presbyterian Church of North America
.135	*Cumberland Presbyterian Church
.136	*Reformed Presbyterian churches
.137	*Presbyterian Church (U.S.A.)
.14–.19	Treatment by continent, country, locality
	Add to base number 285.1 notation 4–9 from Table 2, e.g., the Hudson River Presbytery 285.17473
.2	**Presbyterian churches of British Commonwealth origin**

*Do not use notation 094–099 from Table 1; class in 285.14–285.19

[.209 4–.209 9]	Treatment by specific continents, countries, localities in the modern world
	Do not use; class in 285.24–285.29
.23	Specific denominations
	See Manual at 280: Biography; also at 283–289
[.230 1–.230 9]	Standard subdivisions
	Do not use; class in 285.201–285.209
.232	†United Reformed Church in the United Kingdom
	Class Congregational Church of England and Wales in 285.842
.233	†Church of Scotland
.234	†Free Church of Scotland
.235	†Presbyterian Church of Wales (Welsh Calvinistic Methodist Church)
.24–.29	Treatment by continent, country, locality
	Add to base number 285.2 notation 4–9 from Table 2, e.g., Presbyterianism in Ireland 285.2415, a Church of Scotland parish in Edinburgh 285.24134
	Class United Church of Canada in 287.92; class Uniting Church in Australia in 287.93
.7	**Reformed churches centered in America**
[.709 4–.709 9]	Treatment by specific continents, countries, localities in the modern world
	Do not use; class in 285.74–285.79
.73	Specific denominations
	See Manual at 280: Biography; also at 283–289
[.730 1–.730 9]	Standard subdivisions
	Do not use; class in 285.701–285.709
.731	*Christian Reformed Church
.732	*Reformed Church in America (Dutch)
.733	*Reformed Church in the United States (German)
.734	*Evangelical and Reformed Church
.74–.79	Treatment by continent, country, locality
	Add to base number 285.7 notation 4–9 from Table 2, e.g., First Reformed Church of Schenectady, N.Y. 285.774744

*Do not use notation 094–099 from Table 1; class in 285.74–285.79
†Do not use notation 094–099 from Table 1; class in 285.24–285.29

.8		**Congregationalism**
[.809 4–.809 9]		Treatment by specific continents, countries, localities in the modern world
		Do not use; class in 285.84–285.89
(.82)		(Permanently unassigned)
		(Optional number used to provide local emphasis or a shorter number for Congregational churches in a specific country other than the United States; prefer 285.84–285.89)
.83		Specific denominations centered in the United States
		See Manual at 280: Biography; also at 283–289
[.830 1–.830 9]		Standard subdivisions
		Do not use; class in 285.801–285.809
.832		†Congregational Churches of the United States
.833		†Congregational Christian Churches
.834		†United Church of Christ
		For Evangelical and Reformed Church, see 285.734
.84–.89		Treatment by continent, country, locality
		Class here specific denominations centered outside the United States
		Add to base number 285.8 notation 4–9 from Table 2, e.g., Congregational Church of England and Wales 285.842, Congregational churches in New England 285.874
		Class United Church of Canada in 287.92; class Uniting Church in Australia in 287.93
		(Option: Class Congregational churches in a specific country other than the United States in 285.82)
.9		**Puritanism**

286 Baptist, Disciples of Christ, Adventist churches

Standard subdivisions are added for Baptist, Disciples of Christ, Adventist churches together; for Baptist churches alone

---

> **286.1–286.5 Baptist churches**

Class comprehensive works in 286

(If option under 280 is followed, use 286.001–286.008 for standard subdivisions, 286.02–286.07 for specific elements of Baptist churches)

.1 **Regular (Calvinistic) Baptists**

---

†Do not use notation 094–099 from Table 1; class in 285.84–285.89

[.109 4–.109 9]		Treatment by specific continents, countries, localities in the modern world
		Do not use; class in 286.14–286.19
(.12)		(Permanently unassigned)
		(Optional number used to provide local emphasis or a shorter number for Regular Baptist churches in a specific country other than the United States; prefer 286.14–286.19)
.13		Specific denominations centered in the United States
		See Manual at 280: Biography; also at 283–289
[.130 1–.130 9]		Standard subdivisions
		Do not use; class in 286.101–286.109
.131		*American Baptist Churches in the U.S.A.
		Former name: American (Northern) Baptist Convention
.132		*Southern Baptist Convention
.133		*National Baptist Convention of the United States of America
.134		*National Baptist Convention of America
.135		*Progressive National Baptist Convention
.136		*American Baptist Association
.14–.19		Treatment by continent, country, locality
		Class here specific denominations centered outside the United States
		Add to base number 286.1 notation 4–9 from Table 2, e.g., Association of Regular Baptist Churches of Canada 286.171, a Southern Baptist association in Tennessee 286.1768
		(Option: Class Regular Baptist churches in a specific country other than the United States in 286.12)
.2	**Freewill Baptists**	
.3	**Seventh-Day Baptists**	
.4	**Old School Baptists**	
	Including Antimission, Hard-Shell, Primitive Baptists	
.5	**Other Baptist churches and denominations**	
	Including Baptist General Conference, Church of the Brethren, Dunkers	
.6	**Disciples of Christ (Campbellites)**	

---

*Do not use notation 094–099 from Table 1; class in 286.14–286.19

[.609 4–.609 9]		Treatment by specific continents, countries, localities in the modern world
		Do not use; class in 286.64–286.69
.63		Specific denominations
		Including Christian Church (Disciples of Christ), Churches of Christ
		See Manual at 280: Biography; also at 283–289
[.630 1–.630 9]		Standard subdivisions
		Do not use; class in 286.601–286.609
.64–.69		Treatment by continent, country, locality
		Add to base number 286.6 notation 4–9 from Table 2, e.g., the Christian Church (Disciples of Christ) in Florida 286.6759
.7		**Adventist churches**
[.709 4–.709 9]		Treatment by specific continents, countries, localities in the modern world
		Do not use; class in 286.74–286.79
.73		Specific denominations
		Including Advent Christian Church, Church of God General Conference
		See Manual at 280: Biography; also at 283–289
[.730 1–.730 9]		Standard subdivisions
		Do not use; class in 286.701–286.709
.732		Seventh-Day Adventist Church
[.732 094–.732 099]		Treatment by specific continents, countries, localities in the modern world
		Do not use; class in 286.74–286.79
.74–.79		Treatment by continent, country, locality
		Add to base number 286.7 notation 4–9 from Table 2, e.g., Seventh-Day Adventists in South America 286.78

287 Methodist churches; churches related to Methodism

Standard subdivisions are added for Methodist churches and churches related to Methodism together; for Methodist churches alone

.1   **Wesleyan Methodist Church**

[.109 4–.109 9]   Treatment by specific continents, countries, localities in the modern world

                 Do not use; class in 287.14–287.19

.14–.19		Treatment by continent, country, locality

> Add to base number 287.1 notation 4–9 from Table 2, e.g., Wesleyan Methodist Church in New South Wales 287.1944

.2		**Miscellaneous Methodist churches**

> Including Congregational Methodist Church, Free Methodist Church of North America

.4		**Primitive Methodist Church**
[.409 4–.409 9]		Treatment by specific continents, countries, localities in the modern world

> Do not use; class in 287.44–287.49

.44–.49		Treatment by continent, country, locality

> Add to base number 287.4 notation 4–9 from Table 2, e.g., Primitive Methodist Church in Kent 287.44223

.5		**Methodist churches in British Isles**
[.509 41–.509 42]		British Isles

> Do not use; class in 287.54

.53		Specific denominations

> Including Bible Christians, Methodist New Connexion, Protestant Methodists, United Methodist Church (Great Britain), United Methodist Free Churches, Wesleyan Conference, Wesleyan Reformers, Yearly Conference of People Called Methodists
>
> *For Wesleyan Methodist Church in British Isles, see 287.141; for Primitive Methodist Church in British Isles, see 287.441*
>
> See Manual at 280: Biography; also at 283–289

[.530 1–.530 9]		Standard subdivisions

> Do not use; class in 287.501–287.509

.532		*United Conference of Methodist Churches
.533		*Independent Methodists
.534		*Wesleyan Reform Union
.54		Treatment by country and locality

> Add to base number 287.54 the numbers following —4 in notation 41–42 from Table 2, e.g., Independent Methodists in Wales 287.5429

.6		**United Methodist Church**

> *See also 287.53 for United Methodist Church (Great Britain)*

---

*Do not use notation 0941–0942 from Table 1; class in 287.54

Denominations and sects of Christian church

[.609 4–.609 9]		Treatment by specific continents, countries, localities in the modern world
		Do not use; class in 287.64–287.69
.63		Specific antecedent denominations
		For Methodist Protestant Church, see 287.7; for Evangelical United Brethren Church, see 289.9
		See Manual at 280: Biography; also at 283–289
[.630 1–.630 9]		Standard subdivisions
		Do not use; class in 287.601–287.609
.631		†The Methodist Church (1939–1968)
.632		†Methodist Episcopal Church
.633		†Methodist Episcopal Church, South
.64–.69		Treatment by continent, country, locality
		Add to base number 287.6 notation 4–9 from Table 2, e.g., United Methodist churches in Ohio 287.6771
.7		**Methodist Protestant Church**
.8		**Black Methodist churches of United States origin**
[.809 4–.809 9]		Treatment by specific continents, countries, localities in the modern world
		Do not use; class in 287.84–287.89
.83		Specific denominations
		Including African Methodist Episcopal Church, African Methodist Episcopal Zion Church, Christian Methodist Episcopal Church
		See Manual at 280: Biography; also at 283–289
[.830 1–.830 9]		Standard subdivisions
		Do not use; class in 287.801–287.809
.84–.89		Treatment by continent, country, locality
		Add to base number 287.8 notation 4–9 from Table 2, e.g., Black Methodist churches in Georgia 287.8758, in Liberia 287.86662
.9		**Churches related to Methodism**
		Limited to those listed below
.92		United Church of Canada
.93		Uniting Church in Australia
.94		Church of South India

†Do not use notation 094–099 from Table 1; class in 287.64–287.69

.95		Church of North India
.96		Salvation Army
.99		Church of the Nazarene [*formerly* 289.9]

[288]   [Unassigned]

Most recently used in Edition 19

289   Other denominations and sects

SUMMARY

289.1	**Unitarian and Universalist churches**
.3	**Latter-Day Saints (Mormons)**
.4	**Church of the New Jerusalem (Swedenborgianism)**
.5	**Church of Christ, Scientist (Christian Science)**
.6	**Society of Friends (Quakers)**
.7	**Mennonite churches**
.8	**Shakers (United Society of True Believers in Christ's Second Appearing)**
.9	**Denominations and sects not provided for elsewhere**

.1   Unitarian and Universalist churches

Class here Anti-Trinitarianism, Socinianism, Unitarianism

[.109 4–.109 9]   Treatment by specific continents, countries, localities in the modern world

Do not use; class in 289.14–289.19

.13   Specific denominations

See Manual at 280: Biography; also at 283–289

[.130 1–.130 9]   Standard subdivisions

Do not use; class in 289.101–289.109

.132   *Unitarian Universalist Association

.133   *Unitarian churches

.134   *Universalist churches

.14–.19   Treatment by continent, country, locality

Add to base number 289.1 notation 4–9 from Table 2, e.g., Unitarianism in Boston 289.174461

(.2)   (Permanently unassigned)

(Optional number used to provide local emphasis or a shorter number for a specific denomination or sect; prefer the number for the specific denomination or sect in 281–289)

.3   Latter-Day Saints (Mormons)

---

*Do not use notation 094–099 from Table 1; class in 289.14–289.19

[.309 4–.309 9]		Treatment by specific continents, countries, localities in the modern world
		Do not use; class in 289.34–289.39
.32	Sources (Sacred books)	
.322	Book of Mormon	
.33	Specific branches	

See Manual at 280: Biography; also at 283–289

[.330 1–.330 9]		Standard subdivisions
		Do not use; class in 289.301–289.309
.332	Church of Jesus Christ of Latter-Day Saints	
[.332 094–.332 099]		Treatment by specific continents, countries, localities in the modern world
		Do not use; class in 289.34–289.39
.333	Reorganized Church of Jesus Christ of Latter-Day Saints	
[.333 094–.333 099]		Treatment by specific continents, countries, localities in the modern world
		Do not use; class in 289.34–289.39
.34–.39	Treatment by continent, country, locality	

Add to base number 289.3 notation 4–9 from Table 2, e.g., Mormons in Utah 289.3792

.4   Church of the New Jerusalem (Swedenborgianism)

[.409 4–.409 9]	Treatment by specific continents, countries, localities in the modern world
	Do not use; class in 289.44–289.49
.44–.49	Treatment by continent, country, locality

Add to base number 289.4 notation 4–9 from Table 2, e.g., Swedenborgianism in Europe 289.44

.5   Church of Christ, Scientist (Christian Science)

[.509 4–.509 9]	Treatment by specific continents, countries, localities in the modern world
	Do not use; class in 289.54–289.59
.52	Sources

Writings by Mary Baker Eddy

.54–.59		Treatment by continent, country, locality
		Add to base number 289.5 notation 4–9 from Table 2, e.g., First Church of Christ, Scientist, Boston 289.574461
.6		**Society of Friends (Quakers)**
[.609 4–.609 9]		Treatment by specific continents, countries, localities in the modern world
		Do not use; class in 289.64–289.69
.63		Specific denominations
		See Manual at 280: Biography; also at 283–289
[.630 1–.630 9]		Standard subdivisions
		Do not use; class in 289.601–289.609
.64–.69		Treatment by continent, country, locality
		Add to base number 289.6 notation 4–9 from Table 2, e.g., Quakers in England 289.642
.7		**Mennonite churches**
[.709 4–.709 9]		Treatment by specific continents, countries, localities in the modern world
		Do not use; class in 289.74–289.79
.73		Specific branches
		Including Amish, Church of God in Christ, Defenseless Mennonites, General Conference Mennonites, Hutterian Brethren
		See Manual at 280: Biography; also at 283–289
[.730 1–.730 9]		Standard subdivisions
		Do not use; class in 289.701–289.709
.74–.79		Treatment by continent, country, locality
		Add to base number 289.7 notation 4–9 from Table 2, e.g., Amish churches in Lancaster County, Pennsylvania 289.774815
.8		**Shakers (United Society of Believers in Christ's Second Appearing)**

.9	**Denominations and sects not provided for elsewhere**

> Including Christian and Missionary Alliance, Churches of God, Dukhobors, Evangelical Congregational Church, Evangelical United Brethren Church, Messianic Judaism (Jewish Christians), Plymouth Brethren, United Brethren in Christ
>
> Church of the Nazarene relocated to 287.99
>
> Class nondenominational and interdenominational churches in 280; class Protestant nondenominational and interdenominational churches in 280.4
>
> See Manual at 291: Denominations and sects
>
> (Option: Class a specific denomination or sect requiring local emphasis in 289.2)

.92	Jehovah's Witnesses
.93	African independent churches

> Independent denominations originating in Africa and not connected to another denomination
>
> Including Celestial Church of Christ, Cherubim and Seraphim Church, Eglise de Jésus-Christ sur la terre par le prophète Simon Kimbangu

.94	Pentecostal churches

> Including Assemblies of God, United Pentecostal Church
>
> Class comprehensive works on the pentecostal movement in general church history in 270.82

.95	Independent fundamentalist and evangelical churches

> Including Evangelical Free Church of America, Independent Fundamental Churches of America
>
> Class comprehensive works on fundamentalist, evangelical movements in general church history in 270.82

.96	Unification Church
.97	Unity School of Christianity
.98	New Thought

> Class eclectic New Thought, comprehensive works in 299.93

290 Comparative religion and religions other than Christianity

See Manual at 290

SUMMARY

291		Comparative religion
	.04	Special topics
	.1	Religious mythology, social theology, interreligious relations and attitudes
	.2	Doctrines
	.3	Public worship and other practices
	.4	Religious experience, life, practice
	.5	Moral theology
	.6	Leaders and organization
	.7	Missions and religious education
	.8	Sources
	.9	Sects and reform movements
292		Classical (Greek and Roman) religion
	.001–.009	Standard subdivisions
	.07–.08	Classical religion by specific culture
	.1–.9	Specific elements
293		Germanic religion
294		Religions of Indic origin
	.3	Buddhism
	.4	Jainism
	.5	Hinduism
	.6	Sikhism
295		Zoroastrianism (Mazdaism, Parseeism)
296		Judaism
	.01–.09	Standard subdivisions
	.1	Sources
	.3	Theology, ethics, views of social issues
	.4	Traditions, rites, public services
	.6	Leaders, organization, religious education, outreach activity
	.7	Religious experience, life, practice
	.8	Denominations and movements
297		Islam, Babism, Bahai Faith
	.1	Sources of Islam
	.2	Islamic doctrinal theology ('Aqā'id and Kalām); Islam and secular disciplines; Islam and other systems of belief
	.3	Islamic worship
	.4	Sufism (Islamic mysticism)
	.5	Islamic moral theology and religious experience, life, practice
	.6	Islamic leaders and organization
	.7	Protection and propagation of Islam
	.8	Islamic sects and reform movements
	.9	Babism and Bahai Faith
299		Other religions
	.1–.4	Religions of Indo-European, Semitic, North African, North and West Asian, Dravidian origin
	.5	Religions of East and Southeast Asian origin
	.6	Religions originating among Black Africans and people of Black African descent
	.7	Religions of North American native origin
	.8	Religions of South American native origin
	.9	Religions of other origin

291 Comparative religion

Class here works dealing with various religions, with religious topics not applied to specific religions; syncretistic religious writings of individuals expressing personal views and not claiming to establish a new religion or to represent an old one

Class treatment of religious topics with respect to philosophy of religion, natural theology in 210; class treatment with respect to Christianity in 220–280; class treatment with respect to a specific religion other than Christianity in 292–299

See Manual at at 291; also at 299.93: New Age religions

(Option: To give preferred treatment or shorter numbers to a specific religion other than Christianity, class it in this number, and add to base number 291 the numbers following the base number for that religion in 292–299, e.g., Hinduism 291, Mahabharata 291.923; if the option is followed, class comparative religion in 290, its subdivision 291.04 in 290.04, its subdivisions 291.1–291.9 in 290.1–290.9. Other options are described at 292–299)

SUMMARY

291.04	Special topics
.1	Religious mythology, social theology, interreligious relations and attitudes
.2	Doctrines
.3	Public worship and other practices
.4	Religious experience, life, practice
.5	Moral theology
.6	Leaders and organization
.7	Missions and religious education
.8	Sources
.9	Sects and reform movements

[.01] Philosophy and theory

Relocated to 210

[.011] Systems

Relocated to 200.11

[.012] Classification

Do not use; class in 291.14

[.013] Value

Relocated to 200.13

[.014] Language and communication

Relocated to 210.14

[.015] Scientific principles

Relocated to 200.15

[.019] Psychological principles

Relocated to 200.19

[.02–.03]	Standard subdivisions
	Relocated to 200.2–200.3
.04	Special topics
.042	Prehistoric religions and religions of nonliterate peoples
.046	Religions of 19th and 20th century origin
[.05]	Serial publications
	Relocated to 200.5
[.06]	Organizations and management
	Do not use for management; class in 291.6
	Organizations relocated to 291.65
[.07–.09]	Standard subdivisions
	Relocated to 200.7–200.9
.1	**Religious mythology, social theology, interreligious relations and attitudes**
.13	Mythology and mythological foundations
	Stories of primeval history, beings, origins, and customs archetypally significant in the sacred life, doctrine, and ritual of religions
	Class sources in 291.8. Class myths on a specific subject with the subject, e.g., creation myths 291.24
	See Manual at 398.2 vs. 291.13
.14	General classes of religions
	Including goddess religions; monotheistic, nontheistic, pantheistic, polytheistic religions
	Class here classification of religions [*formerly also* 200.12, 210.12]
	Class philosophic treatment of concepts of God in 211; class concepts of God or the gods in world religions in 291.211
.144	Shamanism
	Class shamanism in a specific religion with the religion, e.g., shamanism in religions of North American native origin 299.7
.17	Social theologies and interreligious relations and attitudes
	Attitudes of religions toward and influences on secular matters, attitudes toward other religions, interreligious relations
.171	Role of organized religions in society
	Class specific socioeconomic problems in 291.178

.172	Interreligious relations	

Including relations of religions with irreligion

.175	Religions and secular disciplines	

Including communications media, literature, medicine, psychology, science, technology

.177	Religions and political affairs	

Attitudes toward and influences on political activities and ideologies

Including civil war and revolution

Class here religions and civil rights

Class secular view of religiously oriented political theories and ideologies in 320.55; class secular view of relation of state to religious organizations and groups in 322.1

> *For religion and international affairs, see 291.1787*

> *See Manual at 322.1 vs. 261.7, 291.177*

.177 2	Religious freedom
.177 3	Theocracy

Supremacy of organized religion over civil government

.178	Religions and socioeconomic problems

> *For religions and political affairs, see 291.177*

> *See also 361.75 for welfare work of religious organizations*

.178 3	Social problems
.178 32	Social welfare problems and services
.178 321–.178 325	Problems of and services to persons with illnesses and disabilities, the poor

Add to base number 291.17832 the numbers following 362 in 362.1–362.5, e.g., attitude of religions toward alcoholism 291.17832292, toward the poor 291.178325

.178 326	Hunger
.178 327	Abuse within the family
.178 327 1	Child abuse and neglect

> *For sexual abuse, see 291.1783272*

.178 327 2	Sexual abuse
.178 327 3	Adults who were victims of abuse as children
.178 328	Refugees and victims of political oppression

.178 33	Crime and punishment

> Add to base number 291.17833 the numbers following 364 in 364.1–364.8, e.g., attitude of religions toward treason 291.17833131, toward capital punishment 291.1783366

.178 34	Relations of age groups, the sexes, social classes, language groups, ethnic groups

> Add to base number 291.17834 the numbers following 305 in 305.2–305.8, e.g., attitude of religions toward women 291.178344; however, for attitudes toward various religions, see 291.172; for attitude toward the poor, see 291.178325

.178 35	Sexual relations, marriage, divorce, family

> Add to base number 291.17835 the numbers following 306 in 306.7–306.8, e.g., attitude of religions toward homosexuality 291.17835766

> Class abuse within the family in 291.178327

.178 36	Ecology and population

> Add to base number 291.17836 the numbers following 304 in 304.2–304.8, e.g., attitude of religions toward ecology 291.178362

.178 5	The economic order

> Including management of business enterprises

.178 7	International affairs
.178 73	War and peace

> Including attitude of religions toward pacifism, conscientious objectors

.178 732	Nuclear weapons and nuclear war
.2	**Doctrines**

Class here beliefs, apologetics, polemics, comprehensive works on theology

For social theologies, see 291.17; for moral theology, see 291.5

.21	Objects of worship and veneration

Class here animism, spiritism

.211	God, gods, goddesses, divinities and deities
.211 2	Attributes of God, of the gods

For attributes of male gods, see 291.2113; for attributes of female goddesses, see 291.2114

.211 3	Male gods

.211 4		Female goddesses
		See also 291.14 for goddess religions
.211 7		Relation to the world
		Including miracles, prophecy, providence, revelation, relation to and action in history
		For creation and cosmology, see 291.24
.211 8		Theodicy
		Vindication of God's justice and goodness in permitting existence of evil and suffering
.212		Nature
		Including fire, sex, sun, trees, water
.213		Persons
		Including ancestors, the dead, heroes, monarchs, saints
.214		Personified abstractions
.215		Good spirits
		Class here angels
.216		Evil spirits
		Class here demons, devils
.218		Images
.22		Humankind
		Including atonement, creation of humankind, repentance, salvation, sin, soul
		Class here comprehensive works on karma
		Class creation of the world in 291.24
		For eschatology, see 291.23. For a specific aspect of karma, see the aspect, e.g., karma as a concept in Buddhist moral theology 294.35
		See Manual at 291: Common terms
.23		Eschatology
		Including death, end of the world, heaven, hell, immortality, other worlds, punishments, purgatory, resurrection, rewards
.237		Reincarnation
.24		Creation and cosmology
		For creation of humankind, see 291.22

.3		**Public worship and other practices**

Practices predominantly public or collective in character

Unless other instructions are given, class a subject with aspects in two or more subdivisions of 291.3 in the number coming first, e.g., religious healing and ceremonies connected with it 291.31 (*not* 291.38)

Class comprehensive works on worship in 291.43; class leaders and organization in 291.6; class missions and religious education in 291.7

.31	Religious healing

See Manual at 615.852 vs. 234.131, 291.31

.32	Divination

Including omens, oracles, prophecies

.33	Witchcraft
.34	Offerings, sacrifices, penances
.35	Pilgrimages and sacred places

Including grottoes, holy buildings, pagodas, shrines, temples

Class monasteries in 291.657

.350 93–.350 99	Treatment by specific continents, countries, localities

Class here pilgrimages to specific sacred places

.351	Pilgrimages [*formerly* 291.446]
[.351 093–.351 099]	Treatment by specific continents, countries, localities

Do not use; class in 291.35093–291.35099

.36	Sacred times

Including holy days, liturgical year, religious calendar, religious festivals

See Manual at 263.9, 291.36 vs. 394.265–394.267

.37	Symbolism, symbolic objects, emblems, sounds

Including mandalas, mantras

Class here religious use, significance, purpose of the arts

See Manual at 291: Common terms

.38	Rites and ceremonies

Conduct and texts

Including liturgy, music, processions, public feasts and fasts, public prayer

Class interdisciplinary works on sacred music in 781.7; class interdisciplinary works on sacred vocal music in 782.22

.4	**Religious experience, life, practice**
	Practices predominantly private or individual in character
	Class here spirituality
	Class moral theology in 291.5
.42	Religious experience
	Including conversion, enlightenment
.422	Mysticism
.43	Worship, meditation, yoga
	Class here description, interpretation, criticism, history; practical works on prayer, on contemplation; comprehensive works on worship
	For public worship, see 291.3
.432	Devotional literature
	Including meditations
.433	Prayer books
.435	Meditation
.436	Yoga
	Religious and spiritual discipline
	Including kundalini yoga
	Class interdisciplinary works on yoga in 181.45
	For Hindu kundalini yoga, see 294.5436
	See also 613.7046 for physical yoga (hatha yoga)
	See Manual at 291: Common terms
.44	Religious life and practice
	For worship, meditation, yoga, see 291.43; for moral theology, see 291.5
[.440 85]	Relatives Parents
	Do not use; class in 291.441
.440 86	Persons by miscellaneous social characteristics
[.440 865 5]	Married persons
	Do not use; class in 291.441

111

.441	Marriage and family life

>Including religious training of children in the home
>
>Class here comprehensive works on marriage
>
>>*For marriage as a concern in social theology, see 291.1783581; for ethics of marriage, see 291.563*

.442	Persons experiencing illness, trouble, addiction, bereavement

>*See Manual at 616.86 vs. 158.1, 248.8629, 291.442, 362.29*

.446	Individual observances

>Not provided for elsewhere
>
>Including almsgiving, ceremonial and ritual observances, observance of restrictions and limitations
>
>Pilgrimages relocated to 291.351

.447	Asceticism

>Including practice of celibacy, fasting and abstinence, poverty, solitude

[.448]	Guides to religious life

>Number discontinued; class in 291.44

.5	**Moral theology**

>Including conscience, sin, vice, virtue

.56	Specific moral issues, sins, vices, virtues

>Add to base number 291.56 the numbers following 17 in 172–179, e.g., morality of discriminatory practices 291.5675

.6	**Leaders and organization**

>Class here management [*formerly also* 200.68]

.61	Leaders and their work

>Variant names: clergy, gurus, messiahs, ministers, pastors, priests, prophets, shamans
>
>Role, function, duties
>
>Including pastoral counseling and preaching
>
>Class here role, function, duties of persons endowed with supernatural power [*formerly* 291.62], divinely inspired persons [*formerly* 291.63], interpreters of religion [*formerly* 291.64]
>
>Class theologians in 291.2. Class a specific activity of a leader with the activity, e.g., religious healing by shamans 291.31
>
>>*For founders of religions, see 291.63*
>>
>>*See Manual at 200.92 and 291–299*

[.610 92]		Persons
		Do not use; class as instructed in Manual at 200.92 and 291–299
[.62]		Persons endowed with supernatural power
		Relocated to 291.61
.63		Founders of religions
		Divinely inspired persons relocated to 291.61
[.630 92]		Persons
		Do not use; class as instructed in Manual at 200.92 and 291–299
[.64]		Interpreters of religion
		Relocated to 291.61
.65		Organizations [*formerly also* 200.6, 291.06] and organization
		Including associations, congregations, institutions, orders, parties; exercise of religious authority
		Class laws and decisions in 291.84
.657		Monasticism and monasteries
.7		**Missions and religious education**
.72		Missions
.75		Religious education
		Class here comprehensive works on religious education and religion as an academic subject
		For education in and teaching of comparative religion, religion as an academic subject, see 200.71
		See Manual at 291.75 vs. 200.71
.8		**Sources**
		Class theology based on sacred sources in 291.2
.82		Sacred books and scriptures
.83		Oral traditions
.84		Laws and decisions
		Class civil law relating to religious matters in 340
		See also 364.188 for offenses against religion as defined and penalized by the state
.85		Sources of sects and reform movements

.9 **Sects and reform movements**

Class specific aspects of sects and reform movements in 291.1–291.8

See Manual at 291: Denominations and sects; also at 299.93: New Age religions

> ## 292–299 Religions other than Christianity

Except for modifications shown under specific entries, add to each subdivision identified by † as follows:

```
01–05    Standard subdivisions
[06]     Organizations and management
             Do not use for management; class in 6
             Organizations relocated to 65
07       Education, research, related topics
071          Education
                 Class here the religion as an academic subject
                 Class comprehensive works on religious education,
                 religious education to inculcate religious faith and practice
                 in 75
                    See Manual at 291.75 vs. 200.71
08–09    Standard subdivisions
1–9      Specific elements
             Add the numbers following 291 in 291.1–291.9, e.g.,
             organizations 65 [formerly —06]
```

Class comprehensive works in 291

See Manual at 291; also at 200.92 and 291–299

(Options: To give preferred treatment or shorter numbers to a specific religion, use one of the following:

(Option A: Class the religion in 230–280, its sources in 220, comprehensive works in 200; in that case class the Bible and Christianity in 298

(Option B: Class in 210, and add to base number 21 the numbers following the base number for the religion in 292–299, e.g., Hinduism 210, Mahabharata 219.23; in that case class philosophy and theory of religion in 200, its subdivisions 211–218 in 201–208, standard subdivisions of religion in 200.01–200.09

(Option C: Class in 291, and add to base number 291 the numbers following the base number for that religion in 292–299, e.g., Hinduism 291, Mahabharata 291.923; in that case class comparative religion in 290, its subdivision 291.04 in 290.04, its subdivisions 291.1–291.9 in 290.1–290.9

(Option D: Class in 298, which is permanently unassigned

(Option E: Place first by use of a letter or other symbol, e.g., Hinduism 2H0 (preceding 220), or 29H (preceding 291 or 292); add to the base number thus derived, e.g., to 2H or to 29H, the numbers following the base number for the religion in 292–299, e.g., Shivaism 2H5.13 or 29H.513)

292 Classical (Greek and Roman) religion

See also 299 for modern revivals of classical religions

See Manual at 291; also at 200.92 and 291–299

.001–.005	Standard subdivisions
[.006]	Organizations and management

          Do not use for management; class in 292.6

          Organizations relocated to 292.65

.007	Education, research, related topics
.007 1	Education

          Class here classical religion as an academic subject

          Class comprehensive works on religious education, religious education to inculcate religious faith and practice in 292.75

          See Manual at 291.75 vs. 200.71

.008–.009	Standard subdivisions

> 292.07–292.08 Classical religion by specific culture

          Class specific elements regardless of culture in 292.1–292.9; class comprehensive works in 292

.07	Roman
.08	Greek
.1–.9	**Specific elements**

          Add to base number 292 the numbers following 291 in 291.1–291.9, e.g., organizations 292.65 [*formerly* 292.006], mythology 292.13

          Class classical religion as an academic subject in 292.0071

293 †Germanic religion

See also 299 for modern revivals of Germanic religion

See Manual at 291; also at 200.92 and 291–299

294 Religions of Indic origin

Including Divine Light Mission, Radha Soami Satsang

See Manual at 200.9 vs. 294, 299.5

---

†Add as instructed under 292–299

SUMMARY

294.3	**Buddhism**
.4	**Jainism**
.5	**Hinduism**
.6	**Sikhism**

.3 Buddhism

See Manual at 291; also at 200.92 and 291–299

[.306]   Organizations and management

Do not use for management; class in 294.36

Organizations relocated to 294.365

.307   Education, research, related topics

.307 1   Education

Class here Buddhism as an academic subject

Class comprehensive works on religious education, religious education to inculcate religious faith and practice in 294.375

See Manual at 291.75 vs. 200.71

.33   Mythology, social theology, interreligious relations and attitudes

Add to base number 294.33 the numbers following 291.1 in 291.13–291.17, e.g., social theology 294.337

.34   Doctrines and practices

.342   Doctrines

For social theology, see 294.337; for moral theology, see 294.35

.342 04   Doctrines of specific branches, sects, reform movements

Add to base number 294.34204 the numbers following 294.39 in 294.391–294.392, e.g., Zen doctrines 294.3420427

.342 1–.342 4   Specific doctrines

Add to base number 294.342 the numbers following 291.2 in 291.21–291.24, e.g., reincarnation 294.34237

.343–.344   Public worship and other practices, religious experience, life, practice

Add to base number 294.34 the numbers following 291 in 291.3–291.4, e.g., religious experience 294.3442

.35–.37   Moral theology, leaders and organization, missions, religious education

Add to base number 294.3 the numbers following 291 in 291.5–291.7, e.g., organizations 294.365 [*formerly also* 294.306], the Buddha 294.363

See Manual at 291.75 vs. 200.71

.38		Sources
.382		Sacred books and scriptures (Tripiṭaka, Tipiṭaka)

> Works sacred to both Theravadins and Mahayanists
>
> Class here comprehensive treatment of Theravadin and Mahayanist sacred texts
>
> *For works sacred only to Mahayanists, see 294.385*

.382 2		Vinayapiṭaka
.382 3		Sūtrapiṭaka (Suttapiṭaka)
.382 32		Khuddakanikāya
.382 322		Dhammapada
.382 325		Jatakas
.382 4		Abhidharmapiṭaka (Abhidhammapiṭaka)
.383		Oral traditions
.384		Laws and decisions
.385		Sources of branches, sects, reform movements

> Including Buddhist Tantras, Mahayanist sacred works

.39		Branches, sects, reform movements

> Class specific aspects of branches, sects, reform movements in 294.33–294.38

.391		Theravada (Southern, Hinayana) Buddhism

> Including Mahasanghika, Saravastivada, Sautrantika schools

.392		Mahayana (Northern) Buddhism

> Including Madhyamika, Yogacara (Vijnana) schools

.392 3		Tibetan Buddhism (Lamaism)

> *See also 299.54 for Bon*

.392 5		Tantric Buddhism
.392 6		Pure Land sects
.392 7		Zen (Ch'an)

> Including Rinzai, Soto

.392 8		Nichiren Shoshu and Sōka Gakkai
.4	**†Jainism**	

> *See Manual at 291; also at 200.92 and 291–299*

---

†Add as instructed under 292–299

.49		Sects and reform movements

Number built according to instructions under 292–299

Class specific aspects of sects and reform movements in 294.41–294.48

.492		Svetambara
.493		Digambara
.5		**Hinduism**

Class here Brahmanism

See Manual at 291; also at 200.92 and 291–299

SUMMARY

294.501–.509	Standard subdivisions
.51–.53	Mythology, relations, doctrines, public worship
.54	Religious experience, life, practice, moral theology
.55	Sects and reform movements
.56–.57	Leaders, organization, missions, religious education
.59	Sources

[.506]	Organizations and management

Do not use for management; class in 294.56

Organizations relocated to 294.565

.507	Education, research, related topics
.507 1	Education

Class here Hinduism as an academic subject

Class comprehensive works on religious education, religious education to inculcate religious faith and practice in 294.575

See Manual at 291.75 vs. 200.71

.509	Historical, geographic, persons treatment
.509 013	3999–1000 B.C.

Class here religion of Vedic period

.51–.53	Mythology, relations, doctrines, public worship

Add to base number 294.5 the numbers following 291 in 291.1–291.3, e.g., attitude toward science 294.5175

.54	Religious experience, life, practice, moral theology

Practices predominantly private or individual in character

Class here spirituality

.542	Religious experience

Including conversion, enlightenment

.542 2		Mysticism
.543		Worship, meditation, yoga

> Class here description, interpretation, criticism, history, practical works on prayer, on contemplation; comprehensive works on worship
>
> *For public worship, see 294.53*

.543 2		Devotional literature

> Including meditations

.543 3		Prayer books
.543 5		Meditation
.543 6		Yoga

> Religious and spiritual discipline
>
> Including bhakti yoga, jnana yoga, karma yoga, kundalini yoga, raja yoga
>
> Class yoga philosophy, raja yoga philosophy, interdisciplinary works on yoga in 181.45
>
> *See also 613.7046 for physical yoga (hatha yoga)*
>
> *See Manual at 291: Common terms*

.544		Religious life and practice

> Add to base number 294.544 the numbers following 291.44 in 291.441–291.447, e.g., asceticism 294.5447

.548		Moral theology

> Including conscience, dharma, sin, vice

.548 6		Specific moral issues, sins, vices, virtues

> Add to base number 294.5486 the numbers following 17 in 172–179, e.g., morality of family relationships 294.54863

.55		Sects and reform movements

> Class Buddhism in 294.3; class Jainism in 294.4; class Sikhism in 294.6. Class a specific aspect of a Hindu sect or reform movement with the subject, e.g., doctrines of Vishnuism 294.52

.551		Early Hindu sects
.551 2		Vishnuism

> Including International Society for Krishna Consciousness

.551 3		Shivaism

> Including Lingayats

.551 4		Shaktaism

.551 4 Shaktaism

> Class here Tantric Hinduism

.551 5 Ganapataism

.551 6 Shanmukaism

.551 7 Sauraism

.555 Ramakrishna movement

.556 Reformed Hinduism

.556 2 Brahma Samaj

.556 3 Arya-Samaj

.56–.57 Leaders, organization, missions, religious education

> Add to base number 294.5 the numbers following 291 in 291.6–291.7, e.g., organizations 294.565 [*formerly also* 294.506], the role of the guru 294.561
>
> Class Hinduism as an academic subject in 294.5071
>
> *See Manual at 291.75 vs. 200.71*

.59 Sources

.592 Sacred books and scriptures

> Add to each subdivision identified by * as follows:
>
> 04 Special topics
> 041 Sanskrit texts
>   Including textual criticism
>   Class Sanskrit texts accompanied by translations in 045; class Sanskrit texts accompanied by commentaries in 047
> 045 Translations
>   Class here Sanskrit texts accompanied by translations
>   Add to 045 notation 1–9 from Table 6, e.g., translations into English 04521
>   Class texts accompanied by commentaries in 047
> 046 Interpretation and criticism
>   *For textual criticism, see 041; for commentaries, see 047*
> 047 Commentaries
>   Criticism and interpretation arranged in textual order
>   Including texts accompanied by commentaries
> 048 Nonreligious subjects treated in sacred books and scriptures
>   Class a religious subject treated in sacred books and scriptures with the subject, e.g., rites and ceremonies 294.538

.592 1 *Vedic literature

---

*Add as instructed under 294.592

	294.592 12–294.592 15	The Vedas

>

Class here Samhitas, Brahmanas, Aranyakas

Class Upanishads in 294.59218; class Vedic religion in 294.509013; class comprehensive works on the Vedas in 294.5921

.592 12	*Rigveda
.592 13	*Samaveda
.592 14	*Yajurveda
.592 15	*Atharvaveda
.592 18	Upanishads
.592 2	*Ramayana
.592 3	*Mahabharata

> For Bhagavad Gita, see 294.5924

.592 4	*Bhagavad Gita
.592 5	Puranas
.592 6	Dharmasastras

> Including Code of Manu

.593	Oral traditions
.594	Laws and decisions
.595	Sources of sects and reform movements

> Including Hindu tantras

.6	†Sikhism

> See Manual at 291; also at 200.92 and 291–299

.663	Founders of Sikhism

> Number built according to instructions under 292–299
>
> Class here role and function of the ten founding gurus

295 †Zoroastrianism (Mazdaism, Parseeism)

Class Mithraism in 299.15

See Manual at 291; also at 200.92 and 291–299

296 Judaism

---

*Add as instructed under 294.592
†Add as instructed under 292–299

SUMMARY

296.01–.09	Standard subdivisions
.1	Sources
.3	Theology, ethics, views of social issues
.4	Traditions, rites, public services
.6	Leaders, organization, religious education, outreach activity
.7	Religious experience, life, practice
.8	Denominations and movements

[.06]   Organizations and management

         Do not use for management; class in 296.6

         Organizations relocated to 296.67

.071   Education

         Class here Judaism as an academic subject

         Class comprehensive works on Jewish religious education, religious education to inculcate religious faith and practice in 296.68

         See Manual at 291.75 vs. 200.71

.071 1   Higher education

         Class here Jewish theological faculties, rabbinical seminaries, yeshivot, education of rabbis

.09   Historical, geographic, persons treatment

         Class here history of specific synagogues [*formerly* 296.8]

         See also 320.54095694 for Zionism, 909.04924 for world history of Jews

---

>   296.090 1–296.090 5   Historical periods

         Add to each subdivision identified by * as instructed under —0901–0905 in Table 1, e.g., museums of ancient Judaism 296.0901074

         Class comprehensive works in 296.09

.090 1   *To 499 A.D.

.090 13   *Earliest Judaism to 586 B.C.

         Including 999–586 B.C. [*formerly* 296.09014]

.090 14   *Second Temple period, 586 B.C.–70 A.D.

         Including 1–70 A.D. [*formerly* 296.09015]

         999–586 B.C. relocated to 296.09013

.090 15   *Early rabbinic period, 70–499

         1–70 A.D. relocated to 296.09014

---

*Add as instructed under 296.0901–296.0905

.090 2–.090 5		6th–21st centuries

Add to base number 296.090 the numbers following —090 in notation 0902–0905 from Table 1, e.g., Judaism in the Middle Ages 296.0902

.092	Persons

Class here persons not associated with one activity or denomination

Class a person associated with one activity or denomination with the activity or denomination with which the person is associated, e.g., a theologian 296.3092, a Reform rabbi 296.8341092

.1	**Sources**

Class Jewish theology based on these sources in 296.3

For Torah and sacred scripture (Tanakh, Old Testament), see 221

See Manual at 221

SUMMARY

296.12	**Talmudic literature**
.14	**Midrash**
.15	**Sources of specific sects and movements**
.16	**Cabalistic literature**
.18	**Halakhah (Legal literature)**
.19	**Aggadah (Nonlegal literature)**

(.11)	Tanakh

(Optional number; prefer 221)

Arranged as found in Jewish Bibles

See Manual at 221: Optional numbers for books of Tanakh

[.110 3]	Dictionaries, encyclopedias, concordances

Do not use for dictionaries and encyclopedias; class in 296.1113. Do not use for concordances; class in 296.1114–296.1115

(.111)	Generalities

(Optional number; prefer 221)

Add to base number 296.111 the numbers following 221 in 221.04–221.9, e.g., criticism and interpretation 296.1116

(.112)	*‡Torah (Pentateuch)
(.112 1)	*‡Genesis
(.112 2)	*‡Exodus

For Ten Commandments, see 296.1126

---

*Add as instructed under 221–229

‡(Optional number; prefer 222–224)

(.112 3)	*‡Leviticus
(.112 4)	*‡Numbers
(.112 5)	*‡Deuteronomy

> For Ten Commandments, see 296.1126

(.112 6)	*‡Ten Commandments (Decalogue)
(.113)	*‡Prophetic books (Nevi'im)
(.113 1)	*Former Prophets (Nevi'im rishonim)

> (Optional number; prefer 222)
>
> For individual books of Former Prophets, see 296.1132–296.1135

(.113 2)	*‡Joshua
(.113 3)	*‡Judges
(.113 4)	*‡Samuel
(.113 41)	*‡Samuel 1
(.113 42)	*‡Samuel 2
(.113 5)	*‡Kings
(.113 51)	*‡Kings 1
(.113 52)	*‡Kings 2
(.113 6)	*Later Prophets (Nevi'im aharonim)

> (Optional number; prefer 224)
>
> For Isaiah, see 296.1137; for Jeremiah, see 296.1138; for Ezekiel, see 296.1139; for Minor Prophets, see 296.114

(.113 7)	*‡Isaiah
(.113 8)	*‡Jeremiah
(.113 9)	*‡Ezekiel
(.114)	*‡Minor Prophets

> For Zephaniah, Haggai, Zechariah, Malachi, see 296.115

(.114 1)	*‡Hosea
(.114 2)	*‡Joel
(.114 3)	*‡Amos
(.114 4)	*‡Obadiah
(.114 5)	*‡Jonah
(.114 6)	*‡Micah

*Add as instructed under 221–229

‡(Optional number; prefer 222–224)

(.114 7)	*‡Nahum
(.114 8)	*‡Habakkuk
(.115)	*‡Zephaniah, Haggai, Zechariah, Malachi
(.115 1)	*‡Zephaniah
(.115 2)	*‡Haggai
(.115 3)	*‡Zechariah
(.115 4)	*‡Malachi
(.116)	*‡Writings (Ketuvim)
(.116 1)	*‡Psalms
(.116 2)	*‡Proverbs
(.116 3)	*‡Job
(.116 4)	*Megillot (Five scrolls)
	(Optional number; prefer 221.044)
(.116 41)	*‡Song of Solomon (Canticle of Canticles, Song of Songs)
(.116 42)	*‡Ruth
(.116 43)	*‡Lamentations
(.116 44)	*‡Ecclesiastes (Kohelet, Qohelet)
(.116 45)	*‡Esther
(.116 5)	*‡Daniel
(.116 6)	*‡Ezra
(.116 7)	*‡Nehemiah
(.116 8)	*‡Chronicles
(.116 81)	*‡Chronicles 1
(.116 82)	*‡Chronicles 2
(.118)	*Apocrypha
	(Optional number; prefer 229)
	For pseudepigrapha, see 229.9
(.118 1)	*Esdras 1 and 2
	(Optional number; prefer 229.1)
	Variant names: Esdras 3 and 4
	See also 296.1166 for Ezra, 296.1167 for Nehemiah

*Add as instructed under 221–229

‡(Optional number; prefer 222–224)

(.118 2)	*Tobit, Judith, Additions to Esther
	(Optional number; prefer 229.2)
(.118 22)	*Tobit
	(Optional number; prefer 229.22)
(.118 24)	*Judith
	(Optional number; prefer 229.24)
(.118 27)	*Additions to Esther
	(Optional number; prefer 229.27)
(.118 3)	*Wisdom of Solomon (Wisdom)
	(Optional number; prefer 229.3)
	Class here Apocryphal wisdom literature
	For Ecclesiasticus, see 296.1184
(.118 4)	*Ecclesiasticus (Sirach)
	(Optional number; prefer 229.4)
(.118 5)	*Baruch and Epistle of Jeremiah
	(Optional number; prefer 229.5)
(.118 6)	*Song of the Three Children, Susanna, Bel and the Dragon
	(Optional number; prefer 229.6)
(.118 7)	*Maccabees (Machabees)
	(Optional number; prefer 229.7)
(.118 73)	*Maccabees 1 and 2 (Machabees 1 and 2)
	(Optional number; prefer 229.73)
(.118 75)	*Maccabees 3 and 4 (Machabees 3 and 4)
	(Optional number; prefer 229.75)
(.118 8)	*Prayer of Manasseh
	(Optional number; prefer 229.6)

*Add as instructed under 221–229

>	296.12–296.14	Talmudic literature and Midrash

Add to each subdivision identified by ‡ as follows:
- 001–009   Standard subdivisions
- 04   Hebrew and Aramaic texts
    - Including textual criticism
    - Class texts accompanied by modern commentaries since 1500 in 07
- 05   Translations
    - Add to 05 notation 1–9 from Table 6, e.g., literature in English 0521
    - Class texts accompanied by modern commentaries since 1500 in 07
- 06   Interpretation and criticism (Exegesis)
    - Add to 06 the numbers following 220.6 in 220.601–220.68, e.g., historical criticism 067
    - *For textual criticism, see 04; for modern commentaries since 1500, see 07*
- 07   Modern commentaries since 1500
    - Criticism and interpretation arranged in textual order
    - Including texts accompanied by modern commentaries
    - Commentaries written before 1500 are classed with the text without addition of 07
    - *See Manual at 296.12–296.14: Add table: 07*
- 08   Nonreligious subjects treated in Talmudic literature and Midrash
    - Add to base number 08 notation 001–999, e.g., natural sciences in Talmudic literature and Midrash 085
    - Class a religious subject treated in Talmudic literature and Midrash with the subject, e.g., Jewish ethics 296.36

Class comprehensive works in 296.1

.12	‡Talmudic literature
.120 092	Persons
	Number built according to instructions under 296.12–296.14
	Class here Soferim, Tannaim, Amoraim, Geonim
.123	‡Mishnah
.123 1	‡Order Zera'im
	Including tractates Berakhot, Bikkurim, Demai, Ḥallah, Kilayim, Ma'aser Sheni, Ma'aserot, Orlah, Pe'ah, Shevi'it, Terumot
.123 2	‡Order Mo'ed
	Including tractates Beẓah, Eruvin, Ḥagigah, Megillah, Mo'ed Katan, Pesaḥim, Rosh Hashanah, Shabbat, Shekalim, Sukkah, Ta'anit, Yoma

‡Add as instructed under 296.12–296.14

.123 3		‡Order Nashim

Including tractates Gittin, Ketubbot, Kiddushin, Nazir, Nedarim, Sotah, Yevamot

.123 4		‡Order Nezikin

Including tractates Avodah Zarah, Bava Batra, Bava Kamma, Bava Meẓia, Eduyyot, Horayot, Makkot, Sanhedrin, Shevu'ot

.123 47		‡Tractate Avot (Pirke Avot)
.123 5		‡Order Kodashim

Including tractates Arakhin, Bekhorot, Ḥullin, Keritot, Kinnim, Me'ilah, Menaḥot, Middot, Tamid, Temurah, Zevaḥim

.123 6		‡Order Tohorot

Including tractates Kelim, Makhshirin, Mikva'ot, Nega'im, Niddah, Oholot (Ahilot), Parah, Tevul Yom, Tohorot, Ukẓin, Yadayim, Zavim

.123 7		Minor tractates
.124		‡Palestinian Talmud (Jerusalem Talmud, Talmud Yerushalmi)
.124 1–.124 7		Individual orders and tractates

Add to base number 296.124 the numbers following 296.123 in 296.1231–296.1237, e.g., Order Zera'im in Palestinian Talmud 296.1241

.125		‡Babylonian Talmud

Often called simply the Talmud

.125 1–.125 7		Individual orders and tractates

Add to base number 296.125 the numbers following 296.123 in 296.1231–296.1237, e.g., tractate Shabbat in Babylonian Talmud 296.1252

.126		Tosefta and Baraita
.126 2		‡Tosefta
.126 21–.126 27		Individual orders and tractates

Add to base number 296.1262 the numbers following 296.123 in 296.1231–296.1237, e.g., order Nezikin in Tosefta 296.12624

.126 3		‡Baraita
.127		Specific types of Talmudic literature
.127 4		‡Halakhah
.127 6		‡Aggadah
.14	‡Midrash	

‡Add as instructed under 296.12–296.14

	.141	‡Midrashic Halakhah
	.142	‡Midrashic Aggadah
	.15	Sources of specific sects and movements
	.155	Writings of Qumran community

> Class here comprehensive works on Dead Sea Scrolls
>
> *For Old Testament texts in Dead Sea Scrolls, see 221.44; for pseudepigrapha in Dead Sea Scrolls, see 229.91*
>
> See also 296.815 for comprehensive works on Qumran community

.16 Cabalistic literature

> Class here interdisciplinary works on cabala
>
> The texts of religious cabalistic works are classed here even if the editor introduces and annotates them from an occult or Christian point of view
>
> Class Jewish mystical experience in 296.712; class Jewish mystical movements in 296.8
>
> *For cabalistic traditions in occultism, see 135.47*

.162 Zohar

[.17] Early rabbinical writings to 1400

> Early rabbinical legal writings, comprehensive works on rabbinical writings to 1400 relocated to 296.18

.18 Halakhah (Legal literature)

> Including early rabbinical legal writings, comprehensive works on rabbinical writings to 1400 [*formerly* 296.17]
>
> Class here commandments (mitzvot) treated as laws, the 613 commandments, comprehensive works on Jewish law
>
> Class commandments (mitzvot) treated as ethical values in 296.36; class Jewish law relating to secular matters in 340.58
>
> *For Torah, see 222.1; for Talmudic Halakhah, see 296.1274; for Midrashic Halakhah, see 296.141. For early rabbinical writings to 1400 on a specific subject, see the subject, e.g., creation 296.34; for laws on a specific religious topic, see the topic, e.g., laws concerning marriage rites 296.444*
>
> See Manual at 296.18 vs. 340.58

.180 92 Persons

> Class here Rishonim, Aharonim

‡Add as instructed under 296.12–296.14

.181	Legal writings of Maimonides

> Class here comprehensive works on writings of Maimonides
>
> *For philosophical writings of Maimonides, see 181.06. For writings on a specific religious topic, see the topic, e.g., the Thirteen Articles of Faith 296.3*

.181 2	Mishneh Torah
.182	Work of Joseph Caro

> Class here Shulḥan 'arukh

.185	Responsa

> Class responsa on a specific religious topic with the topic, e.g., responsa concerning marriage rites 296.444

.185 4	Responsa of reform movements

> Add to base number 296.1854 the numbers following 296.834 in 296.8341–296.8344, e.g., Reform responsa 296.18541

.188	Nonreligious subjects treated in halakhah
.188 000 1–.188 000 9	Standard subdivisions
.188 001–.188 999	Specific nonreligious subjects treated in halakhah

> Add to base number 296.188 notation 001–999, e.g., agriculture in halakhah 296.18863

.19	Aggadah (Nonlegal literature)

> Stories, legends, parables, proverbs, anecdotes, ancient or modern, told for religious edification
>
> Class here comprehensive works on Aggadah
>
> Class Jewish folklore in 398.2089924
>
> *For Talmudic Aggadah, see 296.1276; for Midrashic Aggadah, see 296.142*
>
> *See also 296.45371 for Passover Haggadah*

.3	**Theology, ethics, views of social issues**

> Standard subdivisions are added for theology, ethics, social issues together; for theology alone
>
> Class here Biblical theology, the Thirteen Articles of Faith
>
> *See also 181.06 for Jewish philosophy*
>
> *See Manual at 100 vs. 200; also at 220: Biblical theology*

.31	God and spiritual beings
.311	God

.311 2		Attributes and names of God
.311 4		Relation to the world

> *For revelation, see 296.3115; for miracles, see 296.3116; for relation to and action in history, see 296.3117; for creation, see 296.34*

.311 5		Revelation
.311 55		Prophecy

> Class Biblical prophecy and prophecies in 221.15; class the prophetic books of the Bible in 224; class messianic prophecies in 296.336

.311 6		Miracles
.311 7		Relation to and action in history
.311 72		Relationship to the Jewish people (Covenant relationship)
.311 73		Land of Israel
.311 74		Specific historical events

> Including the Holocaust

.311 8		Theodicy

> Vindication of God's justice and goodness in permitting existence of evil and suffering

.315		Angels
.316		Devils (Demons)
.32		Humankind

> Including atonement, creation of humankind, free will, repentance, salvation, sin, soul

> *For eschatology, see 296.33*

.33		Eschatology

> Including death, resurrection, immortality

.336		Messianism

> *See also 232.906 for Jewish interpretations of Jesus*

.34		Creation

> *For creation of humankind, see 296.32*

.35		Apologetics and polemics

	.36	Ethics [*formerly* 296.385]

Including Biblical precepts, conscience, ethical wills, sin

Class here general works on commandments (mitzvot) treated as ethical values

Add to base number 296.36 the numbers following 17 in 172–179, e.g., morality of family relationships 296.363

Class works on commandments (mitzvot) treated as laws in 296.18; class guides to conduct of life in 296.7

See also 296.12347 for talmudic tractate Avot (Pirke Avot)

	.37	Judaism and secular disciplines [*formerly* 296.3875]

Class here attitudes of Judaism toward and influence on secular issues, religious views and teachings about secular disciplines, works treating relation between Jewish belief and a secular discipline

Class Jewish philosophy of a secular discipline and Jewish theories within a secular discipline with the discipline, e.g., Jewish philosophy 181.06

For Judaism and social issues, see 296.38

See also 296.12–296.14 for nonreligious subjects treated in Talmudic literature and Midrash, 296.188 for nonreligious subjects treated in halakhah

	.371	Judaism and philosophy, paranormal phenomena, psychology
	.375	Judaism and natural sciences, mathematics
	.376	Judaism and technology

Including Judaism and medicine

	.377	Judaism and the arts
	.38	Judaism and social sciences

Attitudes of Judaism toward and influence on social issues

Including Judaism and human ecology

Class here Judaism and socioeconomic problems, Jewish social theology

Class Jewish view of marriage and family in 296.74

	.382	Judaism and politics [*formerly* 296.3877]

Attitude toward and influence on political activities and ideologies

Class here Judaism and civil rights

See Manual at 322.1 vs. 261.7, 291.177; also at 322.1 vs. 296.382, 320.54095694

.382 7		International affairs, war and peace [*formerly* 296.38787]
		Including attitude of Judaism toward civil and revolutionary wars, conscientious objectors, pacifism
.383		Judaism and economics [*formerly* 296.38785]
[.385]		Ethics
		Relocated to 296.36
[.387]		Social theology
		Number discontinued; class in 296.38
[.387 2]		Judaism and other systems of belief
		Relocated to 296.39
[.387 5]		Judaism and secular disciplines
		Relocated to 296.37
[.387 7]		Judaism and politics
		Relocated to 296.382
[.387 835]		Social theology of marriage and family
		Relocated to 296.74
[.387 85]		Judaism and economics
		Relocated to 296.383
[.387 87]		International affairs, war and peace
		Relocated to 296.3827
.39		Judaism and other systems of belief [*formerly* 296.3872]
		Including Judaism and atheism, Judaism and irreligion
.396		Judaism and Christianity
.397		Judaism and Islam
.4		**Traditions, rites, public services**
		Class individual observances not provided for here in 296.7

SUMMARY

	296.41	Sabbath
	.43	Festivals, holy days, fasts
	.44	Rites and customs for occasions that occur generally once in a lifetime
	.45	Liturgy and prayers
	.46	Use of the arts and symbolism
	.47	Sermons and preaching (Homiletics)
	.48	Pilgrimages and sacred places
	.49	**Traditions, rites, public services of ancient Judaism to 70 A.D.**

.41	Sabbath

>   Liturgy and prayers for Sabbath relocated to 296.45

.412	Prohibited activity
[.42]	Sermons and preaching (Homiletics)

>   Relocated to 296.47

> 296.43–296.44 Festivals, holy days, fasts; rites and customs for occasions that occur generally once in a lifetime
>
> Class here personal ritual observances to be performed at specific times or in conjunction with specific rites
>
> Liturgy and prayers for festivals, holy days, fasts; for occasions that occur generally once in a lifetime relocated to 296.453–296.454
>
> Class comprehensive works in 296.43
>
>> *For specific rites of ancient Judaism to 70 A.D. not provided for elsewhere, see 296.49*

.43	Festivals, holy days, fasts

>   *For Sabbath, see 296.41*
>
>   *See Manual at 263.9, 291.36 vs. 394.265–394.267*

.431	High Holy Days

>   *For Yom Kippur (Day of Atonement), see 296.432*

.431 5	Rosh Hashanah (New Year)
.432	Yom Kippur (Day of Atonement)
.433	Sukkot (Feast of Tabernacles)
.433 9	Simḥat Torah
.435	Hanukkah (Feast of the Dedication)
.436	Purim (Feast of Lots)
.437	Pesach (Passover)
.438	Shavuot (Feast of Weeks, Pentecost)
.439	Other festivals, holy days, fasts

>   Including Lag b'Omer, Tishah b'Av

.439 1	Festivals, holy days, fasts associated with the land of Israel

>   Including Sabbatical Year (shemittah)

.44	Rites and customs for occasions that occur generally once in a lifetime

>   *See also 296.7 for rites and customs which continue throughout life*

.442		Special rites for male Jews
.442 2		Berit milah (Circumcision)
.442 3		Pidyon haben (Redemption of first-born male)
.442 4		Bar mitzvah
.443		Special rites for female Jews

Including naming ceremonies

For observance of laws of family purity, see 296.742

.443 4		Bat mitzvah
.444		Marriage and divorce rites and traditions

Standard subdivisions are added for marriage and divorce rites and traditions together, for marriage rites alone, for marriage traditions alone

Including issues concerning who may be married, descent of Jewish identity

For guides to marriage and family life, see 296.74

.444 3		Interreligious marriage
.444 4		Divorce rites and traditions

Standard subdivisions are added for either or both topics in heading

.445		Burial and mourning rites and traditions

Standard subdivisions are added for any or all topics in heading

Including memorial services

.446		Synagogue dedication
.45		Liturgy and prayers

Description, interpretation, conduct, texts of rites and public services; private and public prayers, blessings, benedictions

Including prayer at meals

Class here liturgy and prayers for Sabbath [*formerly* 296.41]; comprehensive works on worship [*formerly* 296.72]; prayer books, e.g., siddurim; Ashkenazic liturgy

Class devotional reading for the individual in 296.72

.450 4		Liturgy of specific groups

Including Ari liturgy

Class Ashkenazic liturgy or liturgy of unspecified group in 296.45

[.450 401–.450 409]		Standard subdivisions

Do not use; class in 296.4501–296.4509

.450 42		Sephardic liturgy
.450 44		Hasidic liturgy
.450 46		Reform liturgy
.450 47		Conservative liturgy
.450 48		Reconstructionist liturgy
.452		Piyyutim

> 296.453–296.454 Liturgy and prayers for festivals, holy days, fasts; for occasions that occur generally once in a lifetime [*formerly* 296.43–296.44]

> Add to each subdivision identified by * the numbers following 296.45 in 296.4504, e.g., Passover Haggadah of the Sephardic rite 296.45371042

> Class comprehensive works in 296.45

.453   *Liturgy and prayers for festivals, holy days, fasts

Class here Mahzorim

.453 1–.453 6   Liturgy and prayers for High Holy Days, Sukkot, Hanukkah, Purim

Add to base number 296.453 the numbers following 296.43 in 296.431–296.436, e.g., liturgy and prayers for High Holy Days 296.4531; then add further as instructed under 296.453–296.454, e.g., Reform prayer books for High Holy Days 296.4531046

.453 7   *Liturgy and prayers for Pesach (Passover)

.453 71   *Passover Haggadah (Seder service)

.453 8–.453 9   Liturgy and prayers for Shavuot, other festivals, holy days, fasts

Add to base number 296.453 the numbers following 296.43 in 296.438–296.439, e.g., prayers for Shavuot 296.4538; then add further as instructed under 296.453–296.454, e.g., prayers for Shavuot of the Sephardic rite 296.4538042

.454   Liturgy and prayers for occasions that occur generally once in a lifetime

Add to base number 296.454 the numbers following 296.44 in 296.442–296.446, e.g., liturgy and prayers for weddings 296.4544; then add further as instructed under 296.453–2296.454, e.g., Reform prayer books for weddings 296.4544046

.46   Use of the arts and symbolism

Including synagogue buildings

.461   Liturgical articles

Including mezuzot, prayer shawls

---

*Add as instructed under 296.453–296.454

.461 2		Phylacteries (Tefillin)
.461 5		Torah scrolls

> Class here scribes (soferim)

.462		Music

> Class here cantors
>
> Class works containing both text and music, interdisciplinary works on Jewish liturgical music in 782.36

.47		Sermons and preaching (Homiletics) [*formerly* 296.42]

> Add to base number 296.47 the numbers following 296.4 in 296.41–296.44, e.g., High Holy Day sermons 296.4731
>
> Class sermons on a specific subject with the subject, e.g., sermons on social issues 296.38

.48		Pilgrimages and sacred places
[.480 93–.480 99]		Specific continents, countries, localities

> Do not use; class in 296.482–296.489

.481		Pilgrimages

> Class pilgrimages to specific sacred places in 296.482–296.489

.482		Jerusalem
.483–.489		Geographic treatment of sacred places in specific continents, countries, localities

> Add to base number 296.48 notation 3–9 from Table 2, e.g., sacred places in Iraq 296.48567; however, for Jerusalem, see 296.482
>
> Class the Land of Israel as a theme in Jewish theology in 296.31173

.49		Traditions, rites, public services of ancient Judaism to 70 A.D.

> Not provided for elsewhere

.491		The Temple
.492		Sacrifices and offerings
.493		Ark of the Covenant
.495		Ancient priesthood
.6		**Leaders, organization, religious education, outreach activity**

.61	Leaders and their work

Role, function, duties

Class here ordination, work of rabbis; activities of leaders and other congregational workers designed to promote religious and social welfare of social groups in community, pastoral care; chaplaincy

For ancient priesthood, see 296.495

See also 296.4615 for scribes, 296.462 for cantors

[.610 92]	Persons

Do not use for persons treatment of religious leaders primarily associated with a specific religious activity; class in 296.1–296.7, e.g., a theologian 296.3092. Do not use for persons treatment of religious leaders primarily associated with a specific denomination or movement; class in 296.8, e.g., a Reform rabbi 296.8341092. Do not use for persons treatment of other religious leaders; class in 296.092

Use of this number for persons treatment of writers on leaders and their work discontinued; class in 296.61

.65	Synagogues and congregations

Role and function

See also 296.46 for synagogue buildings

.650 9	Historical, geographic, persons treatment

Class history of specific synagogues in 296.09

.67	Organizations [*formerly also* 296.06] and organization

Theory and history of organizations other than synagogues and congregations

Including religious authority, excommunication, schism; sanhedrin

Class laws and decisions in 296.18. Class organizations sponsored by one denomination with the denomination in 296.8, e.g., Union of Orthodox Congregations of America 296.83206073

For synagogues and congregations, see 296.65

See also 369.3924 for Jewish service and fraternal associations, e.g., B'nai B'rith

[.673–.675]	Young Men's and Women's Hebrew Associations

Numbers discontinued; class in 296.67

.68	Religious education

Class Judaism as an academic subject in 296.071

For religious education at the level of higher education, see 296.0711

See Manual at 291.75 vs. 200.71

.680 83		History and description with respect to young people

Class here afternoon weekday schools, Hebrew schools, Jewish religious schools, Sunday schools; religious education in Jewish day schools

Class comprehensive works on Jewish day schools in 371.076

.69	Outreach activity for the benefit of converts and nonobservant Jews
.7	**Religious experience, life, practice**

Standard subdivisions are added for religious experience, life, practice together; for religious life and practice together

Practices which continue throughout life

Including asceticism

Class here guides to religious life, spirituality

For ethics, see 296.36; for traditions, rites, public services, see 296.4

[.708 5]		Relatives Parents

Do not use; class in 296.74

.708 6	Persons by miscellaneous social characteristics
[.708 655]	Married persons

Do not use; class in 296.74

.71	Religious experience
.712	Mysticism

Class cabalistic literature in 296.16; class Jewish mystical movements in 296.8

.714	Conversion

Class here conversion of non-Jews to Judaism

Class outreach activity for the benefit of converts and nonobservant Jews in 296.69. Class conversion of Jews to another religion with the religion, e.g., conversion of Jews to Christianity 248.246

.715	Return of Jews from non-observance to religious observance
.72	Devotional reading for the individual

Including meditation and meditations

Worship relocated to 296.45

Class devotional literature in the form of Aggadah in 296.19

.73	Kosher (Kashrut) observance

Observance of dietary laws

Including ritual slaughter (shehitah)

.74		Marriage and family life

> Class here social theology of marriage and family [*formerly* 296.387835], comprehensive works on marriage
>
> Use of this number for religious life and practice discontinued; class in 296.7
>
> > For ethics of marriage, see 296.363; for marriage and divorce rites and traditions, see 296.444

.742		Observance of laws of family purity

> *For ritual bath (mikveh), see 296.75*

.75		Ritual bath (Mikveh)
.8		**Denominations and movements**

> History of specific synagogues relocated to 296.09
>
> Class specific aspects of denominations and movements in 296.1–296.7

.81		Denominations and movements of ancient origin

> Including Hellenistic movement, Karaites, Zealots

.812		Pharisees
.813		Sadducees
.814		Essenes

> *For Qumran community, see 296.815*

.815		Qumran community

> *See also 296.155 for writings of Qumran community*

.817		Samaritans
.82		Medieval and early modern denominations and movements to ca. 1750

> Including Sabbatianism

.83		Modern denominations and movements after ca. 1750
.832		Orthodox Judaism
.833		Mystical Judaism
.833 2		Hasidism
.833 22		Habad Lubavitch Hasidism
.834		Reform movements

> Including Humanistic Judaism

.834 1		Reform Judaism [*formerly* 296.8346]
.834 2		Conservative Judaism

	.834 4	Reconstructionist Judaism
	[.834 6]	Reform Judaism
		Relocated to 296.8341

297 Islam, Babism, Bahai Faith

Standard subdivisions are added for Islam, Babism, Bahai Faith together; for Islam alone

SUMMARY

297.01–.09	Standard subdivisions
.1	**Sources of Islam**
.2	**Islamic doctrinal theology ('Aqā'id and Kalām); Islam and secular disciplines; Islam and other systems of belief**
.3	**Islamic worship**
.4	**Sufism (Islamic mysticism)**
.5	**Islamic moral theology and religious experience, life, practice**
.6	**Islamic leaders and organization**
.7	**Protection and propagation of Islam**
.8	**Islamic sects and reform movements**
.9	**Babism and Bahai Faith**

[.06]   Organizations and management

> Do not use for management; class in 297.6
>
> Organizations relocated to 297.65

.07   Education, research, related topics

.071   Education

> Class here Islamic religion as an academic subject
>
> Class comprehensive works on Islamic religious education, religious education to inculcate religious faith and practice in 297.77
>
> *See Manual at 291.75 vs. 200.71*

.09   Historical, geographic, persons treatment

> Class here comprehensive religious works on Islamic fundamentalism
>
> Class political science aspects of Islam in 320
>
> *For Islamic fundamentalism in a specific sect or reform movement, see 297.8*
>
> See also 909.097671 for Islamic civilization
>
> *See Manual at 320.55 vs. 297.09, 322.1*

.092 Persons

Class interdisciplinary works on caliphs as civil and religious heads of state with the subject in 940–990, e.g., Abu Bakr 953.02092

For Muslims primarily associated with a specific religious activity, see 297.1–297.7; for founders of Sufi orders, see 297.48; for Muhammad the Prophet, see 297.63; for Muhammad's family and companions (including religious biography of the first four caliphs), see 297.64; for Muslims primarily associated with a specific sect or reform movement, see 297.8

See Manual at 297.092

> 297.1–297.8 Islam

Class comprehensive works in 297

> 297.1–297.3 Sources of Islam; Islamic doctrinal theology ('Aqā'id and Kalām); Islam and secular disciplines; Islam and other systems of belief; Islamic worship

Specific aspects of Sufism relocated to 297.4

Class comprehensive works in 297

.1 Sources of Islam

SUMMARY

297.12	Koran and Hadith
.14	Religious and ceremonial laws and decisions
.18	Stories, legends, parables, proverbs, anecdotes told for religious edification

.12 Koran and Hadith

Class theology based on Koran and Hadith in 297.2

.122 Koran

.122 03 Topical dictionaries and encyclopedias

Do not use for concordances or non-topical dictionaries; class in 297.1224–297.1225

.122 09 Historical, geographic, persons treatment

Class here geography, history, chronology of the Middle East in Koran times in relation to the Koran

Class origin of Koran, commentary about historical occasions on which passages of Koran were revealed in 297.1221; class compilation and recording of Koran in 297.1224042; class comprehensive works on geography, history, chronology of the Middle East in Koran times in 939.4

	.122 092	Persons

> For Muḥammad, see 297.63; for Muḥammad's family and companions, see 297.64; for prophets prior to Muḥammad, see 297.246

	.122 1	Origin and authenticity

Including inspiration, revelation, commentary about historic occasions on which passages were revealed; Koranic prophecy and prophecies

Class compilation and recording of Koran in 297.1224042

	.122 2	Koran stories retold

Including picture books

> 297.122 4–297.122 5 Texts

Class comprehensive works in 297.122

For texts accompanied by commentaries, see 297.1227

	.122 4	Arabic texts

Class here textual criticism

Class Arabic texts accompanied by translations in 297.1225

	.122 404	Special topics
	.122 404 2	Compilation and recording of Koran
	.122 404 5	Recitation and readings

Standard subdivisions are added for either or both topics in heading

Class here art of melodic reading, tajwīd (adornment of recitation); qirā'āt (science of the readings, which treats various renditions of the text according to different oral traditions)

	.122 5	Translations

Class here Arabic texts accompanied by translations

Add to base number 297.1225 notation 1–9 from Table 6, e.g., the Koran in English 297.122521

	.122 6	Interpretation and criticism (Exegesis)

Class art of recitation in 297.1224045

For textual criticism, see 297.1224; for commentaries, see 297.1227

.122 601		Philosophy and theory
		Class here hermeneutics, principles and methods of Koranic exegesis
.122 61		General introductions to the Koran
		Including general introductions to the sciences necessary to study the Koran
[.122 64–.122 66]		Symbolism, typology, harmonies, literary criticism
		Numbers discontinued; class in 297.1226
.122 67		Historical criticism
.122 68		Allegorical and numerical interpretations
		Use of this number for mythological, astronomical interpretations discontinued; class in 297.1226
.122 7		Commentaries
		Criticism and interpretation arranged in textual order
		Class here texts accompanied by commentaries
.122 8		Nonreligious subjects treated in the Koran
		Class a religious subject treated in the Koran with the subject, e.g., Islamic ethics 297.5
.122 800 01–.122 800 09		Standard subdivisions
.122 800 1–.122 899 9		Specific nonreligious subjects treated in the Koran
		Add to base number 297.1228 notation 001–999, e.g., natural sciences in the Koran 297.12285
.122 9		Individual suras and groups of suras
		Origins, authenticity; geography, history, chronology of Koran lands in Koran times; texts; criticism, interpretation; commentaries; nonreligious subjects treated in the suras
.124		Hadith (Traditions)
		Including collection by Aḥmad ibn Ḥanbal
.124 001–.124 009		Standard subdivisions
.124 01–.124 08		Generalities
		Add to base number 297.1240 the numbers following 297.122 in 297.1221–297.1228, e.g., origins 297.12401

>	297.124 1–297.124 8	Specific Hadith

Add to each subdivision identified by * as follows:
001–009   Standard subdivisions
01–08   Generalities
        Add to 0 the numbers following 297.122 in
        297.1221–297.1228, e.g., criticism 06

Class comprehensive works in 297.124

.124 1	*Al-Bukhārī, Muḥammad ibn Ismāʿīl
.124 2	*Abū Dāʾūd Sulaymān ibn al-Ashʿath al-Sijistānī
.124 3	*Muslim ibn al-Ḥajjāj al-Qushayrī
.124 4	*Al-Tirmidhī, Muḥammad ibn ʿĪsá
.124 5	*Al-Nasāʾī, Aḥmad ibn Shuʿayb
.124 6	*Ibn Mājah, Muḥammad ibn Yazīd
.124 7	Other Sunni Hadith
.124 8	Hadith of other sects
[.13]	Oral traditions

Number discontinued; class in 297.1

.14   Religious and ceremonial laws and decisions

Class here fiqh in relation to religious and ceremonial laws and decisions [*formerly also* 340.59], sharia in relation to religious and ceremonial laws and decisions

Interdisciplinary works on sharia relocated to 340.59

Class Islamic law relating to secular matters, interdisciplinary works on Islamic law in 340.59. Class religious law on a specific topic with the topic, e.g., religious law concerning ḥajj 297.352

See Manual at 340.59 vs. 297.14

.18   Stories, legends, parables, proverbs, anecdotes told for religious edification

Class here comprehensive works on Islamic legends

Class Islamic folklore in 398.20882971

For Islamic legends on a specific topic, see the topic, e.g., Islamic legends about pre-Islamic prophets 297.246

[.19]   Mythology

Provision discontinued because without meaning in context

---

*Add as instructed under 297.1241–297.1248

[.197] Islam and secular disciplines; Islam and other systems of belief

Relocated to 297.26–297.28

[.197 835 8] Social theology of marriage and family

Relocated to 297.577

.2 **Islamic doctrinal theology ('Aqā'id and Kalām); Islam and secular disciplines; Islam and other systems of belief**

Standard subdivisions are added for Islamic doctrinal theology, Islam and secular disciplines, Islam and other systems of belief together; for Islamic doctrinal theology alone

Class Islamic moral theology in 297.5; class doctrines concerning Muḥammad the Prophet in 297.63

SUMMARY

297.204	Doctrines of specific sects
.21	**God and spiritual beings**
.22	**Humankind**
.23	**Eschatology**
.24	**Other doctrines**
.26	**Islam and secular disciplines**
.27	**Islam and social sciences**
.28	**Islam and other systems of belief**
.29	**Apologetics and polemics**

> 297.204–297.24 Islamic doctrinal theology ('Aqā'id and Kalām)

Class comprehensive works in 297.2

For apologetics and polemics, see 297.29; for shahāda (profession of faith), see 297.34

.204 Doctrines of specific sects

Add to base number 297.204 the numbers following 297.8 in 297.81–297.87, e.g., doctrines of Shiites 297.2042

.21 God and spiritual beings

.211 God

.211 2 Attributes and names of God

Class vindication of God's justice and goodness in permitting existence of evil and suffering in 297.2118

For tawhid (unity of God), see 297.2113

.211 3 Tawhid (Unity of God)

146

.211 4		Relation to the world
		Including relation to and action in history
		For revelation, see 297.2115; for creation, see 297.242
.211 5		Revelation
		Including prophecy
		Class Koranic prophecy in 297.1221; class prophets and prophethood in 297.246
.211 8		Theodicy
		Vindication of God's justice and goodness in permitting existence of evil and suffering
.215		Angels
.216		Devils
.217		Jinn
.22		Humankind
		Including faith, repentance
		For eschatology, see 297.23
.221		Creation
		Class comprehensive works on creation in 297.242
.225		Nature
		Including soul
		Class free will and predestination in 297.227
.227		Free will and predestination
		Class here freedom of choice between good and evil
.23		Eschatology
		Including day of judgment, death, eternity, future life, heaven, hell, punishment, resurrection, rewards
		Class doctrines of Hidden Imam, of Mahdi in 297.24
.24		Other doctrines
		Including doctrines of Hidden Imam, of Mahdi
		Caliphate and imamate relocated to 297.61
.242		Creation
		Including origin of life
		Class here Islamic cosmology
		For creation of humankind, see 297.221

.246	Prophets prior to Muḥammad

        Including Adam, Moses

        Class here comprehensive works on prophets and prophethood in Islam

        For Muḥammad the Prophet, see 297.63

.246 3	Abraham
.246 5	Jesus, son of Mary

> 297.26–297.28 Islam and secular disciplines; Islam and other systems of belief [*formerly* 297.197]

        Class comprehensive works in 297.2

.26	Islam and secular disciplines

        Class here attitudes of Islam toward and influence on secular issues, Islamic views and teachings about secular disciplines

        Class relation of a specific Islamic doctrine and a secular discipline with the doctrine in 297.2, e.g., relation of Islamic doctrine about creation and scientific theories about creation 297.242; class work influenced by Islam and Islamic theories within a secular discipline with the discipline, e.g., Islamic philosophy 181.07, architecture in the Islamic world 720.917671

        For Islam and social sciences, see 297.27

        See also 297.1228 for nonreligious subjects treated in Koran, 297.12408 for nonreligious subjects treated in Hadith

        See Manual at 297.26–297.27

.261	Islam and philosophy, paranormal phenomena, psychology
.265	Islam and natural sciences, mathematics
.266	Islam and technology
.267	Islam and the arts
.27	Islam and social sciences

        Attitudes of Islam toward and influence on social issues

        Including war and peace

        Class here attitudes of Islam toward and influence on social issues, Islam and socioeconomic problems, Islamic social theology

        Class Islamic view of marriage and family in 297.577

        See Manual at 297.26–297.27

.272	Islam and politics	
	Including civil rights, international affairs, nationalism	
	Class political science view of religiously oriented political theories and ideologies in 320.55; class political science view of relation of state to religious organizations and groups in 322.1; class political science view of religious political parties in 324.2182	
	See Manual at 320.55 vs. 297.09, 322.1	
.273	Islam and economics	
	Including Islam and communism	
	See also 297.289 for Islam and atheism	
.28	Islam and other systems of belief	
	Attitudes toward and relations with other systems of belief	
	Class apologetics and polemics in 297.29	
.282	Islam and Judaism	
	Class Biblical figures as prophets prior to Muḥammad in 297.246	
.283	Islam and Christianity	
	Class Biblical figures as prophets prior to Muḥammad in 297.246	
.284	Islam and religions of Indic origin	
	Add to base number 297.284 the numbers following 294 in 294.3–294.6, e.g., Islam and Hinduism 297.2845	
.289	Islam and irreligion	
	Including Islam and atheism	
.29	Apologetics and polemics	
[.291]	Polemics against pagans and heathens	
	Number discontinued; class in 297.29	
.292	Polemics against Judaism	
.293	Polemics against Christianity	
.294	Polemics against religions of Indic origin	
[.295]	Polemics against other religions	
	Number discontinued; class in 297.29	
[.297]	Polemics against rationalists, agnostics, atheists	
	Number discontinued; class in 297.29	
.298	Polemics against scientists and materialists	

.3	**Islamic worship**

>Including use of arts and symbolism in worship
>
>Class here comprehensive works on Islamic worship, on non-Sufi worship, on Islamic private worship, on non-Sufi private worship [*all formerly* 297.43], public worship
>
>Class Pillars of Islam (Pillars of the Faith) in 297.31. Class specific applications of the arts and symbolism in worship with the application in 297.301–297.38, e.g., use of arts and symbolism in mosques 297.351
>
>*For Sufi worship, see 297.43*

.300 1–.300 9	Standard subdivisions
.301–.307	Specific sects

>Add to base number 297.30 the numbers following 297.8 in 297.81–297.87, e.g., Shiite rites 297.302

.31	Pillars of Islam (Pillars of the Faith) [*formerly* 297.5]

>Comprehensive works only
>
>*For shahāda (profession of faith), see 297.34; for ḥajj (pilgrimage to Mecca), see 297.352; for ṣawm Ramaḍān (annual fast of Ramadan), see 297.362; for ṣalāt (prayer five times daily), see 297.3822; for zakat, see 297.54*
>
>See also 297.72 for jihad

[.32–.33]	Divination and occultism

>Relocated to 297.39

.34	Shahāda (Profession of faith) [*formerly* 297.51]
.35	Sacred places and pilgrimages

>Standard subdivisions are added for sacred places and pilgrimages together, for sacred places alone
>
>Including non-Sufi pilgrimages, comprehensive works on Islamic pilgrimages [*both formerly* 297.446]
>
>Class here rites and ceremonies associated with sacred places and pilgrimages [*formerly* 297.38]
>
>Class pilgrimages to specific places in 297.352–297.359
>
>*For Sufi pilgrimages, see 297.435*

[.350 93–.350 99]	Treatment by specific continents, countries, localities

>Relocated to 297.353–297.359

		Comparative religion and non-Christian religions
.351		Mosques
		Class here interdisciplinary works
		For organizational role and function of mosques, see 297.65; for architecture of mosques, see 726.2
[.351 093–.351 099]		Treatment by specific continents, countries, localities
		Do not use; class in 297.352–297.359
.352		Mecca
		Class here ḥajj (pilgrimage to Mecca) [*formerly* 297.55]
.353–.359		Treatment by specific continents, countries, localities [*formerly* 297.35093–297.35099]
		Add to base number 297.35 notation 3–9 from Table 2, e.g., Medina 297.35538, Jerusalem 297.35569442; however, for Mecca, see 297.352
.36		Special days and seasons
		Including Jum'ah (Friday prayer); 'Āshūrā' (Tenth of Muḥarram); Mawlid al-Nabī (Prophet's birthday); 'Īd al-Aḍḥā, 'Īd al-Fiṭr
		Class here rites and ceremonies associated with special days and seasons [*formerly also* 297.38], Islamic religious calendar
		See also 297.37 for sermons for special days and seasons
.362		Ṣawm Ramaḍān (Annual fast of Ramadan) [*formerly also* 297.53]
		Including Laylat al-Qadr
		Class comprehensive works on fasting in 297.53
.37		Sermons and preaching
		Class sermons on a specific subject with the subject, e.g., sermons on day of judgment 297.23
.38		Rites, ceremonies, prayer, meditation
		Conduct and texts
		Including ablutions
		Rites and ceremonies associated with sacred places and pilgrimages relocated to 297.35; rites and ceremonies associated with special days and seasons relocated to 297.36
		Class ablutions associated with prayer and meditations in 297.382; class ablutions associated with burial and mourning in 297.385
		See also 297.37 for sermons and preaching

.382	Prayer and meditation

Standard subdivisions are added for prayer and meditation together, for prayer alone

Including dhikr (remembrance), qiblah (direction of prayer)

Class here practical works on prayer and meditation

Class prayer and meditation associated with sacred places and pilgrimages in 297.35; class prayer and meditation associated with special days and seasons in 297.36. Class prayer and meditation associated with specific rites and ceremonies with the rites and ceremonies, e.g., funerals in 297.385; class prayers and meditations on a specific subject with the subject, e.g., unity of God 297.2113

.382 2	Ṣalāt (Prayer five times daily) [*formerly* 297.52]

For texts of prayers, see 297.3824

.382 4	Texts of prayers and meditations

Class here prayer books

.385	Burial and mourning rites
.39	Popular practices

Including controversial practices, e.g., divination and occultism [*both formerly* 297.32–297.33]

Class occult practices not regarded as Islamic practices in 133; class Islamic views of occultism regarded as a secular topic in 297.261; class sociological studies of Islamic popular practices in 306.69739. Class popular practices associated with a topic provided elsewhere with the topic, e.g., popular practices associated with burial and mourning 297.385

.4	**Sufism (Islamic mysticism)**

Class here specific aspects of Sufism [*formerly* 297.1–297.3, 297.5–297.7]

Non-Sufi and comprehensive works on Islamic religious experience, life, practice relocated to 297.57

See Manual at 297.4

.41	Sufi doctrinal theology; Sufism and secular disciplines; Sufism and non-Islamic systems of belief

Standard subdivisions are added for Sufi doctrinal theology, Sufism and secular disciplines, Sufism and non-Islamic systems of belief together; for Sufi doctrinal theology alone

Add to base number 297.41 the numbers following 297.2 in 297.21–297.29, e.g., Sufi concept of God 297.4111

Class Sufi doctrines concerning Muḥammad the Prophet in 297.4; class Sufi moral theology in 297.45

[.42]		Sufi religious experience
		Number discontinued; class in 297.4
.43		Sufi worship
		Add to base number 297.43 the numbers following 297.3 in 297.3001–297.38, e.g., Sufi pilgrimages 297.435 [*formerly* 297.446], Sufi prayer and meditation 297.4382
		Comprehensive works on Islamic worship, on non-Sufi worship, on Islamic private worship, on non-Sufi private worship relocated to 297.3
.44		Sufi religious life and practice
		Class here guides to Sufi religious life
		Class Sufi moral theology in 297.45
		For Sufi worship, see 297.43
.446		Sufi individual observances
		Including Sufi ascetic practices [*formerly* 297.447], dietary laws and observance
		Non-Sufi pilgrimages, comprehensive works on Islamic pilgrimages relocated to 297.35; Sufi pilgrimages relocated to 297.435
		For Sufi fasting, see 297.45
[.447]		Sufi asceticism
		Sufi ascetic practices relocated to 297.446; Sufi fasting relocated to 297.45
[.448]		Guides to religious life
		Use of this number for guides to Sufi religious life discontinued; class in 297.44
		Non-Sufi and comprehensive guides to religious life relocated to 297.57
.45		Sufi moral theology
		Including Sufi fasting [*formerly* 297.447], almsgiving, ṣadaqah, zakat
		For Sufi observance of ṣawm Ramaḍān, see 297.4362
.48		Sufi orders
		Including Bektashi, Naqshabandiyah, Qādirīyah, Tijānīyah
		See also 297.835 for Kadarites (Islamic sect)
.482		Mevleviyeh

> **297.5–297.7 Islamic moral theology and religious experience, life, practice; Islamic leaders and organization; protection and propagation of Islam**

>> Specific aspects of Sufism relocated to 297.4

>> Class comprehensive works in 297

.5 **Islamic moral theology and religious experience, life, practice**

Standard subdivisions are added for moral theology and religious experience, life, practice together; for moral theology alone

Including conscience; general works on duty, sin, vice, virtue

Pillars of Islam (Pillars of the Faith) relocated to 297.31

Class a specific duty, sin, vice, virtue in 297.56

For jihad, see 297.72

[.51] Shahāda (Profession of faith)

Relocated to 297.34

[.52] Ṣalāt (Prayer five times daily)

Relocated to 297.3822

.53 Ṣawm (Fast)

Class here comprehensive works on fasting

Ṣawm Ramaḍān (Annual Fast of Ramadan) relocated to 297.362

.54 Zakat

Class here almsgiving, ṣadaqah

[.55] Ḥajj (Pilgrimage to Mecca)

Relocated to 297.352

.56 Specific vices, virtues, moral issues

Add to base number 297.56 the numbers following 17 in 172–179, e.g., Islamic sexual ethics 297.566; however, for almsgiving, see 297.54

Class comprehensive works on vices, on virtues in 297.5

.57		Religious experience, life, practice

Standard subdivisions are added for any or all topics in heading

Class here non-Sufi and comprehensive works on Islamic religious experience, life, practice [*all formerly* 297.4]; non-Sufi and comprehensive guides to religious life [*formerly* 297.448]

Class moral theology in 297.5

> *For worship, see 297.3; for mysticism and Sufi religious experience, see 297.4; for Sufi life and practice, see 297.44*

[.570 85]		Relatives Parents

Do not use; class in 297.577

.570 86		Persons by miscellaneous social characteristics
[.570 865 5]		Married persons

Do not use; class in 297.577

.574		Conversion

Class here conversion of non-Muslims to Islam

Class da'wah in 297.74. Class conversion of Muslims to another religion with the religion, e.g., conversion of Muslims to Christianity 248.246

.576		Individual observances

Including ascetic practices, dietary laws and observance, ritual slaughter of animals to conform with dietary laws

> *For pilgrimages, see 297.35; for fasting, see 297.53; for almsgiving, see 297.54*

.577		Marriage and family life

Class here social theology of marriage and family [*formerly* 297.1978358]; comprehensive works on marriage, on family life

> *For ethics of marriage and family, see 297.563*

.6	**Islamic leaders and organization**	
.61		Leaders and their work

Role, function, duties

Class here caliphate, imamate [*both formerly* 297.24, 297.65]; ayatollahs, caliphs, imams, ulama

> *For doctrine of Hidden Imam, see 297.24; for Muḥammad the Prophet, see 297.63; for Muḥammad's family and companions (including first four caliphs), see 297.64*

[.610 92]		Persons

> Do not use for persons treatment of religious leaders primarily associated with a specific religious activity; class in 297.1–297.7, e.g., founders of Sufi orders 297.48. Do not use for persons treatment of Muḥammad; class in 297.63. Do not use for persons treatment of Muḥammad's family and companions (including first four caliphs); class in 297.64. Do not use for persons treatment of Islamic leaders primarily associated with a specific sect or reform movement; class in 297.8. Do not use for persons treatment of other religious leaders; class in 297.092

> Use of this number for persons who study and write about the role, function, duties of religious leaders discontinued; class in 297.61

.63   **Muḥammad the Prophet**

> Class here comprehensive works on Muḥammad and his family and companions

> Class Hadith in 297.124

> *For Muḥammad's family and companions, see 297.64*

.630 92   Persons

> Do not use for Muḥammad the Prophet; class in 297.63

> Class here scholars who specialize in the life and works of Muḥammad the Prophet

.632   **Period prior to call to prophethood**

> Including birth, childhood

> *See also 297.36 for Mawlid al-Nabī (holiday of Prophet's birthday)*

.633   **Period at Mecca**

> Including Isrā' (Night Journey to Jerusalem) and Mi'rāj (Ascent to Heaven)

> Class comprehensive works on prophetic career in 297.635

> *For period prior to call to prophethood, see 297.632*

.634   **Hijrah (Emigration from Mecca)**

.635   **Period at Medina**

> *For emigration from Mecca to Medina, see 297.634*

.64   **Muḥammad's family and companions**

> Standard subdivisions are added for family and companions together, for family alone

> Including descendants of Muḥammad

.642	Wives	
.644	Daughters	
.648	Ṣaḥābah (Companions)	

>   Including religious biography and theological discussion of the first four caliphs
>
>   Class interdisciplinary biographies of the first four caliphs with the subject in 950, e.g., Abu Bakr 953.02092

.65   Organizations [*formerly also* 297.06] and organization

>   Role and function
>
>   Including associations, congregations, mosques
>
>   Caliphate, imamate relocated to 297.61
>
>   Class Islamic organizations in relation to political affairs in 297.272; class a specific organization limited to a specific sect or reform movement in 297.8; class political science view of relation of state to religious organizations and groups in 322.1; class political science view of religious political parties in 324.2182; class interdisciplinary works on mosques in 297.351

.7   **Protection and propagation of Islam**

.72   Jihad

.74   Da'wah

>   Class here call to Islam, missionary work

.77   Islamic religious education

>   Class Islam as an academic subject in 297.071; class comprehensive works on madrasa education, treating both religious education and other subjects, in 371.077
>
>   > *For religious education at the level of higher education, see 297.0711*
>
>   > *See Manual at 291.75 vs. 200.71*

.770 83   Young people

>   > Class here Islamic religious schools, religious education in Islamic schools that teach all subjects
>   >
>   > Class comprehensive works on Islamic schools that teach all subjects in 371.077

.8   **Islamic sects and reform movements**

>   Class specific aspects of sects and reform movements in 297.1–297.7; class secular view of relation of state to religious organizations and groups in 322.1; class secular view of religious political parties in 324.2182
>
>   *For Sufism, see 297.4*

.804		Special topics
.804 2		Relations among sects and reform movements
		Class here relations between Sunni and Shia Islam
.81		**Sunnites**
		Class relations between Sunnites and Shiites in 297.8042
.811		Hanafites
.812		Shafiites
.813		Malikites
.814		Hanbalites and Wahhābīyah
.82		**Shiites**
		Class relations between Shiites and Sunnites in 297.8042
.821		Twelvers (Ithna Asharites)
.822		Seveners (Ismailites)
		Including Mustalians, Nizaris
.824		Zaydites
.83		**Other sects and reform movements**
		Including Kharijites
.833		Ibadites
.834		Motazilites
.835		Kadarites
		See also 297.48 for Qādirīyah (Sufi order)
.837		Murjiites
.85		Druzes
.86		Ahmadiyya movement
.87		Black Muslim movement
		Including American Muslim Mission, Nation of Islam, World Community of al-Islam in the West
.9		**Babism and Bahai Faith**
.92		Babism
.93		†Bahai Faith
		See Manual at 291

†Add as instructed under 292–299

(298) (Permanently unassigned)

(Optional number used to provide local emphasis and a shorter number for a specific religion other than Christianity; prefer the number for the specific religion elsewhere in 292–299; or optional number used for Christianity if option A under 292–299 is chosen. Other options are described at 292–299)

299 Other religions

Including Urantia, modern revivals of long dormant religions, religions based on modern revivals of witchcraft

Class syncretistic religious writings of individuals expressing personal views and not claiming to establish a new religion or to represent an old one in 291

If a religion not named in the schedule claims to be Christian, class it in 289.9 even if it is unorthodox or syncretistic

(Options for giving local emphasis and shorter numbers for a specific religion are described at 292–299)

SUMMARY

299.1–.4	Religions of Indo-European, Semitic, North African, North and West Asian, Dravidian origin
.5	Religions of East and Southeast Asian origin
.6	Religions originating among Black Africans and people of Black African descent
.7	Religions of North American native origin
.8	Religions of South American native origin
.9	Religions of other origin

.1–.4 Religions of Indo-European, Semitic, North African, North and West Asian, Dravidian origin

Not otherwise provided for

Add to base number 299 the numbers following —9 in notation 91–94 from Table 5, e.g., Druidism 299.16

Class modern revivals of long dormant religions in 299

.5 Religions of East and Southeast Asian origin

See Manual at 200.9 vs. 294, 299.5

.51   Religions of Chinese origin

.512   †Confucianism

Interdisciplinary works on Confucianism relocated to 181.112

Class the Four books of Confucius in 181.112

See Manual at 291; also at 200.92 and 291–299

.514   †Taoism

See Manual at 291; also at 200.92 and 291–299

†Add as instructed under 292–299

.54		Religions of Tibetan origin
		Class here Bon
.56		Religions of Japanese and Ryukyuan origin
.561		†Shintoism

See Manual at 291; also at 200.92 and 291–299

.57–.59   Other religions of East and Southeast Asian origin

Add to base number 299.5 the numbers following —95 in notation 957–959 from Table 5, e.g., Caodaism 299.592

.6   Religions originating among Black Africans and people of Black African descent

Unless other instructions are given, class a subject with aspects in two or more subdivisions of 299.6 in the number coming first, e.g., rites of the Yoruba 299.64 (*not* 299.68333)

For Black Muslims, see 297.87; for religions originating among Ethiopians, see 299.28; for religions originating among Cushitic and Omotic peoples, see 299.35; for religions originating among the Hausa, see 299.37

[.609 61–.609 69]   Religions in specific areas in Africa

Do not use; class in 299.691–299.699

.62   Mythology and mythological foundations

Class myths on a specific subject with the subject, e.g., on a god 299.63

See Manual at 398.2 vs. 291.13

.63   Doctrines

Including gods, goddesses, other supernatural beings

.64   Practices [*formerly* 299.65], rites, ceremonies

Including divination, religious healing, zombiism

See Manual at 615.852 vs. 234.131, 291.31

[.65]   Practices

Relocated to 299.64

.67   Specific cults

.672   Umbanda

.673   Candomblé

.674   Santeria

.675   Voodooism

Class voodooism as an occult practice without regard to its religious significance in 133.4

†Add as instructed under 292–299

	.676	Ras Tafari movement
	.68	Religions of specific groups and peoples
	.681	Religions of Khoikhoi and San
	.683–.685	Religions of peoples who speak, or whose ancestors spoke, Niger-Congo, Nilo-Saharan languages

Add to base number 299.68 the numbers following —96 in notation 963–965 from Table 6, e.g., religion of the Yoruba 299.68333

.686–.688   Religions of national groups in Africa

Add to base number 299.68 the numbers following —6 in notation 66–68 from Table 2, e.g., religion of Ugandans 299.68761

Class national groups that predominate in specific areas in Africa in 299.69

.689   Religions of other national groups of largely African descent

Add to base number 299.689 notation 4–9 from Table 2, e.g., African religion of Haitians 299.6897294

Class religions of such national groups in areas where they predominate in 299.609, e.g., African religion of Haitians in Haiti 299.6097294

.69   Religions of specific areas in Africa

Add to base number 299.69 the numbers following —6 in notation 61–69 from Table 2, e.g., religions of West Africa 299.696

.7   Religions of North American native origin

Unless other instructions are given, class a subject with aspects in two or more subdivisions of 299.7 in the number coming first, e.g., rites of Hopi 299.74 (*not* 299.7845)

[.709 71–.709 79]   Religions in specific areas in North America

Do not use; class in 299.791–299.799

.72–.77   Specific aspects

Add to base number 299.7 the numbers following 299.6 in 299.62–299.67, e.g., rites and ceremonies 299.74

.78   Religions of specific groups and peoples

Add to base number 299.78 the numbers following —97 in notation 971–979 from Table 5, e.g., Hopi religion 299.7845

.79   Religions of specific areas in North America

Add to base number 299.79 the numbers following —7 in notation 71–79 from Table 2, e.g., religions of Indians of Mexico 299.792

.8	**Religions of South American native origin**

Unless other instructions are given, class a subject with aspects in two or more subdivisions of 299.8 in the number coming first, e.g., rites of Guaranís 299.84 (*not* 299.88382)

[.809 81–.809 89]   Religions of specific areas in South America

Do not use; class in 299.891–299.899

.82–.87   Specific aspects

Add to base number 299.8 the numbers following 299.6 in 299.62–299.67, e.g., gods and goddesses 299.83

.88   Religions of specific groups and peoples

Add to base number 299.88 the numbers following —98 in notation 982–984 from Table 5, e.g., religion of Guaranís 299.88382

.89   Religions of specific areas in South America

Add to base number 299.89 the numbers following —8 in notation 81–89 from Table 2, e.g., religions of Indians of the Amazon 299.8911

.9   Religions of other origin

.92   Religions of other ethnic origin

Add to base number 299.92 the numbers following —99 in notation 991–999 from Table 5, e.g., religion of Polynesians 299.924

.93   Religions of eclectic and syncretistic origin

Religions and applied religious philosophies of eclectic, syncretistic, universal nature

Including Eckankar, a Course in Miracles, Great White Brotherhood, New Age religions, New Thought, systems of Bhagwan Shree Rajneesh and Meher Baba, United Church of Religious Science

Class syncretistic religious writings of individuals expressing personal views and not claiming to establish a new religion or to represent an old one in 291

See also 289.98 for Christian New Thought

See Manual at 299.93: New Age religions

.932   Gnosticism

Including Manicheism

Class Christian Gnosticism in 273.1; class Christian Manicheism in 273.2

.933   Subud

.934   Theosophy

.935	Anthroposophy
.936	Scientology
	Including dianetics [*formerly* 158.9]

Manual Notes for 200 Religion

MANUAL NOTES FOR 200 RELIGION

133 vs. 200

Parapsychology and occultism vs. Religion

If the author of a work about parapsychological or occult phenomena describes them as religious, or the believers and practitioners consider them to be religious, the work is classed in 200. If parapsychological and occult phenomena are not presented as religious, or if in doubt as to whether they have been so presented, prefer 133.

Class knowledge reputedly derived from secret and ancient religious texts but not applied for religious purposes in 133; however, class editions of the texts in 200, even if annotated from an occultist viewpoint, e.g., discussion of occult traditions derived from the Zohar 135.47, but the text of the Zohar 296.162.

200 vs. 100

Religion vs. Philosophy, paranormal phenomena, psychology

Both philosophy and religion deal with the ultimate nature of existence and relationships, but religion treats them within the context of revelation, deity, worship. Philosophy of religion (210) does not involve revelation or worship but does examine questions within the context of deity.

Any work that emphasizes revelation, deity, or worship is classed in 200, even if it uses philosophical methods, e.g., a philosophical proof of the existence of God 212.1. Sometimes the thought of a religious tradition is used to examine the questions of philosophy without reference to deity or religious topics, e.g., Jewish philosophy 181.06, Christian philosophy 190. However, class ethics based on a religion in 200. If in doubt, prefer 200.

200.9 vs. 294, 299.5

Historical, geographic, persons treatment [of religion] vs. Religions of Indic origin [and] Religions of East and Southeast Asian origin

294 and 299.5 refer to religions that originated in particular geographic areas. Most of these religions have spread beyond the area where they originated. The areas also have adherents of religions that originated elsewhere, e.g., Buddhism (which originated in India) is present in China. If a work covers various religious traditions in an area, not just the religions that originated there, class it in 200.9. For example, class the religions of India (including Christianity and Islam) in 200.954, of China (including Christianity and Buddhism) in 200.951.

200.92 and 291–299

Persons [associated with religion] and Comparative religion, Religions other than Christianity

Persons associated with the religions in 292–299 are often identified with a number of religious functions and activities. A Hindu guru, for example, may be thought of as a theologian, a teacher, a missionary, or a clergyman. If a religious leader cannot be identified primarily with one function, activity, or sect, class the leader's biography in the base number for the religion and add notation 092 from Table 1. Class collected biography of persons from many religions who are not identified with one function or activity in 200.922. For persons associated with a specific religion, use a number that corresponds to the number given in the table below, e.g., a Buddhist member of a religious order 294.365 (corresponds to 291.65 in the table below). For comprehensive biographies of persons primarily identified with one function, activity, or sect, use the following table of preference:

Founders of religions	291.63
Founders of sects	291.9
Founders of religious orders	291.65
Religious leaders (high ranking officials)	200.92
Of specific sects	291.9
Theologians	291.2092
Moral theologians	291.5092
Missionaries	291.72092
Martyrs, heretics, saints	200.92
Of specific sects	291.9
Teachers	291.75092
Members of religious orders	291.65
Clergy	200.92
Of specific sects	291.9

Except for founders of religions (291.63) and founders of religious orders (291.65), the subdivisions of 291.6 are not used for biography, but for the nature, role, and function of religious leaders.

Works dealing with only one aspect of a person's career are classed with the aspect, e.g., Muḥammad as a moral theologian 297.5092 (*not* 297.63).

220

Bible

Biblical theology

Biblical theology usually means using the Bible for the basis of Christian or Jewish doctrine and is classed as directed at 220. But if a book on Biblical theology does no more than interpret the text of the Bible, it is classed in 220.6 and cognate numbers in 221–229. The key difference is whether the author adheres to the Biblical text and its meaning, or whether the author uses the Biblical text as a springboard to the interpretation of theological concepts.

220.92

Collected persons [in Bible]

Class a comprehensive biography of a Biblical character with the book or books with which the character is most closely associated. In many cases this is the historical part of the Bible in which persons' lives are narrated, e.g., Solomon, King of Israel, in 1st Kings 222.53092. Solomon's association with 223 Poetic books is weaker. However, some Biblical characters are more closely associated with non-historical books. For example, class Isaiah and Timothy with the books that bear their names, 224.1092 and 227.83092, respectively. They appear briefly in historical narratives, but their lives are not narrated in full there. Class the apostles John, Peter, and Paul at 225.92 since each is associated with a number of books in the New Testament, but class the rest of the original Apostles, associated primarily with Gospels and Acts, in 226.092.

See also discussion at 230–280: Biography.

221

Old Testament (Tanakh)

Optional numbers for books of Tanakh

Alphabetical index

Each of the books of the Old Testament (Tanakh) and the combination of them can have one of three different numbers depending on whether one chooses the preferred arrangement at 222–224 or one of the two optional arrangements. Optional numbers showing the books in the order found in Jewish Bibles appear in appendix A (Option A) and at 296.11 (Option B). The following alphabetical listing gives the three numbers for each book or combination of books:

Book	Preferred	Option A	Option B
Amos	224.8	223.63	296.1143
Canticle of Canticles	223.9	224.41	296.11641
Chronicles	222.6	224.8	296.1168
Chronicles 1	222.63	224.81	296.11681
Chronicles 2	222.64	224.82	296.11682
Daniel	224.5	224.5	296.1165
Deuteronomy	222.15	222.5	296.1125
Ecclesiastes	223.8	224.44	296.11644
Exodus	222.12	222.2	296.1122
Esther	222.9	224.45	296.11645
Ezekiel	224.4	223.5	296.1139
Ezra	222.7	224.6	296.1166
Five scrolls	221.044	224.4	296.1164
Former Prophets	222	223.1	296.1131
Genesis	222.11	222.1	296.1121
Habakkuk	224.95	223.68	296.1148

Haggai	224.97	223.72	296.1152
Hosea	224.6	223.61	296.1141
Isaiah	224.1	223.3	296.1137
Jeremiah	224.2	223.4	296.1138
Job	223.1	224.3	296.1163
Joel	224.7	223.62	296.1142
Jonah	224.92	223.65	296.1145
Joshua	222.2	223.11	296.1132
Judges	222.32	223.12	296.1133
Ketuvim	223	224	296.116
Kings	222.5	223.14	296.1135
Kings 1	222.53	223.141	296.11351
Kings 2	222.54	223.142	296.11352
Kohelet	223.8	224.44	296.11644
Lamentations	224.3	224.43	296.11643
Later Prophets	224	223.2	296.1136
Leviticus	222.13	222.3	296.1123
Malachi	224.99	223.74	296.1154
Megillot	221.044	224.4	296.1164
Micah	224.93	223.66	296.1146
Minor Prophets	224.9	223.6	296.114
Nahum	224.94	223.67	296.1147
Nehemiah	222.8	224.7	296.1167
Nevi'im	224	223	296.113
Numbers	222.14	222.4	296.1124
Obadiah	224.91	223.64	296.1144
Pentateuch	222.1	222	296.112
Prophetic books	224	223	296.113
Proverbs	223.7	224.2	296.1162
Pslams	223.2	224.1	296.1161
Qohelet	223.8	224.44	296.11644
Ruth	222.35	224.42	296.11642
Samuel	222.4	223.13	296.1134
Samuel 1	222.43	223.131	296.11341
Samuel 2	222.44	223.132	296.11342
Song of Solomon	223.9	224.41	296.11641
Song of Songs	223.9	224.41	296.11641
Torah	222.1	222	296.112
Writings	223	224	296.116
Zechariah	224.98	223.73	296.1153
Zephaniah	224.96	223.71	296.1151

230–280

Christianity

Biography

Use the following table of preference for comprehensive biographies:

Jesus Christ, Mary, Joseph, Joachim, Anne, John the Baptist	232.9
Other persons in the Bible	220
Founders of denominations	280
Founders of religious orders	271
Higher clergy (e.g., popes, metropolitans, archbishops, bishops) prior to 1054	270.1–.3
Higher clergy subsequent to 1054	280
Theologians	230
Moral theologians	241
Missionaries	266
Evangelists	269.2
Persons noted for participation in associations for religious work	267
Martyrs	272
Heretics	273
Saints	270
Saints prior to 1054	270.1–.3
Saints subsequent to 1054	280
Mystics	248.22
Hymn writers	264.23
Religious educators	268
Members of religious orders	271
Clergy prior to 1054	270.1–.3
Clergy subsequent to 1054	280
Members of the early church to 1054	270.1–.3
Members of denominations	280
Christian biography of persons who fall in none of the above categories	270

Class in 270 biographies of persons known not to be members of any church or for whom it has not been possible to determine whether there is church membership or not. Use the historical period that most closely matches the individual's life span or the time period of his greatest prominence, e.g., biography of a twentieth century Christian 270.82092. Class in 280 without subdivision church members whose affiliation is not known and members of nondenominational and interdenominational churches.

Do not use 248.2 Religious experience or its subdivisions except 248.22 for comprehensive biographies, e.g., a biography of Teresa of Avila's religious life 282.092, not 248.2092. However, biographical accounts written for devotional purposes, not as comprehensive accounts of a person's life, may be classed in 248.2, e.g., the story of one's conversion 248.246092.

253, 255, and 262.1 are not used for biographies of the kinds of persons listed above in the table of preference.

Certain numbers in the range 220–269 other than those listed in the table of preference above may be used for comprehensive biographies of persons with specialized religious careers, but are more commonly used for books treating only one aspect of a person's life and work, e.g., 220.092 for a Biblical scholar.

Examples:

270.0922	(Collected biography of saints)
225.92	(New Testament biography) Paul the Apostle
230.2092	(Catholic theology) Saint Thomas Aquinas
232.94	(John the Baptist) John the Baptist
266.2092	(Catholic missions) Saint Francis Xavier
269.2092	(Evangelism) Billy Graham
271.12502	(Trappist order in church history) Thomas Merton
270.2092	(Church history, 325–787) Pope Gregory the Great
283.092	(Anglican churches) Thomas Cranmer
287.092	(Methodist churches) John Wesley

See also discussion at 220.92; also at 230.04 vs. 230.092, 230.1–.9; also at 232; also at 280: Biography.

230

Christianity   Christian theology

Contextual theology

Contextual theology refers to the study of the doctrines of Christian theology within the context of an area or of a group of people. Usually, specific examples are classed with theology using standard subdivisions T1—08 or T1—09. For example, feminist theology, 230.082; black theology 230.08996; theology in the Asian context 230.095.

The relation of a group of people to Christianity, the church, or to church history is classed in 270.08, e.g., women in Christianity through the centuries 270.082, in the 20th century 270.82082.

230.04 vs. 230.092, 230.1–.9

Specific types of Christian theology vs. [Persons treatment of theology] vs. Doctrines of specific denominations and sects

Use these subdivisions with notation 092 from Table 1 for biography and criticism of individual theologians, e.g., criticism of a United Methodist theologian

230.76092. Class Protestant theologians who are not connected with a specific denomination or who are important and influential enough to transcend their own denominations in 230.044092, e.g., Karl Barth 230.044092. Class theologians not connected with any specific type of theology in 230.092. If in doubt, prefer 230.092. Class critical appraisal of an individual theologian's thought on a specific topic with the topic, e.g., on justification 234.7092.

230.15–.2

[Doctrines of Eastern churches, of Roman Catholic Church]

Class here theology of Eastern and Roman Catholic churches after 1054; for earlier theology, use 230.11–.14.

231.7652 vs. 213, 500, 576.8

Relation of scientific and Christian viewpoints of origin of universe vs. Creation [in philosophy of religion] vs. Natural sciences and mathematics vs. Evolution

Evolution versus creation

Most works on creation science or creationism are classed in 231.7652 because they are written by Christians who assume that the Bible provides a chronology of natural history and who rely upon religious premises in responding to theories from the natural sciences. On the other hand, works by creationist authors that attempt to refute evolution theory by examining the writings, hypotheses, and findings of scientists are classed in 500 with the branch of science criticized. Similarly, works that attempt to refute creation science are usually classed in 231.7652, unless they take the writings of creationists as a starting point from which to demonstrate the case for evolution.

The difficulty stems from the fact that on the question of evolution the *pro* and *con* positions differ so radically that they normally belong in different disciplines, science and religion, respectively. However, when a religious author is trying to enlighten scientists on a specific scientific matter, class the work with science, while if a scientist is trying to enlighten the religious on a specific religious matter, class the work with religion. The place in the classification is determined by the intent of the author, and the interest of the readers that the author is seeking to reach, not by the truth, falsity, or validity of interpretations and premises.

Class comprehensive works including both religion and science in 231.7652.

Among the works that belong in 500, the most common focus of interest is on biological evolution. Class these works in 576.8. If the emphasis of a work is mainly on stellar evolution, class in 523.88; if on basic physical principles, in 530; if on historical geology, in 551.7; and if on paleontology, in 560. If there is no clear emphasis on a specific branch of science, then class in the broad number, 500.

Works that consider the relation between divine creation and evolution as a philosophical problem, without appealing to a particular religion or scripture, are classed in 213. If in doubt between 213 and 231.7652, prefer 231.7652.

232

Jesus Christ and his family   Christology

Class doctrine and theories about Jesus Christ in 232.1–.8, events in the life of Jesus in 232.9, e.g., the doctrine of the resurrection 232.5, historicity and narration of events surrounding the resurrection 232.97.

Use notation 092 from Table 1 for criticism, biography of Christologists (232.092) and Mariologists (232.91092). Class biography of Jesus, Mary, Joseph, Joachim, Anne, and John the Baptist in 232.9, without use of notation 092 from Table 1.

241 vs. 261.8

[Christian] Moral theology vs. Christianity and socioeconomic problems

Some topics are covered in both moral and social theology, e.g., family relationships (241.63, 261.83587). Works classed in 241 focus on what conduct is right or wrong. Works classed in 261.8 may discuss right and wrong, but they treat the topic in a broader context as a problem in society and discuss Christian attitudes toward and influence on the problem. Class in 241 works that emphasize what is right and wrong, or what the individual should do. Class in 261.8 works that stress what the church's stance should be, what response the church or Christian community should make to alleviate the problem, or the church's view on problems transcending individual conduct. If in doubt, prefer 241.

241.3–.4 vs. 241.6

[Sin, vices, virtues] vs. Specific moral issues

Class in 241.3–.4 works about sin, about vices and virtues in general, and about specific vices and virtues. Class in 241.6 works treating specific moral issues in such a way that the works cannot be viewed as being about specific vices or virtues. Vices and virtues are habits, e.g., gluttony, temperance. Works on specific moral issues discuss the morality or immorality of specific actions, e.g., whether it is right to eat meat 241.693. In case of doubt, prefer 241.3–.4.

260 vs. 251–254, 259

Christian social and ecclesiastical theology vs. Local church [and] Pastoral care of specific kinds of persons

The local church is the group in which individual believers can meet regularly face to face for worship, fellowship, and church activities—for example, a congregation, a college church group.

Among the more recent forms of the local church are the small groups called basic Christian communities or basic ecclesial communities. These are smaller than parishes or congregations, but, like other forms of the local church, are organized for the general religious welfare of their members, not just for special projects or functions. They are classed in the same way as parishes, i.e., comprehensive works are classed in 250 (or in 262.26 when treated as part of ecclesiology) and specific aspects are classed with the aspect in the subdivisions of 250.

Activities undertaken by the church may be classed in 250 or 260, depending on the context. Most of the works in 250 are intended for the individual practitioner in the local setting. The local setting may be as small as a parish youth group or as large as a counseling program that serves a metropolitan area. Class the church's attitude to cultural and social problems, and its activities regarding them in 261 unless the context is limited to the local church, e.g., a practical work for the prison chaplain 259.5, but the church's attitude to the treatment of criminals 261.8336. If in doubt, prefer 260.

Some activities that can be conducted by the local church are classed in 260, e.g., public worship (264–265), religious education (268), spiritual renewal and evangelism (269). The context of works on these subjects is often broader than that of the local church.

Class church organization in 262, unless the scope is limited to administration of the local church (254).

261.5

Christianity and secular disciplines

Class here personal Christian views and church teachings about secular disciplines as a whole, their value, how seriously a Christian should take them, how far the disciplines should affect faith. Class Christian philosophy of a secular discipline or Christian theories within a discipline with the discipline, e.g., a Christian philosophy of psychology 150.1. Be alert for specific uses of secular disciplines for religious purposes, e.g., use of drama 246.72. If in doubt, class with the secular discipline.

261.5 vs. 231–239

Christianity and secular disciplines vs. Christian doctrinal theology

Class in 261.5 works treating generally antagonism between and reconciliation of Christian belief and another discipline. Class antagonism of a specific Christian doctrine and another discipline with the doctrine in 231–239. For example, class the relation between Christian doctrines in general and science in 261.55; but class the relation between Christian doctrine on the soul and modern biology in 233.5.

263.9, 291.36 vs. 394.265–.267

Church year and other days and times [of Christian religious observance] and Sacred times [among religions] vs. [Religious holidays]

Class in 263.9, 291.36, and cognate numbers in 290 the religious customs associated with religious holidays, e.g., sunrise Easter services 263.93. Class in 394.265–.267 the secular customs associated with religious holidays, e.g., Easter egg hunts 394.266. If in doubt, prefer 263.9, 291.36, and cognate numbers in 290.

268 vs. 230.071

[Christian] Religious education vs. Education in Christianity, in Christian theology

Class education in and teaching of Christianity as an academic subject in 230.071, e.g., a course on Christianity in secular secondary schools 230.0712. Class in 268 religious education as a ministry of the church for the purpose of confirming believers in Christian faith and life, and religious education programs sponsored by the local church. If in doubt, prefer 268.

Higher education in Christianity and Christian theology usually takes place in divinity schools, theological seminaries, and graduate departments of theology or ministry in universities. Students and scholars in such institutions may be preparing for the ordained ministry or they may be following a course of studies in the academic discipline of theology, or they may be doing both simultaneously. Such institutions are usually engaged both in religious education as a ministry of the church and in the academic study of Christianity and Christian theology. Class all such institutions with higher education in theology, i.e., in 230.0711, rather than in 268. Education or training of the clergy for specialized work is classed with the specialty, e.g., courses in Biblical studies 220.0711, programs in pastoral counseling 253.50711.

Christian religious education of adults, other than in the setting of formal higher education, is provided for at 268.434. Examples of works to be classed in 268.434 are works about adult education in parish religious education programs or Sunday schools.

Study and teaching with regard to any specific topic in Christianity are classed as follows:

> For religious education of children of elementary-school age, class a work on teaching a specific topic with works on religious education of children in general in 268.432.

> For religious education of persons of secondary-school age and older, class a work on teaching a specific topic with the topic, plus notation 071 from Table 1, e.g., study and teaching of church history 270.071.

See also discussion at 291.75 vs. 200.71.

280

Denominations and sects of Christian church

Biography

The kinds of biographies to be classed here are shown in the table of preference for biographies under 230–280: Biography.

The Decimal Classification Division classifies biographies with the main branch of the denomination rather than with the most specific organization or area, e.g., a biography of a clergyman of the Lutheran Church in America 284.1092, not 284.133092; of the African Methodist Episcopal Church 287.8092, not 287.83; of a Russian clergyman of the Eastern Orthodox Church 281.9092, not 281.947092; collected biography of Catholics in the United States 282.092273.

280.042 vs. 262.0011

Relations between denominations vs. Ecumenism

Class the ecumenical movement and interdenominational cooperation in 280.042. Also class in 280.042 relations between two or more specific denominations having notation that differs in the first three digits, e.g., relations between Roman Catholics (282) and Lutherans (284.1). Class works about relations among denominations having the same notation in the first three digits in the most specific number that includes them all, e.g., relations among the various Baptist denominations, between Baptists and Disciples of Christ 286. Class works about relations between one denomination and several others with the denomination emphasized, e.g., relations of Baptists with other denominations 286. Class theoretical works on ecumenism at 262.0011. Class discussions among denominations with respect to a specific subject with the subject, e.g., the Eucharist 234.163. If in doubt, class in 280.042.

281.1–.4

Early church

The early church is considered to be undivided by denominations until the schism of 1054. Therefore, the history of the Church prior to 1054 is classed in 270.1–.3, not here. The history of specific churches prior to 1054 is classed in 274–279.

The early history of the Eastern and Roman Catholic churches is also classed in 270. The history of these churches before 1054 is classed in 270.1–.3 or 274–279. Works on later history or works that cover both the early and later history are classed in 281.5–.9 or 282.

283–289

Protestant and other denominations

Notation for specific denominations is provided under the general name of some denominations, e.g., Presbyterian churches of United States origin 285.1, specific denominations 285.13. A specific denomination here means a named church body uniting a number of individual local churches, e.g., the Presbyterian Church (U.S.A.) 285.137, the Associate Presbyterian Church of North America 285.13 (the latter denomination is not listed in the schedule). In these cases, there is a special span for treatment of the denomination by continent, country, or locality, e.g., 285.14–.19. Class specific denominations in the notation provided for them (under the heading "specific denominations") if they are treated with regard to all or nearly all the geographic area they cover. Class works on a specific denomination covering a smaller area in the span for treatment by continent, country, or locality. For example, the Southern Baptist Convention is classed in 286.132, but a state association of Southern Baptist churches in Tennessee is classed in 286.1768 (286.1 plus notation 768 for Tennessee from Table 2). Class individual local churches in the special area span, regardless of the specific denomination to which they belong. Also class a work about several specific denominations in one country by area, e.g., a work describing the various Presbyterian denominations in the United States 285.173, not 285.13.

In several cases, the notation for specific denominations is limited to churches centered in the United States or the United Kingdom, e.g., the numbers following 284.1, 285.1, 285.2 and 287.5. In these cases, specific denominations in other countries are classed by dividing by area. For example, the Evangelical Lutheran Church in America is classed in 284.135, but the Lutheran Church of Sweden is classed in 284.1485 (284.1 plus notation 485 for Sweden from Table 2).

Churches which are centered in the United States or the United Kingdom may have branches in other countries; thus, there are usually instructions to add any area from Table 2, e.g., at 285.14–.19.

284.143

Lutheran church in Germany

Class here Evangelische Kirche in Deutschland, even though some non-Lutheran churches have joined with it.

290

Comparative religion and religions other than Christianity

290 by itself will never be used, since 291 has been designated as the number for comprehensive works on the non-Christian religions, on Christian and non-Christian religions, and for works on comparative religion.

291

Comparative religion

Except for 296 Judaism and 297 Islam, the subdivisions of the various religions in 292–299 are based on the subdivisions of 291. The order is sometimes different, but all topics in 291 are provided for either explicitly, by synthesis, or by implication under the separate religions included in 292–299. What is said about 291, therefore, will also be true of 292–299.

A comparison of the topics in 291 with the subdivisions of Christianity can sometimes be helpful in determining what goes where. A comparative list follows:

Social theologies	291.17	261
Doctrinal theologies	291.2	230
Public worship	291.3	246–247, 263–265
Religious experience, life, practice	291.4	242, 248
Moral theology	291.5	241
Leaders and organizations	291.6	250, 262, 267
Pastoral theology and work	291.61	253
Missions, religious education	291.7	266, 268
Sources	291.8	220
Denominations, sects, reform movements	291.9	280

A comparison of 291.211 (God, gods, goddesses, divinities and deities) with 231 (God) shows that 291.211 includes the topics listed at 231 that are not limited to Christianity: ways of knowing God, general concepts of God, attributes, providence, love and wisdom, relation to human experience, justice, and goodness.

Denominations and sects

In some cases, there is disagreement as to whether a specific sect should be listed under a religion or whether it should be considered a separate religion. The majority or mainstream members of the religion may not consider it a part of their religion. The criterion used in the Classification is that a denomination or sect is listed in the schedule with the religion to which its members say it belongs.

Treat the early history of a specific religion before its division into sects as general history of the religion, but class a comprehensive survey of the various sects in the number for the sects of the religion, e.g., the sects and reform movements of Buddhism 294.39. A work dealing with both early history and sects is classed in the general number for history of the religion.

Class the history of a specific congregation in the number for the sect to which it belongs, if this can be determined. ("Congregation" here refers to organizations in other religions analogous to the local church in Christianity.) If the sect cannot be determined, class the work in the broadest number for the sects of the religion.

Class religious orders in 291.65 and cognate numbers in 292–299, and not with any sect within the religion to which they may belong.

Common terms

Some terms that have their origin in a particular religion have become commonly used in other religions. Such terms as "karma" and "yoga" originated in Hinduism or other religions of Indic origin. These terms appear in the schedule under 291, because they may be discussed from a point of view not limited to the religion of origin. However, a work on yoga from a Hindu point of view should be classed with Hinduism in 294.5436 rather than in 291.436.

291.75 vs. 200.71

Religious education vs. Education [in religion]

Class in 200.71 education in and teaching of comparative religion, the religions of the world, and religion as an academic subject. 291.75 is meant for discussion of how various religions educate their members (especially young members) to be good followers of their own religions. Such education stresses knowledge of the faith and living as a member of a religion. It is meant to instill the values of a particular religion, not to study it in a detached manner. This type of education is usually termed "religious education" in contrast to the study of religion or "religious studies". In case of doubt as to which type of education is being treated, prefer 291.75.

At the level of higher education, students may be studying their own religion as an academic subject or they may be studying in order to become members of the clergy or they may be doing both at the same time. Religious education at the level of higher education is classed in 200.711 rather than in 291.75. Works about the education of the clergy are also classed with higher education in 200.711.

With regard to any specific topic in comparative religion or the specific religions in 292–299, study and teaching are classed as follows:

> For religious education of children of elementary-school age, class a work on teaching a specific topic with works on religious education of children in general, e.g., Jewish religious education courses on the Tanakh (scriptures) for children 296.68.

> For religious education of persons of secondary-school age and older, class a work on teaching a specific topic with the topic using notation 071 from Table 1, e.g., study of the Tanakh in Jewish colleges and universities 221.0711.

See also discussion at 268 vs. 230.071.

296.12–.14

Talmudic literature and Midrash

Add table

07 Modern commentaries since 1500

> Most editions of the Talmud include the commentaries of ancient and medieval commentators along with the text. Use 07 only for works where the focus is on a commentary written by a modern author. Do not use 07 for works where there are some notes by a modern author but where the focus is on the original text or a translation of the text.

296.18 vs. 340.58

Halakhah (Legal literature) vs. Oriental law

Jewish law concerns itself with most of the issues of life, but its basis is religious. Also, it has rarely been the law of the land of any country. When it addresses secular matters, it is often from a religious perspective, because it is not the civil or criminal law of the land. For these reasons, comprehensive works on Jewish law are classed in 296.18. Class in 340.58 only works proposing or treating Jewish law as the law of a country, or comparing Jewish and other Oriental systems of law.

Class Jewish law on a specific religious topic with the topic elsewhere in 296, e.g., laws of marriage 296.444. Most works on this topic emphasize religious obligations, since they do not discuss the marriage law of a country.

If the law of a country is discussed, class the work with the law in 340, e.g., marriage law of Israel 346.5694016.

297.092

Persons

If a Muslim cannot be identified primarily with one function, activity, or sect, class his biography in 297.092.

For comprehensive biographies of persons of an identifiable function, activity, or sect, use the following table of preference:

Muḥammad the Prophet	297.63
Muḥammad's family	297.64
Muḥammad's companions	297.648
Prophets prior to Muḥammad	297.246092
Other persons in Koran	297.122092
Founders of sects and reform movements	297.8
Founders of Sufi orders	297.48
Higher non-Sufi religious leaders	297.092
Of specific sects and movements	297.8
Theologians	297.2092
Moral theologians	297.5092
Daʻwah workers	297.74
Leaders and members of Sufi orders	297.48
Other Sufis (mystics)	297.4
Religious educators	297.77092
Mosque officers	297.092
Of specific sects and movements	297.8
Members of sects and movements	297.8

Use 297.61 Leaders and their work for the role, function, and duties of religious leaders, not for biography of religious leaders.

Works dealing with only one specialized aspect of a person's career or religious experience are classed with the aspect, e.g., an account of conversion to Islam 297.574092.

297.26–.27

[Islam and secular disciplines]

Class in 297.26–.27 works that focus on theological issues in relation to secular disciplines. Class with the secular discipline works that focus on issues of importance to practitioners of the discipline, works that describe achievements of Muslims working within the discipline. For example, class in 297.267 Islamic attitudes toward the arts, e.g., what kinds of music and visual arts are consistent with Islamic belief. Class works describing achievements of Islamic arts with art. Class a work on Islam and politics that emphasizes Islamic religious issues in 297.272, but class a work on Islam and politics that emphasizes issues primarily of concern to political scientists in 320.917671 (political situation and conditions in the Islamic world) or another subdivision of 320. Class a general theological discussion about what kind of economic system is appropriate for an Islamic country in 297.273, but class a discussion of how to run an interest-free bank that would be of practical interest to a banker in 332.1. If in doubt, prefer a number outside 297.

297.4

Sufism (Islamic mysticism)

All works on Sufism are classed in 297.4 or one of its subdivisions, e.g., Sufi concepts of God 297.4111, Sufi worship 297.43, Sufi religious life and practice 297.44, Sufi orders 297.48. Comprehensive and non-Sufi works on Islam are classed in 297 and its subdivisions other than 297.4, e.g., comprehensive works on Sufi and non-Sufi Islamic views of God 297.211.

If in doubt, prefer a number outside 297.4.

299.93

Religions of eclectic and syncretistic origin

New Age religions

The "New Age" is a term that can be used to describe a great variety of works. There are New Age perspectives on health and medicine, environmentalism, gardening, and other activities and areas of knowledge. Class such works with the subject and discipline under discussion, even if the discussion rejects some of the main tenets of the discipline, e.g., using mental energy to cure illness 615.851.

Some New Age literature is mostly concerned with psychic and paranormal phenomena and is classed in 130 and its subdivisions.

Much of the New Age literature is religious. If a work is concerned with several New Age religions, class it in 299.93, unless it includes sects of the more established religions, e.g., sects of Buddhism, Hinduism, Native American religion, etc. In that case, class the work in 291, with other works on comparative religion.

In some cases, a writer will address some aspect of religion from a New Age perspective without attempting to speak for a particular known religion or to establish a new religion or sect. Class such works in 291, e.g., a New Age perspective on spirituality 291.4.

Class comprehensive works on the New Age as a whole or as a movement in 299.93.

320.55 vs. 297.09, 322.1

Religiously oriented [political] theories and ideologies vs. Historical, geographic, persons treatment [of Islam] vs. [Relation of the state to] Religious organizations and groups

Islamic fundamentalism

Class in 297.09 and other subdivisions of 297 only works that emphasize religious aspects of Islamic fundamentalism, such as a concern to maintain and hand down a pure version of the Islamic faith, a mindfulness to follow the strict letter of the Koran and Hadith, an attempt to generate a religious reawakening through preaching, teaching, and other forms of religious communication. Class in 297.272 Islam and politics only works that treat politics from the religious point of view.

Many works about Islamic fundamentalism, however, emphasize political aspects from a secular viewpoint; such works are classed in political science. Works emphasizing the religiously oriented political ideologies of Islamic fundamentalism are classed in 320.55. Works emphasizing the political role of Islamic fundamentalist organizations and groups in relation to the state are classed in 322.1.

If in doubt between a political science number and a subdivision of 297, prefer a political science number. If in doubt between 320.55 and 322.1, prefer 320.55.

322.1 vs. 261.7, 291.177

[Relation of the state to] Religious organizations and groups vs. Christianity and political affairs [and] Religions and political affairs

261.7, 291.177 and related numbers in 292–299 are in social theology, and are used for works on the position that religious people and organizations take or should take toward political affairs (including the state). 322.1 is used for works with a secular perspective, discussing the relationships between religious organizations or movements and states or governments. If in doubt, class in 322.1.

322.1 vs. 296.382, 320.54095694

[Relation of state to] Religious organizations and groups vs. Judaism and politics vs. [Nationalism in] Palestine Israel

Class in 296.382 works concerning politics and the state from the point of view of the religion of Judaism, e.g., whether it is a religious duty to support civil rights, whether Judaism encourages political freedom. Class political ideologies which are inspired by Judaism with Zionism in 320.54095694. Class the relation of religious groups to the state from a secular viewpoint in 322.1, e.g., religion and the state in Israel 322.1095694.

If in doubt between 296.382 and a political science number, prefer a political science number. If in doubt between 320.54095694 and 322.1, prefer 322.1.

340.59 vs. 297.14

Islamic law vs. [Islamic] Religious and ceremonial laws and decisions

Class in 297.14 comprehensive works on Islamic law concerning religious matters, such as ritual purification, ritual prayer, fasting, zakat, the hajj, sacred places. Class Islamic law on a specific religious topic with the topic, e.g., fasting 297.53. Class Islamic law on religious topics in religion even if the laws are being enforced by the state rather than just by religious organizations.

Class in 340.59 comprehensive works on Islamic law concerning secular matters, such as contract law, criminal law, social welfare law, law of inheritance. Class Islamic law on a specific secular topic with the topic in 342–347, e.g., law of inheritance in Saudi Arabia 346.538052.

Class in 340.59 interdisciplinary works about Islamic law covering both religious and secular topics. If in doubt, prefer 340.59.

Some topics, such as family and marriage, have both religious and secular aspects. Works on the Islamic law of such topics are rarely limited to the religious aspects and thus rarely classed in religion. In particular, always class in 340 works about laws on such topics if the laws under discussion are enforced by the state. For example, class family law of Pakistan in 346.549015, marriage law of Pakistan in 346.549016.

398.2 vs. 291.13

Folk literature vs. Mythology and mythological foundations [of religions]

Works on the mythology of a people or on mythologies from around the world are usually concerned with the most basic beliefs of people and with religious beliefs and practices. Such works are predominantly concerned with religion and are classed in 291.13. But mythology may refer also to beliefs and stories that can be referred to as superstitions, legends, fairy tales, etc., where the religious content or interest is not apparent. Class in 398.2 mythology having a nonreligious basis. Interdisciplinary works on mythology are classed in 398.2, since this number includes folk narratives with a broader focus than religion alone. If in doubt, prefer 398.2.

Religious myths are classed either in 398.2 or 291.13 according to content, mode of presentation, or author's or editor's intention. Mythology presented from a strictly theological point of view or presented as an embodiment of the religion of a people is classed in 291.13. However, myths or mythology presented in terms of cultural entertainment or, especially, as representatives of the early literary expression of a society are classed in 398.2, even if they are populated by gods and goddesses. Often the literary or religious focus is clear. For example, almost all Greco-Roman myths retold for a juvenile audience are classed in 398.2; but Jataka tales are usually classed in 294.382325 because they illustrate the character of the Buddha.

Specific myths and legends presented as examples of a people's religion are classed with the subject in religion, e.g., legends of Jesus' coming to Britain 232.9.

615.852 vs. 234.131, 291.31

Religious and psychic therapy vs. [the Christian gift of] healing [and] Religious healing

In many cultures, medicine and healing involve rites and ceremonies and religious beliefs, as well as physical practices. Class a work on healing and medicine in 615.852 if it focuses on religious practices as a part of the medical practice.

Also class in 615.852 works on the use of psychic and paranormal powers in healing that do not mention a religious context.

Class in 291.31 or 234.131 healing as a religious practice, including such topics as religious beliefs about illness, rituals and prayers for healing, miraculous cures by charismatic leaders or saints. Often, works on this topic are also concerned with emotional or spiritual healing as well as physical healing, or in place of physical healing.

If in doubt, prefer 615.852.

Other numbers used for works concerning illness or medicine and religion should be kept in mind:

Religion and health and illness and the social questions and programs concerning them	291.178321
Christianity	261.8321
Religion and the art and science of medicine	291.175
Christianity	261.561
Discussion of whether cures are miracles	291.2117
Christianity	231.73
Philosophy of religion	212

616.86 vs. 158.1, 248.8629, 291.442, 362.29

[Medical aspects of] Substance abuse (Drug abuse) vs. [Applied psychology aspects of] Personal improvement and analysis vs. [Guides to Christian life for persons experiencing substance abuse and Religious life for] Persons experiencing illness, trouble, addiction, bereavement vs. Substance abuse [as a social problem]

Recovery from addiction

Class in 616.86 self-help programs for individuals recovering from substance abuse and interdisciplinary works about recovery programs that focus on the individual's life with addiction, covering the individual's experience with both social and medical aspects. Class in 362.29 the organization providing the program, including administration of the program, and interdisciplinary works that cover both organizational and therapeutic aspects of recovery programs. Class in 248.8629, 291.442, and related numbers in 290 religious guides and inspirational works for the recovering addict. If in doubt, class in 616.86.

As a kind of medical service, recovery programs for persons recovering from a specific kind of substance abuse are classed with the substance, plus notation 03 Rehabilitation or notation 06 Therapy from the add table under 616.1–.9. No distinction is made between programs run by professionals, such as psychiatrists or clinical psychologists, and self-help programs run by laypersons; both kinds of recovery programs are classed as therapy for or rehabilitation from a medical problem. Notation 06 is used for programs, such as twelve step programs, to stop or cure the illness. Notation 03 is used for programs to help the individual remain cured. If in doubt, prefer notation 06.

As a kind of social service, recovery programs for those recovering from a specific kind of substance abuse are classed with the substance in 362.29, plus notation 86 Counseling and guidance from the add table under 362–363. Works classed in 362.29 typically emphasize the organizational or institutional aspects of the program.

For example, interdisciplinary works on life as a recovering alcoholic are classed in 616.86103. The twelve step Alcoholics Anonymous program is classed in 616.86106. Comprehensive works on Alcoholics Anonymous, the organization which provides the program and places for individuals in the program to meet, are classed in 362.29286. A general guide to a recovering alcoholic on how to live a religious life is classed in 291.442; a Christian life, 248.86292.

Works on recovery from addiction are not classed in 158.1 Personal improvement and analysis in applied psychology because psychology applied to a medical problem is classed with the medical problem, not in 150.

Appendixes

Appendix A

**Optional numbers for books of Bible as arranged in Tanakh
(Jewish Bible, Hebrew Bible) (Option A)**

The following schedule is an optional arrangement for books of the Bible as found in Jewish Bibles. The preferred arrangement is at 222-224 in the regular schedule. Option B is given as 296.11 in the regular schedule. The see references and footnote instructions in this optional arrangement refer to numbers in the schedules, not to other numbers found in the Manual entries.

> **(222–224) Optional numbers for books of Bible as arranged in Tanakh (Jewish Bible, Hebrew Bible)**

　　　　Class comprehensive works in 221

　　　　For Apocrypha, pseudepigrapha, see 229

　　　　See Manual at 221: Optional numbers for books of Tanakh

(222) ***Torah (Pentateuch)**

　　　　(Optional number; prefer standard 222.1)

(.1) ***Genesis**

　　　　(Optional number; prefer standard 222.11)

(.2) ***Exodus**

　　　　(Optional number; prefer standard 222.12)

　　　　For Ten Commandments, see 222.6

(.3) ***Leviticus**

　　　　(Optional number; prefer standard 222.13)

(.4) ***Numbers**

　　　　(Optional number; prefer standard 222.14)

(.5) ***Deuteronomy**

　　　　(Optional number; prefer standard 222.15)

　　　　For Ten Commandments, see 222.6

(.6) ***Ten Commandments (Decalogue)**

　　　　(Optional number; prefer standard 222.16)

---

*Add as instructed under 221–229

(223) *Prophetic books (Nevi'im)

(Optional number; prefer standard 224)

(.1) *Former Prophets (Nevi'im rishonim)

(Optional number; prefer standard 222)

(.11) *Joshua

(Optional number; prefer standard 222.2)

(.12) *Judges

(Optional number; prefer standard 222.32)

(.13) *Samuel

(Optional number; prefer standard 222.4)

(.131) *Samuel 1

(Optional number; prefer standard 222.43)

(.132) *Samuel 2

(Optional number; prefer standard 222.44)

(.14) *Kings

(Optional number; prefer standard 222.5)

(.141) *Kings 1

(Optional number; prefer standard 222.53)

(.142) *Kings 2

(Optional number; prefer standard 222.54)

(.2) *Later Prophets (Nevi'im aharonim)

(Optional number; prefer standard 224)

For Isaiah, see 223.3; for Jeremiah, see 223.4; for Ezekiel, see 223.5; for Minor Prophets, see 223.6

(.3) *Isaiah

(Optional number; prefer standard 224.1)

(.4) *Jeremiah

(Optional number; prefer standard 224.2)

(.5) *Ezekiel

(Optional number; prefer standard 224.4)

---

*Add as instructed under 221–229

(.6)	***Minor prophets**	

        (Optional number; prefer standard 224.9)

        For Zephaniah, Haggai, Zechariah, Malachi, see 223.7

(.61)   *Hosea

        (Optional number; prefer standard 224.6)

(.62)   *Joel

        (Optional number; prefer standard 224.7)

(.63)   *Amos

        (Optional number; prefer standard 224.8)

(.64)   *Obadiah

        (Optional number; prefer standard 224.91)

(.65)   *Jonah

        (Optional number; prefer standard 224.92)

(.66)   *Micah

        (Optional number; prefer standard 224.93)

(.67)   *Nahum

        (Optional number; prefer standard 224.94)

(.68)   *Habakkuk

        (Optional number; prefer standard 224.95)

(.7)   ***Zephaniah, Haggai, Zechariah, Malachi**

        (Optional number; prefer standard 224.9)

(.71)   *Zephaniah

        (Optional number; prefer standard 224.96)

(.72)   *Haggai

        (Optional number; prefer standard 224.97)

(.73)   *Zechariah

        (Optional number; prefer standard 224.98)

(.74)   *Malachi

        (Optional number; prefer standard 224.99)

---

*Add as instructed under 221–229

(224)   *Writings (Ketuvim)

(Optional number; prefer standard 223)

(.1)   *Psalms

(Optional number; prefer standard 223.2)

(.2)   *Proverbs

(Optional number; prefer standard 223.7)

(.3)   *Job

(Optional number; prefer standard 223.1)

(.4)   *Megillot (Five scrolls)

(Optional number; prefer standard 221.044)

(.41)   *Song of Solomon (Canticle of Canticles, Song of Songs)

(Optional number; prefer standard 223.9)

(.42)   *Ruth

(Optional number; prefer standard 222.35)

(.43)   *Lamentations

(Optional number; prefer standard 224.3)

(.44)   *Ecclesiastes (Kohelet, Qohelet)

(Optional number; prefer standard 223.8)

(.45)   *Esther

(Optional number; prefer standard 222.9)

(.5)   *Daniel

(Optional number; prefer standard 224.5)

(.6)   *Ezra

(Optional number; prefer standard 222.7)

(.7)   *Nehemiah

(Optional number; prefer standard 222.8)

---

*Add as instructed under 221–229

(.8)	***Chronicles**
	(Optional number; prefer standard 222.6)
(.81)	*Chronicles 1
	(Optional number; prefer standard 222.63)
(.82)	*Chronicles 2
	(Optional number; prefer standard 222.64)

*Add as instructed under 221-229

Appendix B:
170 Ethics

Some entries in the index have been built by adding *unabridged* numbers from *outside the 200 class*.

Since many of these entries have been built with numbers from 172-179 Applied ethics, class 170 from Edition 21 has been included for your use. An example of such a built number follows:

              Civil disobedience
                 ethics
                    religion   291.562 1

The built number 291.5621 is made up of two elements: 291.56 Specific moral issues + 21 (last two digits from 172.1 Relation of individuals to state).

Instructions on how to build such numbers are provided in the 200 schedule.

170 Ethics (Moral philosophy)

Class here ethics of specific subjects and disciplines, interdisciplinary works on social ethics

For religious ethics, see 291.5; for social ethics as a method of social control, see 303.372. For ethics of a specific religion, see the religion, e.g., Christian moral theology 241

See Manual at 170; also at 170 vs. 303.372

SUMMARY

170.1–.9	Standard subdivisions and special topics
171	Ethical systems
172	Political ethics
173	Ethics of family relationships
174	Occupational ethics
175	Ethics of recreation, leisure, public performances, communication
176	Ethics of sex and reproduction
177	Ethics of social relations
178	Ethics of consumption
179	Other ethical norms

- **.4** **Special topics**

- .42 Metaethics

    Class bases for specific systems in 171

- .44 Normative ethics

- [.440 8] History and description with respect to kinds of persons

    Do not use; class in 170.8

- **.8** **History and description with respect to kinds of persons**

- [.88] Occupational and religious groups

    Do not use for ethics of occupational groups; class in 174. Do not use for ethics of religious groups; class in 291.5

- .92 Persons

    See Manual at 170.92 vs. 171

171 Ethical systems

Regardless of time or place

Class a specific topic in ethics, regardless of the system within which it is treated, with the topic in 172–179, e.g., professional ethics 174

See Manual at 170.92 vs. 171

.1 Systems based on authority

.2 Systems based on intuition, moral sense, reason

Including empiricism, existentialism, humanism, natural law, naturalism, stoicism

For systems and doctrines based on conscience, see 171.6

See also 171.7 for systems based on biology, genetics, evolution; 340.112 for natural law in legal theory

.3 Perfectionism

Systems based on self-realization, personal fulfillment

.4 Hedonism

Systems based on achievement of individual pleasure or happiness

.5 Utilitarianism and consequentialism

Standard subdivisions are added for either or both topics in heading

.6 Systems based on conscience

Including casuistry, conflict of duties

.7 Systems based on biology, genetics, evolution, education, social factors

Including communist ethics, relativism, situation ethics, sociobiological ethics

See also 171.2 for systems based on natural law, naturalism

.8 Systems based on altruism

For utilitarianism, see 171.5

.9 Systems based on egoism

For hedonism, see 171.4

> **172–179 Applied ethics (Social ethics)**

Ethics of specific human qualities, relationships, activities

Class comprehensive works in 170

172 Political ethics

.1	**Relation of individuals to the state**
	Including civic and political activity, military service, obedience to law, payment of taxes, resistance, revolution, civil war
.2	**Duties of the state**
	Duties of government toward citizens, e.g., education, freedom, personal security, welfare; duties of officeholders and officials
	Class here justice
.4	**International relations**
	Including conduct of foreign affairs, disarmament, espionage
.42	War and peace
	Standard subdivisions are added for either or both topics in heading
	Including conscientious objection, just war theory, pacifism, ways and means of conducting warfare
	Class occupational ethics of military personnel in 174.9355
	For civil war, see 172.1
.422	Nuclear weapons and nuclear war
	Standard subdivisions are added for either or both topics in heading

173 Ethics of family relationships

Including ethics of marriage, divorce, separation, parent-child relationships, sibling relationships

Class ethics of sex and reproduction in 176

174 Occupational ethics

Class here economic, professional ethics; ethics of work

.1	**Clergy**
	See Manual at 174.1
.2	**Medical professions**
	Class medical ethics related to human reproduction in 176
.22	Hippocratic oath
.24	Questions of life and death
	For euthanasia, see 179.7; for abortion, see 179.76
.25	Innovative procedures
	Including genetic engineering, organ transplants
	Class comprehensive works on bioethics in 174.957

	.26	Economic questions
		Including advertising, fee splitting
	.28	Experimentation
		Class here experimentation on human subjects
		For experimentation on animals, see 179.4
	.3	**Legal professions**
	.4	**Business ethics**
		Including industrial espionage
		Class here ethics of finance, manufacturing, trade
	.6	**Gambling business**
		Including lottery management
		See also 175 for gambling
	.9	**Other professions and occupations**
		Add to base number 174.9 notation 09–99 from Table 7, e.g., ethics of genetic engineering 174.957; however, for ethics of public administration and public office, see 172.2
175		**Ethics of recreation, leisure, public performances, communication**
		Including ethics of dancing, gambling, music, television; fair play, sportsmanship
		Ethics of hunting relocated to 179.3
		Class occupational ethics for those involved in the recreation industry with the industry in 174, e.g., occupational ethics for professional athletes 174.9796
[.1–.9]		**Ethics of specific types of recreation**
		Numbers discontinued; class in 175
176		**Ethics of sex and reproduction**
		Including artificial insemination, celibacy, chastity, contraception, embryo transplant, homosexuality, premarital and extramarital relations, promiscuity, surrogate motherhood
		Class abortion in 179.76
		See also 177.65 for ethics of courtship, 177.7 for ethics of love
	.5	**Prostitution**
	.7	**Obscenity and pornography**
		Standard subdivisions are added for either or both topics in heading
		For obscenity and pornography in literature, see 176.8; for obscenity in speech, see 179.5

	.8	**Obscenity and pornography in literature**
		Standard subdivisions are added for either or both topics in heading
177		**Ethics of social relations**
		Limited to the topics provided for below
	.1	**Courtesy, hospitality, politeness**
		Class etiquette in 395
	.2	**Conversation**
		Including gossip
	.3	**Truthfulness, lying, slander, flattery**
	.4	**Personal appearance**
		Including exposure of person, ostentatious dress
	.5	**Slavery and discriminatory practices**
		Standard subdivisions are added for either or both topics in heading
	.6	**Friendship and courtship**
	.62	Friendship
	.65	Courtship
		Class sexual ethics in courtship in 176
	.7	**Love**
		Including benevolence, caring, charity, kindness, liberality, philanthropy
		See also 128.46 for love as human experience
178		**Ethics of consumption**
		Including abstinence, gluttony, greed, overindulgence, temperance
		Class here use of natural resources, of wealth
		Class environmental and ecological ethics, respect for nature in 179.1; class consumption of meat in 179.3
	.1	**Consumption of alcoholic beverages**
	.7	**Consumption of tobacco**
	.8	**Consumption of narcotics**
179		**Other ethical norms**
		Class here cruelty
	[.01–.09]	Standard subdivisions
		Do not use; class in 170

.1	**Respect for life and nature**

Standard subdivisions are added for either or both topics in heading

Class here environmental and ecological ethics

> *For ethics of consumption, see 178; for treatment of animals, see 179.3; for respect for human life, see 179.7*

.2	**Treatment of children**

> *For parent-child relationships, see 173*

.3	**Treatment of animals**

Including ethics of hunting [*formerly* 175], vegetarianism

> *For experimentation on animals, see 179.4*

.4	**Experimentation on animals**

Including vivisection

.5	**Blasphemy, profanity, obscenity in speech**

Standard subdivisions are added for any or all topics in heading

.6	**Courage and cowardice**
.7	**Respect and disrespect for human life**

Standard subdivisions are added for either or both topics in heading

Including capital punishment, dueling, euthanasia, genocide, homicide, suicide

Class here comprehensive works on ethics of violence, of nonviolence

Class medical ethics in 174.2; class ethics of contraception in 176

> *For ethics of violence, of nonviolence in political activity, see 172; for ethics of civil war, see 172.1; for ethics of war, see 172.42; for treatment of children, see 179.2*

76	Abortion
.8	**Vices, faults, failings**

Not otherwise provided for

Including anger, cheating, covetousness, envy, hatred, jealousy, pride, sloth

.9	**Virtues**

Not otherwise provided for

Including cheerfulness, gentleness, gratitude, honesty, humility, modesty, patience, prudence, self-control, self-reliance, toleration

Class here virtue

Relative Index

Use of the Relative Index

Alphabetizing is word by word. A hyphenated word is filed as two words. Initialisms and acronyms are entered without punctuation and are filed as if spelled as one word. Entries beginning with the same word or phrase are arranged as follows:

>Term
>Term. Subheading
>Term (Parenthetical qualifier)
>Term, inverted term qualifier
>Term as part of phrase

In the Relative Index, topics are arranged alphabetically, with the terms identifying the discipline or subdiscipline in which they are treated subarranged alphabetically under them. The first class number displayed in an index entry (opposite the unindented term) is the number for interdisciplinary works. See-also references or see-Manual references come at the end of the alphabet of subentries or under the subentry to which the reference applies. See-Manual references follow see-also references under the same term.

Digits are printed in groups of three for ease in reading and copying. The spaces are not part of the numbers, and the groups are not related to the segmentation shown in DDC numbers on Library of Congress cataloging records.

Two abbreviations are used in the index:

>O.T.   Old Testament
>N.T.   New Testament

Relative Index

A

Abbeys	
church history	271
religious significance of buildings	246.97
Abdias (Biblical book)	224.91
Abel (Biblical person)	
Bible stories	222.110 950 5
Abhidhammapiṭaka	294.382 4
Abhidharmapiṭaka	294.382 4
Ablutions	
Islam	297.38
Abodah Zarah	296.123 4
Babylonian Talmud	296.125 4
Mishnah	296.123 4
Palestinian Talmud	296.124 4
Abortion	
ethics	
religion	291.569 76
Buddhism	294.356 976
Christianity	241.697 6
Hinduism	294.548 697 6
Islam	297.569 76
Judaism	296.369 76
social theology	291.178 366 67
Christianity	261.836 667
Judaism	296.38
Aboth	296.123 47
Abraham (Patriarch)	
Bible	222.110 92
Islam	297.246 3
Absolution (Christian rite)	234.166
public worship	265.64
theology	234.166
Abstinence	
religious practice	291.447
Buddhism	294.344 47
Christianity	248.47
Hinduism	294.544 7
Islam	297.576
Judaism	296.7
Abū Dā'ūd Sulaymān ibn al-Ash'ath al-Sijistānī	
Hadith	297.124 2
Abused children	
social theology	291.178 327 1
Christianity	261.832 71
Accountability	
Christian doctrines	233.4
Acts of the Apostles	226.6
pseudepigrapha	229.925
Actual grace	234.1
Adam	
Bible stories	222.110 950 5
Islam	297.246
Addiction	
devotional literature	291.432
Christianity	242.4
pastoral theology	291.61
Christianity	259.429
religious guidance	291.442
Christianity	248.862 9
social theology	291.178 322 9
Christianity	261.832 29
Adi Granth	294.682
Adolescents	
religion	200.835
Christianity	270.083 5
devotional literature	242.63
guides to Christian life	248.83
pastoral care of	259.23
religious education	268.433
sermons	252.55
social theology	261.834 235
guides to life	291.440 835
Judaism	296.083 5
guides to life	296.708 35
religious education	296.680 835
social theology	291.178 342 35
Adoration of magi	232.923
Adoration of shepherds	232.922
Adult baptism	234.161 3
public worship	265.13
theology	234.161 3
Adult child abuse victims	
social theology	291.178 327 3
Christianity	261.832 73
Adult child sexual abuse victims	
social theology	291.178 327 3
Christianity	261.832 73
Adultery	
ethics	
religion	291.566
see also Sexual relations—ethics—religion	
social theology	291.178 357 36
Christianity	261.835 736
Adults	
religion	200
Christianity	230
guides to Christian life	248.84
religious education	268.434
social theology	261.834 24
social theology	291.178 342 4

Dewey Decimal Classification

Advent	263.912
devotional literature	242.332
sermons	252.612
Advent Christian Church	286.73
see also Adventists	
Adventists	286.7
biography	286.709 2
church government	262.067
parishes	254.067
church law	262.986 7
doctrines	230.67
catechisms and creeds	238.67
guides to Christian life	248.486 7
missions	266.67
moral theology	241.046 7
public worship	264.067
religious associations	267.186 7
religious education	268.867
seminaries	230.073 67
theology	230.67
African American Methodist churches	287.8
see also Methodist Church	
African independent churches	289.93
see also Christian denominations	
African Methodist Episcopal Church	287.83
see also Methodist Church	
African Methodist Episcopal Zion Church	287.83
see also Methodist Church	
African religions	299.6
Agama	294.482
Agapes (Christian rites)	265.9
Aggadah	296.19
Midrash	296.142
Talmud	296.127 6
Aggeus (Biblical book)	224.97
Agnosticism	211.7
Christian polemics	239.7
philosophy of religion	211.7
Agnostics	211.709 2
Agnus Dei	264.36
Agrapha	229.8
Aharonim	296.180 92
Ahilot	296.123 6
Ahimsa	294.548 697
Buddhism	294.356 97
Hinduism	294.548 697
Jainism	294.456 97
Ahmadiyya movement	297.86
doctrines	297.204 6

AIDS (Disease)	
church work with patients	259.419 697 92
social theology	291.178 321 969 792
Christianity	261.832 196 979 2
Albigensianism	273.6
denomination	284.4
see also Christian denominations	
persecution of	272.3
Alcoholic beverages	
ethics	
religion	291.568 1
Christianity	241.681
Islam	297.568 1
Judaism	296.368 1
Alcoholism	
pastoral theology	291.61
Christianity	259.429 2
social theology	291.178 322 92
Christianity	261.832 292
Allah	297.211
Allegory	
Biblical	220.68
Koran	297.122 68
Almsgiving	291.446
Christianity	248.46
Islam	297.54
Altar railings	247.1
Altar screens	247.1
Altars	291.37
Christianity	247.1
American Baptist Association	286.136
see also Baptists	
American Baptist Churches in the U.S.A.	286.131
see also Baptists	
American Baptist Convention	286.131
see also Baptists	
American Evangelical Lutheran Church	284.133 2
see also Lutheran church	
American Lutheran Church	284.131
see also Lutheran church	
American Muslim Mission	297.87
American native peoples	
religion	299.7
North America	299.7
South America	299.8
American Reformed Church	285.7
see also Reformed Church (American Reformed)	
American Revised version Bible	220.520 4
American Standard version Bible	220.520 4
Amish	
biography	289.709 2

Amish churches	289.73	Animism	
see also Mennonite Church		comparative religion	291.21
Amoraim	296.120 092	Anne (Mother of the Virgin	
Amos (Biblical book)	224.8	Mary), Saint	232.933
Amulets		private prayers to	242.75
Islamic popular practices	297.39	Annihilationism	236.23
religious significance	291.37	Annunciation to Mary	232.912
Anabaptists	284.3	Anointing of the sick	234.167
see also Christian		public worship	265.7
denominations		theology	234.167
Ancestors		Ante-Nicene church	270.1
objects of worship	291.213	Anthropology	
Angels	291.215	theological	291.22
Christianity	235.3	Christianity	233
Islam	297.215	philosophy of religion	218
Judaism	296.315	see also Humans—religion	
Anger		Anthropomorphism	
ethics		comparative religion	291.211 2
religion	291.5	philosophy of religion	211
see also Vices—religion		Anthroposophy	299.935
Anglican Communion	283	Anti-mission Baptists	286.4
church government	262.03	see also Baptists	
parishes	254.03	Anti-Semitism	
church law	262.983	social theology	291.172
doctrines	230.3	Christianity	261.26
catechisms and creeds	238.3	Anti-Trinitarianism	289.1
general councils	262.53	Antichrist	236
guides to Christian life	248.483	Antimission Baptists	286.4
liturgy	264.03	see also Baptists	
missions	266.3	Antinomianism	273.6
moral theology	241.043	Antinuclear movement	
persecution by Queen Mary	272.6	social theology	291.178 732
public worship	264.03	see also Nuclear warfare	
religious associations	267.183	Antonines	255.18
religious education	268.83	church history	271.18
religious orders	255.83	Apocalypse (Biblical book)	228
church history	271.83	Apocalypses (Biblical literature)	220.046
women	255.983	New Testament	
church history	271.983	pseudepigrapha	229.94
seminaries	230.073 3	Old Testament pseudepigrapha	229.913
theology	230.3	Apocrypha (Bible)	229
Anglican sacred music		Apocryphal wisdom literature	229.3
public worship		Apologetics	291.2
religion	264.030 2	Christianity	239
Anglicans		Islam	297.29
biography	283.092	Judaism	296.35
Animal sacrifice	291.34	Apostates	
Animals		Christian polemics	239.7
ethical treatment of		Apostles	225.92
religion	291.569 3	Apostles' Creed	238.11
Buddhism	294.356 93	Apostleship (Spiritual gift)	234.13
Christianity	241.693	Apostolic Church	270.1
Hinduism	294.548 693	Apostolic succession	262.11
Judaism	296.369 3	Apostolicity	262.72
religious worship	291.212	Apparitions of Mary	232.917
Animals in Bible	220.859	'Aqā'id (Islam)	297.2

Arabic language		Arts and religion	291.175
Biblical texts	220.46	Buddhism	294.337 5
Hadith texts	297.124 04	Christianity	261.57
Koran texts	297.122 4	Hinduism	294.517 5
Arakhin	296.123 5	Islam	297.267
Babylonian Talmud	296.125 5	Judaism	296.377
Mishnah	296.123 5	Arya-Samaj	294.556 3
Aramaic languages		Ascension of Jesus Christ	232.97
Biblical texts	220.42	Ascension of Mary	232.914
Midrashic texts	296.140 4	Ascensiontide	263.93
Talmudic texts	296.120 4	devotional literature	242.36
Aranyakas	294.592 1	sermons	252.63
Archaeology		Ascent to Heaven of Muhammad	297.633
Bible	220.93	Asceticism	291.447
Archbishops	270.092	Buddhism	294.344 47
biography	270.092	Christianity	248.47
specific denominations	280	Hinduism	294.544 7
see Manual at 230–280		Islam	297.576
ecclesiology	262.12	Sufi	297.446
Architecture		Judaism	296.7
religious significance	291.37	Ash Wednesday	263.925
Christianity	246.9	devotional literature	242.35
see also Arts—religious		sermons	252.625
significance		Ashkenazic liturgy	296.45
Ari liturgy	296.450 4	'Āshūrā'	297.36
Arianism	273.4	Assemblies of God	289.94
Ark of the Covenant	296.493	see also Christian	
Armageddon	236.9	denominations	
Armenian Church	281.62	Assisted suicide	
see also Eastern churches		ethics	
Armenian language		religion	291.569 7
Biblical texts	220.49	see also Right to die—	
Arminians	284.9	ethics—religion	
see also Christian		Associations for religious work	291.65
denominations		Christianity	267
Arms race		Judaism	296.67
ethics		Assumption of Mary	232.914
religion	291.562 422	Astrolatry	291.212
social theology	291.178 732	Astrology and religion	291.175
see also Nuclear warfare		Christianity	261.513
Art and religion	291.175	Astronomical interpretation	
see also Arts and religion		Bible	220.68
Artificial insemination		Astronomy and religion	291.175
ethics		Christianity	261.55
religion	291.566	philosophy of religion	215.2
Christianity	241.66	Athanasian Creed	238.144
Judaism	296.366	Atharvaveda	294.592 15
Arts		Atheism	211.8
religious significance	291.37	Christian polemics	239.7
Buddhism	294.343 7	Islamic view	297.289
Christianity	246	Atheistic religions	291.14
Hinduism	294.537	Atheists	211.809 2
Islam	297.3	Atonement	291.22
Judaism	296.46	Christianity	234.5
		Islam	297.22
		Judaism	296.32

Relative Index

Atonement Day	
Judaism	296.432
liturgy	296.453 2
Atonement of Jesus Christ	232.3
Attributes of God	212.7
Christianity	231.4
comparative religion	291.211 2
Islam	297.211 2
Judaism	296.311 2
philosophy of religion	212.7
Attributes of the Church	262.72
Audiovisual materials	
Christian religious education	268.635
Augsburg Confession	238.41
Augustana Evangelical Lutheran Church	284.133 3
see also Lutheran church	
Augustinians	255.4
church history	271.4
Australian aborigines	
religion	299.921 5
Authority	
ethical systems	
Christianity	241.2
religion	291.65
Christianity	262.8
Judaism	296.67
Authorized version (Bible)	220.520 3
Authorship of Bible	220.66
Avarice	
moral theology	291.568
see also Greed—moral theology	
Ave Maria	242.74
Avesta	295.82
Avodah Zarah	296.123 4
Babylonian Talmud	296.125 4
Mishnah	296.123 4
Palestinian Talmud	296.124 4
Avot	296.123 47
Ayatollahs	297.092
biography	297.092
specific sects	297.8
role and function	297.61
see Manual at 297.092	

B

Baba Batra	296.123 4
Babylonian Talmud	296.125 4
Mishnah	296.123 4
Palestinian Talmud	296.124 4
Baba Kamma	296.123 4
Babylonian Talmud	296.125 4
Mishnah	296.123 4
Palestinian Talmud	296.124 4
Baba Mezia	296.123 4
Babylonian Talmud	296.125 4
Mishnah	296.123 4
Palestinian Talmud	296.124 4
Babism	297.92
Babists	
biography	297.920 92
Babylonian Talmud	296.125
Bahai Faith	297.93
Bahais	
biography	297.930 92
Baptism	234.161
public worship	265.1
theology	234.161
Baptism in the Holy Spirit	234.13
Baptism of Jesus Christ	232.95
Baptismal fonts	247.1
Baptist General Conference of America	286.5
see also Baptists	
Baptist sacred music	
public worship	
religion	264.060 2
Baptists	286
biography	286.092
church government	262.06
parishes	254.06
church law	262.986
doctrines	230.6
catechisms and creeds	238.6
general councils	262.56
guides to Christian life	248.486
missions	266.6
moral theology	241.046
persecution of	272.8
public worship	264.06
religious associations	267.186
religious education	268.86
seminaries	230.073 6
theology	230.6
Bar mitzvah	296.442 4
liturgy	296.454 24
Baraita	296.126 3
Barnabites	255.52
church history	271.52
Baruch (Bible)	229.5
Basic Christian communities	250
ecclesiology	262.26
see Manual at 260 vs. 251–254, 259	

Basilians	255.17	Berit milah	296.442 2
church history	271.17	liturgy	296.454 22
Bat mitzvah	296.443 4	Bezah	296.123 2
liturgy	296.454 34	Babylonian Talmud	296.125 2
Bava Batra	296.123 4	Mishnah	296.123 2
Babylonian Talmud	296.125 4	Palestinian Talmud	296.124 2
Mishnah	296.123 4	Bhagavad Gita	294.592 4
Palestinian Talmud	296.124 4	Bhakti Yoga	294.543 6
Bava Kamma	296.123 4	Bible	220
Babylonian Talmud	296.125 4	English	220.52
Mishnah	296.123 4	American Revised	220.520 4
Palestinian Talmud	296.124 4	American Standard	220.520 4
Bava Mezia	296.123 4	Authorized	220.520 3
Babylonian Talmud	296.125 4	Challoner	220.520 2
Mishnah	296.123 4	Confraternity	220.520 5
Palestinian Talmud	296.124 4	Coverdale	220.520 1
Beatification of saints	235.24	Douay	220.520 2
Beatitudes	226.93	English Revised	220.520 4
Christian moral theology	241.53	Good News Bible	220.520 82
Bekhorot	296.123 5	Jerusalem Bible	220.520 7
Babylonian Talmud	296.125 5	King James	220.520 3
Mishnah	296.123 5	Living Bible	220.520 83
Bektashi	297.48	New American	220.520 5
Bel and the Dragon (Bible)	229.6	New English	220.520 6
Benedictines	255.1	New International Version	220.520 81
church history	271.1	New Jerusalem Bible	220.520 7
women	255.97	New King James	220.520 8
church history	271.97	New Revised Standard	220.520 43
Benedictions	291.38	Revised	220.520 4
Christianity	264.13	Revised English	220.520 6
Judaism	296.45	Revised standard	220.520 42
Benedictus	264.36	Rheims	220.520 2
Berakhot	296.123 1	Today's English	220.520 82
Babylonian Talmud	296.125 1	Tyndale	220.520 1
Mishnah	296.123 1	Wycliffe	220.520 1
Palestinian Talmud	296.124 1	homiletical use	251
Bereavement		use in public worship	264.34
religion	291.442	see Manual at 220.92	
Christianity		Bible. N.T.	225
devotional literature	242.4	Acts of the Apostles	226.6
pastoral theology	259.6	Apocalypse	228
personal religion	248.866	Catholic epistles	227.9
rites	265.85	Colossians	227.7
devotional literature	291.432	Corinthians	227.2
Judaism		Ephesians	227.5
pastoral theology	296.61	Epistles	227
personal religion	296.7	Epistles of John	227.94
rites	296.445	Epistles of Paul	227
liturgy	296.454 5	Galatians	227.4
sermons	296.47	Gospels	226
pastoral theology	291.61	Hebrews	227.87
personal religion	291.442	James	227.91
rites	291.38	John	226.5
		Jude	227.97

Bible. N.T. (continued)		Bible. O.T. (continued)	
Luke	226.4	Jonah	224.92
Mark	226.3	Joshua	222.2
Matthew	226.2	Judges	222.32
Pastoral Epistles	227.83	Ketuvim	223
Peter	227.92	Kings	222.5
Philemon	227.86	Kohelet	223.8
Philippians	227.6	Lamentations	224.3
Revelation	228	Later Prophets	224
Romans	227.1	Leviticus	222.13
Thessalonians	227.81	Malachi	224.99
Timothy	227.83	Micah	224.93
Titus	227.85	Minor Prophets	224.9
Bible. O.T.	221	Nahum	224.94
Amos	224.8	Nehemiah	222.8
Apocrypha	229	Nevi'im	224
Baruch	229.5	Numbers	222.14
Bel and the Dragon	229.6	Obadiah	224.91
Ecclesiasticus	229.4	Pentateuch	222.1
Epistle of Jeremiah	229.5	Poetic books	223
Esdras	229.1	Prophets	224
Esther	229.27	Proverbs	223.7
Judith	229.24	Psalms	223.2
Maccabees	229.73	Qohelet	223.8
Prayer of Manasseh	229.6	Ruth	222.35
Sirach	229.4	Samuel	222.4
Song of the Three Children	229.6	Song of Solomon	223.9
Susanna	229.6	Song of Songs	223.9
Tobit	229.22	Ten Commandments	222.16
Wisdom of Solomon	229.3	Torah	222.1
Canticle of Canticles	223.9	Twelve prophets	224.9
Chronicles	222.6	Wisdom literature	223
Daniel	224.5	Zechariah	224.98
Deuteronomy	222.15	Zephaniah	224.96
Ecclesiastes	223.8	see Manual at 221	
English	221.52	Bible Christians (Methodist denomination)	287.53
Jewish Publication Society Bible	221.520 8	see also Methodist Church	
see also Bible—English		Bible colleges	230.071 1
Esther	222.9	Bible meditations	242.5
Exodus	222.12	Bible prayers	242.722
Ezekiel	224.4	Bible stories	220.950 5
Ezra	222.7	Bible study	220.07
Former Prophets	222	Biblical moral precepts	
Genesis	222.11	Christianity	241.5
Habakkuk	224.95	Judaism	296.36
Haggai	224.97	Biblical theology	
Hexateuch	222.1	Christianity	230.041
Historical books	222	Judaism	296.3
Hosea	224.6	see Manual at 220: Biblical theology	
Isaiah	224.1	Bikkurim	296.123 1
Jeremiah	224.2	Mishnah	296.123 1
Job	223.1	Palestinian Talmud	296.124 1
Joel	224.7		

Bioethics	
religion	291.564 957
Christianity	241.649 57
Judaism	296.364 957
see also Ethical problems—	
religion	
Biological warfare	
ethics	
religion	291.562 42
Christianity	241.624 2
social theology	291.178 73
Christianity	261.873
see also War	
Biology and religion	291.175
Christianity	261.55
philosophy of religion	215.7
Birth control	
ethics	
religion	291.566
Buddhism	294.356 6
Christianity	241.66
Hinduism	294.548 66
Islam	297.566
Judaism	296.366
social theology	291.178 366 66
Christianity	261.836 666
Judaism	296.38
Birth of Jesus Christ	232.92
Bishops	270.092
biography	270.092
specific denominations	280
see Manual at 230–280	
ecclesiology	262.12
Bishops' thrones	247.1
Black Methodist churches	287.8
see also Methodist Church	
Black Muslim religion	297.87
Black Muslims	
biography	297.870 92
Black theology	291.208 996
Christianity	230.089 96
United States	230.089 960 73
Blasphemy	291.569 5
Christianity	241.695
Islam	297.569 5
Judaism	296.369 5
Blessings	291.38
Christianity	264.13
Judaism	296.45
Bo tree	
Buddhism	294.343 5
Body (Human)	
religion	291.22
Christianity	233.5
see also Humans—religion	
Body and soul	
religion	291.22
Christianity	233.5
Islam	297.225
Judaism	296.32
philosophy of religion	218
see also Humans—religion	
Bon (Tibetan religion)	299.54
Book of Common Prayer	264.03
Book of Mormon	289.322
Books of Hours	242
Brahma Samaj	294.556 2
Brahmanas	294.592 1
Brahmanism	294.5
Brahmans	
biography	294.509 2
Breviaries	264.15
Roman Catholic	264.020 15
texts	264.024
Brothers (Christian religious	
orders)	255.092
biography	271.092 02
church history	271.092
Brothers Hospitallers of St. John	
of God	255.49
church history	271.49
Buddha	294.363
Buddhism	294.3
Islamic polemics	297.294
Buddhism and Islam	294.337 2
Buddhist view	294.337 2
Islamic view	297.284 3
Buddhist education	294.375
Buddhist ethics	294.35
Buddhists	
biography	294.309 2
Bukhārī, Muḥammad ibn Ismāʻīl	
Hadith	297.124 1
Burial of Jesus Christ	232.964
Business	
social theology	291.178 5
Christianity	261.85
Judaism	296.383
Business ethics	
religion	291.564 4
Christianity	241.644
Islam	297.564 4
Judaism	296.364 4
see also Ethical problems—	
religion	
Byzantine art	
religious significance	246.1
Byzantine rite churches	281.5
see also Eastern churches	

C

Cabala	296.16
Jewish mysticism	
experience	296.712
movement	296.833
Jewish religious sources	296.16
Cain (Biblical person)	
Bible stories	222.110 950 5
Calendars	
religion	291.36
Christianity	263.9
Islam	297.36
Judaism	296.43
Calendars (Liturgical books)	264
Anglican	264.031
Roman Catholic	264.021
Caliphate	297.61
Caliphs	
companions of Muḥammad	297.648
role and function	297.61
Call to Islam	297.74
Calvinistic Baptists	286.1
see also Baptists	
Calvinistic churches	284.2
see also Reformed Church	
Calvinists	
biography	284.209 2
Camillians	255.55
church history	271.55
Camp meetings	
Christian religious practices	269.24
Camp programs	
church work	253.7
Jewish religious work	296.67
Campbellites	286.6
biography	286.609 2
see also Disciples of Christ	
Campus Crusade for Christ	267.61
Campus ministry	259.24
Candomblé	299.673
Canon law	262.9
Canon of Bible	220.12
Canonization of saints	235.24
Canons regular	255.08
church history	271.08
women	255.908
church history	271.908
Canticle of Canticles	223.9
Cantors (Judaism)	
biography	296.462 092
Capital punishment	
ethics	
religion	291.569 7
Buddhism	294.356 97
Christianity	241.697
Hinduism	294.548 697
Islam	297.569 7
Judaism	296.369 7
social theology	291.178 336 6
Christianity	261.833 66
Capitalism	
social theology	291.178 5
Christianity	261.85
Islam	297.273
Judaism	296.383
Capuchins	255.36
church history	271.36
Caracciolini	255.56
church history	271.56
Cardinal sins	241.3
Cardinals (Clergy)	282.092
biography	282.092
ecclesiology	262.135
Caring	
ethics	
religion	291.567 7
Buddhism	294.356 77
Christianity	241.4
Hinduism	294.548 677
Islam	297.567 7
Judaism	296.367 7
Carmelite Nuns	255.971
church history	271.971
Carmelites	255.73
church history	271.73
women	255.971
church history	271.971
Caro, Joseph	
Jewish legal codes	296.182
Carthusians	255.71
church history	271.71
women	255.97
church history	271.97
Catechetics	268
Catechisms	291.2
Christianity	238
Catechists	268.092
biography	268.092
see Manual at 230–280	
role and function	268.3
Catechumenate	265.13

Catharism	273.6
denomination	284.4
see also Christian denominations	
persecution of	272.3
Cathedral systems	
Christian ecclesiology	262.3
Cathedrals	
religious significance	246.96
Catholic Church	282
see also Roman Catholic Church	
Catholic epistles	227.9
Catholicity	262.72
Celestial Church of Christ	289.93
see also Christian denominations	
Celestines	255.16
church history	271.16
Celibacy	
ethics	
religion	291.566
Buddhism	294.356 6
Christianity	241.66
Hinduism	294.548 66
religious practice	291.447
Buddhism	294.344 47
Christianity	248.47
clergy	253.25
Hinduism	294.544 7
Celtic religion	299.16
Ceremonials	264.022
Ceremonies	
religion	291.38
see also Rites—religion	
Chabad Lubavitch Hasidism	296.833 22
Chaldeans (Religious order)	255.18
church history	271.18
Challoner Bible	220.520 2
Ch'an Buddhism	294.392 7
Chancel railings	247.1
Chanukah	296.435
liturgy	296.453 5
Chaplaincy	291.61
Christianity	253
Judaism	296.61
Charismatic gifts	234.13
Charismatic movement	270.82
Charismatic spiritual renewal	269
Charity	
ethics	
religion	291.567 7
Buddhism	294.356 77
Christianity	241.4
Charity	
ethics	
religion (continued)	
Hinduism	294.548 677
Islam	297.567 7
Judaism	296.367 7
Chastity	
ethics	
religion	291.566
Buddhism	294.356 6
Christianity	241.66
Hinduism	294.548 66
Judaism	296.366
religious practice	291.447
Buddhism	294.344 47
Christianity	248.47
Hinduism	294.544 7
Cheerfulness	
ethics	
religion	291.5
see also Virtues—religion	
Cherubim and Seraphim Church	289.93
see also Christian denominations	
Child abuse	
social theology	291.178 327 1
Christianity	261.832 71
Child rearing	
personal religion	291.441
Christianity	248.845
Judaism	296.74
Childhood of Jesus Christ	232.927
Children	
religion	200.83
Christianity	270.083
devotional literature	242.62
guides to Christian life	248.82
pastoral care of	259.22
prayer books	242.82
religious education	268.432
sermons	252.53
social theology	261.834 23
guides to life	291.440 83
Judaism	296.083
guides to life	296.708 3
religious education	296.680 83
social theology	291.178 342 3
Children's church	264.008 3
Chinese religions	299.51
Choir stalls	247.1
Chosen people (Judaism)	296.311 72
Christening	265.1

Relative Index

Christian and Missionary Alliance	289.9
see also Christian denominations	
Christian art	
religious significance	246
Christian biography	270.092
specific denominations	280
Christian Brothers	255.78
church history	271.78
Christian calendars	
religion	263.9
Christian church	260
history	270
local	250
specific denominations	280
see Manual at 260 vs. 251–254, 259	
Christian Church (Disciples of Christ)	286.63
see also Disciples of Christ	
Christian denominations	280
church government	262.01–.09
parishes	254.01–.09
church law	262.98
doctrines	230.1–.9
catechisms and creeds	238.1–.9
general councils	262.51–.59
guides to Christian life	248.48
missions	266.1–.9
moral theology	241.04
public worship	264.01–.09
religious associations	267.18
religious education	268.8
religious orders	255
church history	271
women's	255.9
seminaries	230.073
theology	230.1–.9
see Manual at 283–289	
Christian doctrine	230
Christian education	268
see Manual at 268 vs. 230.071	
Christian ethics	241
Christian holidays	263.9
devotional literature	242.3
sermons	252.6
Christian initiation	265.1
Christian leadership	262.1
local church	253
Christian life	248.4
Christian-Marxist dialogue	
Christian theology	261.21
Christian Methodist Episcopal Church	287.83
see also Methodist Church	
Christian Reformed Church	285.731
see also Reformed Church (American Reformed)	
Christian sacred music	
public worship	
religion	264.2
religious symbolism	246.75
Christian Science	289.5
see also Christian denominations	
Christian Scientists	
biography	289.509 2
Christianity	230
art representation	
religious significance	246
Islamic polemics	297.293
Christianity and anti-Semitism	261.26
Christianity and atheism	261.21
Christianity and culture	261
Christianity and Islam	261.27
Christian view	261.27
Islamic view	297.283
Christianity and Judaism	261.26
Christian view	261.26
Jewish view	296.396
Christianity and occultism	261.513
Christianity and other religions	261.2
Christianity and politics	261.7
Christianity and secular disciplines	261.5
see Manual at 261.5; also at 261.5 vs. 231–239	
Christians	270.092
specific denominations	280
see Manual at 280: Biography	
see Manual at 230–280	
Christmas	263.915
devotional literature	242.335
sermons	252.615
Christmas story	232.92
Christology	232
see Manual at 232	
Chronicles (Biblical books)	222.6
Church	260
ecclesiology	262
history	270
specific denominations	280
local	250
Church administration	262
local church	254

Church and state	
social theology	291.177
Christianity	261.7
see Manual at 322.1 vs. 261.7, 291.177	
Church and the poor	261.832 5
Church authority	262.8
Church buildings	
management	254.7
religious significance	246.9
Church calendar	263.9
Church controversies	262.8
local church	250
specific denominations	280
Church fathers	270
biography	270.092
Church finance	262.006 81
local church	254.8
Church furniture	247.1
Church government	262
local church	254
Church group work	253.7
Church growth	
local church	254.5
missionary work	266
Church history	270
specific denominations	280
Church holidays	263.9
devotional literature	242.3
sermons	252.6
Church law	262.9
Church membership	
local church	254.5
Church of Christ, Scientist	289.5
see also Christian denominations	
Church of England	283.42
church government	262.034 2
parishes	254.034 2
church law	262.983 42
doctrines	230.3
catechisms and creeds	238.3
guides to Christian life	248.483
liturgy	264.03
missions	266.3
moral theology	241.043
persecution by Queen Mary	272.6
religious associations	267.183 42
religious education	268.834 2
religious orders	255.83
church history	271.83
women	255.983
church history	271.983
seminaries	230.073 342
theology	230.3
Church of God General Conference	286.73
see also Adventists	
Church of God in Christ, Mennonites	289.73
see also Mennonite Church	
Church of Jesus Christ of Latter-Day Saints	289.332
see also Mormon Church	
Church of North India	287.95
see also Christian denominations	
Church of Scotland	285.233
see also Presbyterian Church	
Church of South India	287.94
see also Christian denominations	
Church of the Brethren	286.5
see also Baptists	
Church of the Nazarene	287.99
see also Christian denominations	
Church of the New Jerusalem	289.4
see also Christian denominations	
Church organization	262
Church polity	262
Church renewal	262.001 7
Church services	264
Church work with disabled persons	259.44
Church work with families	259.1
Church work with juvenile delinquents	259.5
Church work with the aged	259.3
Church work with the sick	259.4
Church work with young adults	259.25
Church work with youth	259.23
Church year	263.9
devotional literature	242.3
sermon preparation	251.6
sermons	252.6
Church youth groups	259.23
Churches of Christ	286.63
see also Disciples of Christ	
Churches of Christ in Christian Union	289.9
see also Christian denominations	
Churches of God	289.9
see also Christian denominations	
Circumcision	
Jewish rites	296.442 2
liturgy	296.454 22
Circumcision of Jesus Christ	232.92

Cistercians	255.12	Clergy	200.92
church history	271.12	biography	200.92
women	255.97	Christian	270.092
church history	271.97	biography	270.092
Citizenship		specific denominations	280
ethics		see Manual at 280	
religion	291.562 1	see Manual at 230–280	
Christianity	241.621	ecclesiology	262.1
Judaism	296.362 1	occupational ethics	241.641
social theology	291.177	pastoral theology	253
Christianity	261.7	personal religion	248.892
Judaism	296.382	training	230.071 1
City churches	250.917 32	occupational ethics	
administration	254.22	religion	291.564 1
pastoral theology	253.091 732	role and function	291.61
Civil disobedience		see also Rabbis; Religious	
ethics		leaders	
religion	291.562 1	see Manual at 200.92 and	
Buddhism	294.356 21	291–299	
Christianity	241.621	Clergymen's wives	
Hinduism	294.548 621	biography	270.092
Islam	297.562 1	specific denominations	280
Judaism	296.362 1	pastoral theology	253.22
social theology	291.177	Clerical celibacy	253.25
Buddhism	294.337 7	Clerks regular	255.5
Christianity	261.7	church history	271.5
Hinduism	294.517 7	Clerks Regular of Somaschi	255.54
Islam	297.272	church history	271.54
Judaism	296.382	Clerks Regular of the Mother of	
Civil rights		God	255.57
social theology	291.177	church history	271.57
Buddhism	294.337 7	Cluniacs	255.14
Christianity	261.7	church history	271.14
Hinduism	294.517 7	Code of Manu	294.592 6
Islam	297.272	Codependency	
Judaism	296.382	devotional literature	291.432
Civil war		Christianity	242.4
ethics		pastoral theology	291.61
religion	291.562 1	Christianity	259.429
Buddhism	294.356 21	religious guidance	291.442
Christianity	241.621	Christianity	248.862 9
Hinduism	294.548 621	social theology	291.178 322 9
Islam	297.562 1	Christianity	261.832 29
Judaism	296.362 1	Codes of conduct	
social theology	291.177	moral theology	291.5
Buddhism	294.337 7	Christianity	241.5
Christianity	261.7	Judaism	296.36
Hinduism	294.517 7	Codex iuris canonici (1917)	262.93
Islam	297.272	Codex iuris canonici (1983)	262.94
Judaism	296.382	College students	
Civilization		guides to Christian life	248.834
Bible	220.95	pastoral care	259.24
Classical religion	292		

Color	
religious significance	291.37
Christianity	246.6
see also Symbolism—	
religious significance	
Colossians (Biblical book)	227.7
Commandments	
Jewish law	296.18
moral theology	291.5
Christianity	241.5
Judaism	296.36
Common lectionary	264.34
preaching	251.6
Common of the mass	264.36
Communication	
ethics	
religion	291.565
Christianity	241.65
Communications media	
religion	291.175
Christianity	261.52
evangelism	269.26
use by local church	253.78
administration	254.3
Judaism	296.37
Communion (Part of service)	264.36
Communion of saints	262.73
Communion service	264.36
Communism and Christianity	261.21
Communism and Islam	297.273
Companions of Muḥammad	297.648
Comparative religion	291
see Manual at 291	
Compline	264.15
see also Liturgy of the hours	
Condemnation of Jesus Christ	232.962
Conditional immortality	236.23
Conduct of life	
ethics	
religion	291.5
Buddhism	294.35
Christianity	241
Hinduism	294.548
Islam	297.5
Judaism	296.36
personal religion	291.44
Buddhism	294.344 4
Christianity	248.4
Hinduism	294.544
Islam	297.57
Sufi	297.44
Judaism	296.7

Confederated Benedictines	255.11
church history	271.11
Confession (Christian rite)	234.166
public worship	265.62
theology	234.166
Confessionals	247.1
Confessions of faith	291.2
Christianity	238
Confirmation (Religious rite)	291.38
Christianity	234.162
theology	234.162
public worship	265.2
Judaism	296.442 4
liturgy	296.454 24
women's	296.443 4
liturgy	296.454 34
Confraternities	267
Confraternity Bible	220.520 5
Confucianism	
religion	299.512
Confucianists	
biography	
religion	299.512 092
Congregational Christian	
Churches of the United	
States	285.833
see also Congregationalism	
Congregational Churches of the	
United States	285.832
see also Congregationalism	
Congregational Methodist	
Church	287.2
see also Methodist Church	
Congregational systems	
Christian ecclesiology	262.4
Congregationalism	285.8
church government	262.058
parishes	254.058
church law	262.985 8
doctrines	230.58
catechisms and creeds	238.58
general councils	262.558
guides to Christian life	248.485 8
missions	266.58
moral theology	241.045 8
public worship	264.058
religious associations	267.185 8
religious education	268.858
seminaries	230.073 58
theology	230.58
Congregationalists	
biography	285.809 2

Congregations	
Christianity	
denominations	280
local church	250
papal administration	262.136
Judaism	296.65
religion	291.65
Conscience	
religion	291.5
Buddhism	294.35
Christianity	241.1
Hinduism	294.548
Islam	297.5
Judaism	296.36
Conscientious objection	
ethics	
religion	291.562 42
Christianity	241.624 2
social theology	291.178 73
Christianity	261.873
see also War	
Consecrations (Christian rites)	265.92
Conservative Judaism	296.834 2
liturgy	296.450 47
Consolatory devotions	291.432
Christianity	242.4
Judaism	296.72
Constantinopolitan Creed	238.14
Constitutional Church	284.8
Consumption	
ethics	
religion	291.568
Buddhism	294.356 8
Christianity	241.68
Hinduism	294.548 68
Islam	297.568
Judaism	296.368
Contemplation	291.43
Christianity	248.34
Contemplative religious orders	255.01
church history	271.01
women	255.901
church history	271.901
Contextual theology	291.2
Christianity	230
ethnic context	230.089
feminist context	230.082
geographic context	230.09
see Manual at 230	
Contraception	
ethics	
religion	291.566
Christianity	241.66
Islam	297.566
Judaism	296.366

Contraception (continued)	
social theology	291.178 366 66
Christianity	261.836 666
Judaism	296.38
Contrition (Christian rite)	234.166
public worship	265.61
theology	234.166
Convents	291.657
Christianity	255.9
church history	271.9
religious significance of	
buildings	246.97
Conventuals	255.37
church history	271.37
Conversation	
ethics	
religion	291.567 2
Christianity	241.672
Judaism	296.367 2
see also Ethical	
problems—religion	
Conversion (Religious	
experience)	291.42
Christianity	248.24
Islam	297.574
Judaism	296.714
Converts	291.42
Judaism	296.714
outreach activity for	296.69
missions for	291.72
Coptic Church	281.72
see also Eastern churches	
Coptic language	
Biblical texts	220.49
Corinthians (Biblical books)	227.2
Corpus iuris canonici	262.923
Cosmology	
religion	291.24
Buddhism	294.342 4
Christianity	231.765
comparative religion	291.24
Hinduism	294.524
Islam	297.242
Judaism	296.3
philosophy of religion	215.2
Councils	
Christian ecclesiology	262.5
Counseling	
pastoral theology	291.61
Christianity	253.5
Judaism	296.61
Counter-Reformation	270.6
Course in Miracles	299.93

Courtship	
ethics	
religion	291.567 65
Christianity	241.676 5
Judaism	296.367 65
Covenant relationship with God	
Christianity	231.76
Judaism	296.311 72
Coverdale Bible	220.520 1
Creation	
religion	291.24
Christianity	231.765
comparative religion	291.24
Islam	297.242
Judaism	296.34
philosophy of religion	213
Creation science	231.765 2
see Manual at 231.7652 vs. 213, 500, 576.8	
Creationism	231.765 2
see Manual at 231.7652 vs. 213, 500, 576.8	
Credibility	
Christian church	262.72
Credo	264.36
Creeds	291.2
Christianity	238
Crime	
social theology	291.178 33
Christianity	261.833
Crosier Fathers	255.19
church history	271.19
Crosses	
religious significance	246.558
Crucifixes	
religious significance	246.558
Crucifixion of Jesus Christ	232.963
Cruelty to animals	
ethics	
religion	291.569 3
see also Animals—ethical treatment of—religion	
Crusades	
church history	270.4
Cults	291.9
see Manual at 291: Denominations and sects; *also at* 299.93: New Age religions	
Cumberland Presbyterian Church	285.135
see also Presbyterian Church	
Curia Romana	262.136

D

Daily devotions	291.446
Christianity	242.2
Judaism	296.45
Dancing	
religious significance	291.37
Christianity	246.7
see also Arts—religious significance	
Daniel (Biblical book)	224.5
David, King of Israel	
Biblical leader	222.409 2
David and Goliath story	222.430 950 5
Da'wah	297.74
Day of the Lord	
Christianity	236.9
Deacons	270.092
biography	270.092
specific denominations	280
see Manual at 230–280	
ecclesiology	262.14
pastoral theology	253
see also Clergy—Christian	
Dead	
objects of worship	291.213
Dead Sea Scrolls	296.155
Old Testament works in	221.44
pseudepigrapha	229.91
Qumran community writings	296.155
Death	
ethics	
religion	291.569 7
Buddhism	294.356 97
Christianity	241.697
Hinduism	294.548 697
Islam	297.569 7
Judaism	296.369 7
medical ethics	
religion	291.564 24
Christianity	241.642 4
Judaism	296.364 24
religion	291.23
Buddhism	294.342 3
Christianity	236.1
Hinduism	294.523
Islam	297.23
Judaism	296.33
philosophy of religion	218
religious rites	291.38
Christianity	265.85
Islam	297.385
Judaism	296.445
liturgy	296.454 5
see also Rites—religion	

Relative Index

Death of Jesus Christ	232.963
Decalogue	222.16
moral theology	
Christianity	241.52
Judaism	296.36
Dedications (Christian rites)	265.92
Defenseless Mennonites	289.73
biography	289.709 2
see also Mennonite Church	
Deism	211.5
Deists	211.509 2
Deities	291.211
see also Gods and goddesses	
Demai	296.123 1
Mishnah	296.123 1
Palestinian Talmud	296.124 1
Demoniac possession	
religion	291.42
Demonology	
religion	291.216
Demons	
religion	291.216
Demythologizing (Bible)	220.68
Denominations	291.9
Christianity	280
see also Christian denominations	
Judaism	296.8
see Manual at 291: Denominations and sects	
Descent into hell of Jesus Christ	232.967
Destiny	
religion	291.22
Christianity	234.9
Determinism	
religion	
Islam	297.227
Deuteronomy (Bible)	222.15
Devil	291.216
Christianity	235.4
Islam	297.216
Judaism	296.316
Devil worship	291.216
Devotional calendars	242.2
Devotional literature	291.432
Buddhism	294.344 32
Christianity	242
Hinduism	294.543 2
Islam	297.382
Sufi	297.438 2
Judaism	296.72
Devotional theology	291.4
Buddhism	294.344
Christianity	240
Hinduism	294.54
Islam	297.57
Sufi	297.4
Judaism	296.7
Dhammapada	294.382 322
Dharma	
Hinduism	294.548
Dharmasastras	294.592 6
Dhikr	297.382
Dianetics	299.936
Diatessaron	226.1
Dietary laws	
Islam	297.576
Judaism	296.73
Dietary limitations	
religion	291.446
Hinduism	294.544 6
Judaism	296.73
Digambara (Jainism)	294.493
Dioceses	
Christian ecclesiology	262.3
Directors of religious education	291.750 92
biography	291.750 92
see Manual at 230–280	
Christianity	268.092
biography	268.092
role and function	268.3
Judaism	296.680 92
biography	296.680 92
role and function	296.68
Disarmament	
ethics	
religion	291.562 4
social theology	291.178 7
see also International relations	
Disciples of Christ	286.6
biography	286.609 2
church government	262.066
parishes	254.066
church law	262.986 6
doctrines	230.66
catechisms and creeds	238.66
guides to Christian life	248.486 6
missions	266.66
moral theology	241.046 6
public worship	264.066
religious associations	267.186 6
religious education	268.866
seminaries	230.073 66
theology	230.66

Discrimination			Doctrinal controversies	
ethics			Christian church history	273
religion	291.567 5		Doctrinal theology	291.2
Christianity	241.675		Buddhism	294.342
Judaism	296.367 5		Christianity	230
see also Ethical			see Manual at 261.5 vs.	
problems—religion			231–239	
social theology	291.178 34		Hinduism	294.52
Christianity	261.834		Islam	297.2
Judaism	296.38		Sufi	297.41
Diseases (Human)			Judaism	296.3
pastoral theology	291.61		philosophy of religion	210
Christianity	259.41		Documentary hypothesis	
religious rites	291.38		(Pentateuchal criticism)	222.106 6
Christianity	265.82		Dominican Sisters	255.972
social theology	291.178 321		church history	271.972
Christianity	261.832 1		Dominicans	255.2
Dispensationalist theology	230.046 3		church history	271.2
Dissenters (Protestant churches)	280.4		women	255.972
see also Protestantism			church history	271.972
Distributive justice			Dominion theology	230.046
ethics			Donatism	273.4
religion	291.562 2		Douay Bible	220.520 2
Buddhism	294.356 22		Doxologies	
Christianity	241.622		Christian private prayer	242.72
Hinduism	294.548 622		Drama in Christian education	268.67
Islam	297.562 2		Druidism	299.16
Judaism	296.362 2		Druzes (Islamic sect)	297.85
Divination			Dualism (Concept of God)	211.33
religion	291.32		classes of religions	291.14
African religions	299.64		philosophy of religion	211.33
Divine law			Dukhobors	289.9
Christianity	241.2		see also Christian	
Divine Light Mission	294		denominations	
Divine office (Religion)	264.15		Dunkers	286.5
Anglican	264.030 15		see also Baptists	
Roman Catholic	264.020 15		Dutch Reformed Church in	
texts	264.024		North America	285.732
Divinity of Jesus Christ	232.8		see also Reformed Church	
Divinity schools	230.071 1		(American Reformed)	
Divorce			Duty	
ethics			religion	291.5
religion	291.563		Islam	297.5
Buddhism	294.356 3		Dying patients	
Christianity	241.63		pastoral theology	291.61
Hinduism	294.548 63		Christianity	259.417 5
Islam	297.563		social theology	291.178 321 75
Judaism	296.363		Christianity	261.832 175
Judaism	296.444 4		Dysfunctional families	
social theology	291.178 358 9		pastoral theology	291.61
Christianity	261.835 89		Christianity	259.1
Divorced persons			social theology	291.178 358 5
Christian devotional literature	242.646		Christianity	261.835 85
guides to Christian life	248.846			

E

E document (Biblical criticism)	222.106 6
Early Christian art	
religious significance	246.2
Early Church	270.1
see Manual at 281.1–281.4	
Easter	263.93
devotional literature	242.36
sermons	252.63
Easter story	232.97
Eastern churches	281.5
church government	262.015
parishes	254.015
church law	262.981 5
doctrines	230.15
catechisms and creeds	238.19
general councils	262.515
guides to Christian life	248.481 5
liturgy	264.015
missions	266.15
monasticism	255.81
church history	271.81
women	255.981
church history	271.981
moral theology	241.041 5
public worship	264.015
religious associations	267.181 5
religious education	268.815
seminaries	230.073 15
theology	230.15
see Manual at 281.1–281.4	
Eastern Orthodox Christians	
biography	281.909 2
Eastern Orthodox Church	281.9
church government	262.019
parishes	254.019
church law	262.981 9
doctrines	230.19
catechisms and creeds	238.19
general councils	262.519
guides to Christian life	248.481 9
liturgy	264.019
missions	266.19
monasticism	255.819
church history	271.819
women	255.981 9
church history	271.981 9
moral theology	241.041 9
public worship	264.019
religious associations	267.181 9
religious education	268.819
seminaries	230.073 19
Eastern Orthodox Church (continued)	
theology	230.19
see Manual at 281.1–281.4	
Eastern Orthodox sacred music	
public worship	
religion	264.019 02
Eastern rite Catholics	281.5
see also Eastern churches	
Eastern rite churches	281.5
see also Eastern churches	
Eastertide	263.93
devotional literature	242.36
sermons	252.63
Ecclesiastes	223.8
Ecclesiastical law	262.9
Ecclesiasticus (Bible)	229.4
Ecclesiology	
Christianity	262
Eckankar	299.93
Ecology	
ethics	
religion	291.569 1
Buddhism	294.356 91
Christianity	241.691
Hinduism	294.548 691
Islam	297.569 1
Judaism	296.369 1
social theology	291.178 362
Christianity	261.836 2
Judaism	296.38
Economics	
social theology	291.178 5
Christianity	261.85
Islam	297.273
see Manual at 297.26–297.27	
Judaism	296.383
Ecumenical councils	262.5
Christian church history	270.2
modern period	270.82
Ecumenical movement	280.042
see Manual at 280.042 vs. 262.0011	
Ecumenism	262.001 1
see Manual at 280.042 vs. 262.0011	
Eddy, Mary Baker	
Christian Science writings	289.52
Eduyyot	296.123 4
Babylonian Talmud	296.125 4
Mishnah	296.123 4
Palestinian Talmud	296.124 4

Eglise de Jésus-Christ sur la terre par le prophète Simon Kimbangu	289.93
see also Christian denominations	
Egyptians (Ancient)	
religion	299.31
Election (Christian doctrine)	234
Embryo transplant	
ethics	
religion	291.566
Christianity	241.66
Judaism	296.366
Emigration from Mecca	297.634
Encyclicals	262.91
End of the world	
religion	291.23
Christianity	236.9
Islam	297.23
English Revised version Bible	220.520 4
Enlightenment	
religion	291.42
Buddhism	294.344 2
Hinduism	294.542
Islam	297.57
Enoch (Pseudepigrapha)	229.913
Environment	
ethics	
religion	291.569 1
Buddhism	294.356 91
Christianity	241.691
Hinduism	294.548 691
Islam	297.569 1
Judaism	296.369 1
Environmental abuse	
social theology	291.178 362 8
Christianity	261.836 28
Envy	
ethics	
religion	291.5
see also Vices—religion	
Ephesians (Biblical book)	227.5
Epiphany	263.915
devotional literature	242.335
sermons	252.615
Episcopacy	262.12
Episcopal Church	283.73
church government	262.037 3
parishes	254.037 3
church law	262.983 73
doctrines	230.3
catechisms and creeds	238.3
guides to Christian life	248.483
liturgy	264.03
missions	266.3
Episcopal Church (continued)	
moral theology	241.043
religious associations	267.183 73
religious education	268.837 3
religious orders	255.83
church history	271.83
women	255.983
church history	271.983
seminaries	230.073 373
theology	230.3
Episcopal systems	
Christian ecclesiology	262.3
Episcopalians	
biography	283.092
Epistle of Jeremiah (Bible)	229.5
Epistles (Bible)	227
pseudepigrapha	229.93
Equality	
social theology	291.178 34
Christianity	261.834
Judaism	296.38
Equipment	
local Christian parishes	254.7
Eremitical religious orders	255.02
church history	271.02
women	255.902
church history	271.902
Eruvin	296.123 2
Babylonian Talmud	296.125 2
Mishnah	296.123 2
Palestinian Talmud	296.124 2
Eschatology	291.23
Buddhism	294.342 3
Christianity	236
Hinduism	294.523
Islam	297.23
Judaism	296.33
philosophy of religion	218
Esdras (Deuterocanonical book)	229.1
Espionage	
ethics	
religion	291.562 4
social theology	291.178 7
see also International relations	
Essenes	296.814
Esther (Biblical book)	222.9
Esther (Deuterocanonical book)	229.27
Eternity	
religion	291.23
Christianity	236.21
Islam	297.23
Judaism	296.33

Relative Index

Ethical problems
  religion   291.56
    Buddhism   294.356
    Christianity   241.6
      see Manual at
        241.3–241.4 vs.
        241.6
    Hinduism   294.548 6
    Islam   297.56
    Judaism   296.36
Ethical wills
  Judaism   296.36
Ethics
  religion   291.5
    Buddhism   294.35
    Christianity   241
    Hinduism   294.548
    Islam   297.5
      Sufi   297.45
    Judaism   296.36
Ethics of the Fathers   296.123 47
Ethiopian Church   281.75
  see also Eastern churches
Ethiopic language
  Biblical texts   220.46
Ethnic groups
  social theology   291.178 348
    Christianity   261.834 8
Eucharist   234.163
  public worship   264.36
    Anglican   264.030 36
      texts   264.03
    Roman Catholic   264.020 36
      texts   264.023
  theology   234.163
Eucharistic Liturgy   264.36
  see also Eucharist—public
      worship
Euthanasia
  ethics
    religion   291.569 7
      Buddhism   294.356 97
      Christianity   241.697
      Hinduism   294.548 697
      Islam   297.569 7
      Judaism   296.369 7
Eutychian Church   281.6
  see also Christian
      denominations
Evangelical and Reformed
    Church   285.734
  see also Reformed Church
      (American Reformed)

Evangelical churches   289.95
  see also Christian
      denominations
Evangelical Congregational
    Church   289.9
  see also Christian
      denominations
Evangelical Free Church of
    America   289.95
  see also Christian
      denominations
Evangelical Lutheran Church   284.131 2
  see also Lutheran church
Evangelical Lutheran Church in
    America   284.135
  see also Lutheran church
Evangelical Lutheran Synodical
    Conference of North
    America   284.132
  see also Lutheran church
Evangelical theology   230.046 24
Evangelical United Brethren
    Church   289.9
  see also Christian
      denominations
Evangelicalism   270.82
  independent denominations   289.95
  Protestantism   280.4
Evangelische Kirche in
    Deutschland   284.143
  see also Lutheran church
  see Manual at 284.143
Evangelism   269.2
Evangelistic sermons   252.3
Evangelistic writings   243
Evangelization   266
Eve (Biblical person)
  Bible stories   222.110 950 5
Evening prayer   264.15
  Anglican   264.030 15
    texts   264.034
Evensong   264.030 15
  texts   264.034
Evil (Concept)
  ethics
    religion   291.5
      Christianity   241.3
      Islam   297.5
      Judaism   296.36
  religion   291.211 8
    Christianity   231.8
      freedom of choice   233.7
    comparative religion   291.211 8
    Islam   297.211 8
    Judaism   296.311 8
    philosophy of religion   214

Evil spirits	
religion	291.216
Evolution versus creation	291.24
Christianity	231.765 2
see Manual at 231.7652 vs. 213, 500, 576.8	
Islam	297.242
Judaism	296.34
philosophy of religion	213
Exegesis	
sacred books	291.82
Bible	220.6
Koran	297.122 6
Talmud	296.120 6
Existence of God	212.1
Christianity	231
comparative religion	291.211
Islam	297.211
Judaism	296.311
philosophy of religion	212.1
Existentialist theology	230.046
Exodus (Bible)	222.12
Exorcism	
religious rite	291.38
Christianity	265.94
see also Rites—religion	
Exorcists	200.92
biography	200.92
religious role and function	291.61
see Manual at 200.92 and 291–299	
Experience	
religion	291.42
see also Religious experience	
Extramarital relations	
ethics	
religion	291.566
see also Sexual relations—ethics—religion	
social theology	291.178 357 36
Christianity	261.835 736
Extreme unction	234.167
public worship	265.7
theology	234.167
Ezekiel (Biblical book)	224.4
Ezra (Biblical book)	222.7

F

Faith	
religion	291.22
Christianity	234.23
knowledge of God	231.042
Islam	297.22
Judaism	296.32
philosophy of religion	218
Faith and reason	210
Christianity	231.042
Judaism	296.311
philosophy of religion	210
Faith healing	
religion	291.31
Christianity	234.131
see also Spiritual healing—religion	
see Manual at 615.852 vs. 234.131, 291.31	
Fall of humankind	233.14
Families	
religion	
guides to life	291.441
Christianity	248.4
see also Family life—religion	
pastoral theology	291.61
Christianity	259.1
social theology	291.178 358 5
Christianity	261.835 85
worship	291.43
Christianity	249
Judaism	296.45
Families of clergymen	
pastoral theology	253.22
Family counseling	
Christian pastoral counseling	259.12
Family ethics	
religion	291.563
Buddhism	294.356 3
Christianity	241.63
Hinduism	294.548 63
Islam	297.563
Judaism	296.363
Family life	
religion	291.441
Buddhism	294.344 41
Christianity	248.4
Hinduism	294.544 1
Islam	297.577
Judaism	296.74

Relative Index

Family planning	
ethics	
religion	291.566
Buddhism	294.356 6
Christianity	241.66
Hinduism	294.548 66
Islam	297.566
Judaism	296.366
social theology	291.178 366 66
Christianity	261.836 666
Judaism	296.38
Family purity	
Judaism	296.742
Family violence	
social theology	291.178 327
Christianity	261.832 7
Fast days	291.36
Christianity	263.9
devotional literature	242.3
sermons	252.6
Islam	297.53
see also Holy days	
Fasting	
religious practice	291.447
Buddhism	294.344 47
Christianity	248.47
Hinduism	294.544 7
Islam	297.53
Sufi	297.45
Judaism	296.7
Fatalism	
religion	291.22
Islam	297.227
Father (God)	
Christian doctrines	231.1
Jewish doctrine	296.311 2
Fathers	
Christian devotional literature	242.642 1
guides to Christian life	248.842 1
Feast days	
Christianity	263.9
devotional literature	242.3
sermons	252.6
religion	291.36
see also Holy days	
Femininity of God	291.211 4
Christianity	231.4
Judaism	296.311 2
Feminism	
social theology	291.178 344 2
Christianity	261.834 42
Judaism	296.38
Feminist theology	291.208 2
Christianity	230.082
Judaism	296.308 2
Fertilization in vitro	
ethics	
religion	291.566
Christianity	241.66
Judaism	296.366
Festivals	
religion	291.36
Christianity	263
Judaism	296.43
see also Holy days	
Fetishism	
religion	291.21
Finance	
churches	262.006 81
local church	254.8
Finnish Evangelical Lutheran	
Church	284.133 4
see also Lutheran church	
Fiqh	
religious law	297.14
see Manual at 340.59 vs. 297.14	
Fire	
religious worship	291.212
Five Confucian Classics	299.512 82
Five pillars of Islam	297.31
Five scrolls (Bible)	221.044
Flight from Mecca	297.634
Flight into Egypt	232.92
Food taboos	
religion	291.446
Hinduism	294.544 6
Islam	297.576
Judaism	296.73
Foot washing	
Christian rite	265.9
Foreign missions	
Christianity	266.023
Foreordination (Christian doctrine)	234.9
Forgiveness (Christian doctrine)	234.5
Form criticism	
sacred books	291.82
Bible	220.663
Talmud	296.120 663
Forty Hours devotion	
Roman Catholic liturgy	264.027 4
Founders of religions	291.63
Franciscans	255.3
church history	271.3
women	255.973
church history	271.973
Free Church of Scotland	285.234
see also Presbyterian Church	

Free churches	280.4
see also Protestantism	
Free Methodist Church of North America	287.2
see also Methodist Church	
Free thought	211.4
Free will	
religion	291.22
Christianity	233.7
soteriology	234.9
Islam	297.227
Judaism	296.32
Freewill Baptists	286.2
see also Baptists	
Friaries	
church history	271
religious significance of buildings	246.97
Friday	
Islamic observance	297.36
Friends (Religious society)	289.6
biography	289.609 2
see also Society of Friends	
Friendship	
ethics	
religion	291.567 62
Christianity	241.676 2
Islam	297.567 62
Judaism	296.367 62
Fringes (Judaism)	296.461
Fund raising	
local Christian church	254.8
synagogues	296.65
Fundamental theology (Christianity)	230.01
Fundamentalism	
Christianity	270.82
independent denominations	289.95
Protestantism	280.4
Islam	297.09
see Manual at 320.55 vs. 297.09, 322.1	
Fundamentalist theology	230.046 26
Funeral sermons	
Christianity	252.1
Funerals	
Buddhist rites	294.343 8
Christian rites	265.85
Hindu rites	294.538
Islamic rites	297.385
Jewish rites	296.445
liturgy	296.454 5
religious rites	291.38

Future life	
religion	291.23
Buddhism	294.342 3
Christianity	236.2
Hinduism	294.523
Islam	297.23
Judaism	296.33
Future punishment	291.23
Islam	297.23

G

Galatians (Biblical book)	227.4
Gallican schismatic churches	284.8
see also Old Catholic churches	
Gambling	
ethics	
religion	291.565
Christianity	241.65
Islam	297.565
Judaism	296.365
Ganapataism	294.551 5
Gaonim	296.120 092
Gathas	295.82
Gautama Buddha	294.363
Gays	
religion	200.866 4
Christianity	270.086 64
pastoral theology	259.086 64
social theology	261.835 766
Judaism	296.086 64
social theology	291.178 357 66
General Conference Mennonite Church	289.73
see also Mennonite Church	
Genesis (Bible)	222.11
Genetics	
social theology	291.178 365
Christianity	261.836 5
Gentleness	
ethics	
religion	291.5
see also Virtues—religion	
Geography	
Bible	220.91
Geonim	296.120 092
German Reformed Church (U.S.)	285.733
see also Reformed Church (American Reformed)	
Germanic religion	293
Gestures	
preaching	251.03
Gifts of the Holy Spirit	234.13

Gittin	296.123 3	Good and evil	
Babylonian Talmud	296.125 3	ethics	
Mishnah	296.123 3	religion	291.5
Palestinian Talmud	296.124 3	Christianity	241
Gloria	264.36	Islam	297.5
Glossolalia	234.132	Judaism	296.36
Gluttony		religion	291.211 8
moral theology	291.568	Christianity	231.8
Buddhism	294.356 8	freedom of choice	233.7
Christianity	241.3	comparative religion	291.211 8
Hinduism	294.548 68	Islam	297.2
Islam	297.568	freedom of choice	297.227
Judaism	296.368	theodicy	297.211 8
Gnosticism	299.932	Judaism	296.311 8
Christian heresy	273.1	freedom of choice	296.32
God	211	philosophy of religion	214
Buddhism	294.342 11	Good Friday	263.925
Christianity	231	devotional literature	242.35
comparative religion	291.211	sermons	252.625
Hinduism	294.521 1	Good News Bible	220.520 82
Islam	297.211	Goodness of God	214
Judaism	296.311	Christianity	231.8
philosophy of religion	211	comparative religion	291.211 2
Goddess religions	291.14	Islam	297.211 2
Goddesses	291.211 4	Judaism	296.311 2
see also Gods and goddesses		philosophy of religion	214
Gods	291.211	Gospel of Thomas	229.8
see also Gods and goddesses		Gospel stories retold	226.095 05
Gods and goddesses	291.211	Gospels (Bible)	226
African	299.63	pseudepigrapha	229.8
Australian	299.921 5	Gossip	
Buddhist	294.342 11	ethics	
Celtic	299.16	religion	291.567 2
Chinese	299.51	Christianity	241.672
classical	292.211	Judaism	296.367 2
Egyptian	299.31	see also Ethical	
Germanic	293.211	problems—religion	
Greek	292.211	Gothic art	
Hawaiian	299.924 2	religious significance	246.1
Hindu	294.521 1	Grace (Religious doctrine)	291.22
Native American	299.73	Christianity	234
North American	299.73	Gradual	264.36
South American	299.83	Gratitude	
Norse	293.211	ethics	
Polynesian	299.924	religion	291.5
Roman	292.211	see also Virtues—religion	
Scandinavian	293.211	Great schism, 1054	270.38
Semitic	299.2	Great White Brotherhood	299.93
Shinto	299.561 211		
Golden Rule			
Christianity	241.54		
Judaism	296.36		

Greed	
moral theology	291.568
Buddhism	294.356 8
Christianity	241.3
Hinduism	294.548 68
Islam	297.568
Judaism	296.368
Greek language	
Biblical texts	220.48
Greek religion	292.08
Grief	
at death	
Christianity	
pastoral theology	259.6
personal religion	248.866
prayers and meditations	242.4
see also Bereavement—	
religion	
Guides to religious life	291.44
Buddhism	294.344 4
Christianity	248.4
Hinduism	294.544
Islam	297.57
Sufi	297.44
Judaism	296.7
Guilt	
religion	291.22
Christianity	233.4
Judaism	296.32
Guru Granth	294.682
Gurus	200.92
biography	200.92
Buddhist	294.309 2
biography	294.309 2
specific sects	294.39
role and function	294.361
Hindu	294.509 2
biography	294.509 2
specific sects	294.55
role and function	294.561
role and function	291.61
Sikh	294.609 2
biography	294.609 2
role and function	294.663
see Manual at 200.92 and 291–299	

H

Habad Lubavitch Hasidism	296.833 22
Habakkuk (Biblical book)	224.95
Hades	291.23
see also Hell	
Hadith	297.124
Ḥadj	297.352
Haggadah (Passover)	296.453 71
Haggai (Biblical book)	224.97
Ḥagigah	296.123 2
Babylonian Talmud	296.125 2
Mishnah	296.123 2
Palestinian Talmud	296.124 2
Hagiographa (Bible)	223
Hail Mary	242.74
Ḥajj	297.352
Halakhah	296.18
Midrash	296.141
Talmud	296.127 4
see Manual at 296.18 vs. 340.58	
Ḥallah	296.123 1
Mishnah	296.123 1
Palestinian Talmud	296.124 1
Hanafites (Islamic sect)	297.811
Hanbalites (Islamic sect)	297.814
Hanukkah	296.435
liturgy	296.453 5
Hard-Shell Baptists	286.4
see also Baptists	
Harmonies of Bible	220.65
Harmonies of Gospels	226.1
Hasidism	296.833 2
liturgy	296.450 44
Hatred	
religion	291.5
see also Vices—religion	
Hawaiian religion	299.924 2
Healing	
religion	291.31
Christianity	234.131
see also Spiritual healing— religion	
see Manual at 615.852 vs. 234.131, 291.31	
Health	
social theology	291.178 321
Christianity	261.832 1
Judaism	296.38
Health services	
pastoral theology	291.61
Christianity	259.41
social theology	291.178 321
Christianity	261.832 1
Heaven	291.23
Christianity	236.24
Islam	297.23
Judaism	296.33

Hebrew language	
Biblical texts	220.44
Midrashic texts	296.140 4
Talmudic texts	296.120 4
Hebrew schools	296.680 83
Hebrews (Biblical book)	227.87
Hegirah	297.634
Hell	291.23
Christianity	236.25
Islam	297.23
Hellenistic movement (Judaism)	296.81
Heresy	
Christianity	262.8
church history	273
polemics	239
Islam	
polemics	297.29
Judaism	296.67
polemics	296.35
religious authority	296.67
Hermeneutics	
sacred books	291.82
Bible	220.601
Koran	297.122 601
Talmud	296.120 601
Hexateuch (Bible)	222.1
Hidden Imam	297.24
High Holy Days	296.431
liturgy	296.453 1
Higher criticism	
Bible	220.66
Hijrah	297.634
Hinayana Buddhism	294.391
Hindu education	294.575
Hindu ethics	294.548
Hinduism	294.5
Islamic polemics	297.294
Hinduism and Islam	294.517 2
Hindu view	294.517 2
Islamic view	297.284 5
Hindus	
biography	294.509 2
Historians of religion	200.92
Historical books (Old Testament)	222
Historical books (Pseudepigrapha)	229.911
Historical criticism	
sacred books	291.82
Bible	220.67
Koran	297.122 67
Talmud	296.120 67
Historicity of Jesus Christ	232.908
History	
Biblical events	220.95
History (Theology)	291.211 7
Christianity	231.76
Islam	297.211 4
Judaism	296.311 7
Holidays	
religion	291.36
see also Holy days	
Holiness	291.22
Christian church attribute	262.72
Christian doctrine	234.8
Holocaust, 1933–1945	
Christian theology	231.76
interreligious relations	261.26
Jewish theology	296.311 74
Holy, The	211
Holy Communion	234.163
public worship	264.36
Anglican	264.030 36
texts	264.03
Roman Catholic	264.020 36
texts	264.023
theology	234.163
Holy days	291.36
Buddhism	294.343 6
Christianity	263.9
devotional literature	242.3
sermons	252.6
Hinduism	294.536
Islam	297.36
Judaism	296.43
liturgy	296.453
see Manual at 263.9, 291.36 vs. 394.265–394.267	
Holy Family	232.92
Holy Ghost	231.3
Holy Hours	264.7
Holy Orders	234.164
public worship	265.4
theology	234.164
Holy places	291.35
see also Sacred places	
Holy Roman Empire	
church history	270
Holy Shroud	232.966
Holy Spirit	231.3
baptism in	234.13
Holy war (Islam)	297.72
Holy Week	263.925
devotional literature	242.35
Roman Catholic liturgy	264.027 2
sermons	252.625
Home missions	266.022

Homeless persons		Hospitals	
social theology	291.178 325	pastoral theology	291.61
Christianity	261.832 5	Christianity	259.411
Homiletic illustrations		Judaism	296.610 877
Christianity	251.08	social theology	291.178 321 1
Homiletics		Christianity	261.832 11
Christianity	251	Judaism	296.38
see also Preaching		House churches	250
Homilies	291.43	Huguenots	284.5
Christianity	252	biography	284.509 2
Homosexuality		persecution of	272.4
ethics		see also Christian	
religion	291.566	denominations	
Buddhism	294.356 6	Ḥullin	296.123 5
Christianity	241.66	Babylonian Talmud	296.125 5
Hinduism	294.548 66	Mishnah	296.123 5
Islam	297.566	Human ecology	
Judaism	296.366	social theology	291.178 362
social theology	291.178 357 66	Christianity	261.836 2
Christianity	261.835 766	Judaism	296.38
Homosexuals		Human life	
religion	200.866 4	origin	
Christianity	270.086 64	religion	291.22
pastoral theology	259.086 64	Christianity	233.11
social theology	261.835 766	Islam	297.221
Judaism	296.086 64	Judaism	296.32
social theology	291.178 357 66	philosophy of religion	213
Honesty		Human sacrifice	
moral theology	291.5	religion	291.34
see also Virtues—religion		Humanism	
Hope		philosophy of religion	211.6
Christianity	234.25	Humanistic Judaism	296.834
Horayot	296.123 4	Humanity of Jesus Christ	232.8
Babylonian Talmud	296.125 4	Humans	
Mishnah	296.123 4	religion	291.22
Palestinian Talmud	296.124 4	Buddhism	294.342 2
Hosea (Biblical book)	224.6	Christianity	233
Hospices (Terminal care		Hinduism	294.522
facilities)		Islam	297.22
pastoral theology	291.61	Judaism	296.32
Christianity	259.417 56	philosophy of religion	218
Judaism	296.610 877	Humility	
social theology	291.178 321 756	moral theology	291.5
Christianity	261.832 175 6	see also Virtues—religion	
Judaism	296.38	Hunger	
Hospital chaplaincy	291.61	social theology	291.178 326
Christianity	259.411	Christianity	261.832 6
Judaism	296.610 877	Hunting	
Hospitalers of St. John of		ethics	
Jerusalem	255.791 2	religion	291.569 3
church history	271.791 2	Christianity	241.693
		Judaism	296.369 3
		Husbands	
		guides to Christian life	248.842 5

Relative Index

Hussites	284.3
see also Christian denominations	
Hutterite Brethren	289.73
biography	289.709 2
see also Mennonite Church	
Hymns	
religion	291.38
Christianity	264.23
Judaism	296.462
private devotions	291.43
Hypostatic union	232.8

I

Ibadites	297.833
Iblīs	297.216
Ibn Ḥanbal, Aḥmad ibn Muḥammad	
Hadith	297.124
Ibn Mājah, Muḥammad ibn Yazīd	
Hadith	297.124 6
Ibrāhīm (Patriarch)	
Islam	297.246 3
Icons	
religious significance	291.37
Christianity	246.53
see also Symbolism—religious significance	
'Īd al-Aḍhā	297.36
'Īd al-Fiṭr	297.36
Idolatry	291.218
Idols	291.218
Images	
religious significance	291.37
Christianity	246.53
see also Symbolism—religious significance	
religious worship	291.218
Imamate	297.61
Imams	297.092
biography	297.092
specific sects	297.8
role and function	297.61
see Manual at 297.092	
Immaculate Conception of Mary	232.911
Immorality	
religion	291.5
Christianity	241
see also Moral theology	

Immortality	
religion	291.23
Christianity	236.22
Islam	297.23
Judaism	296.33
philosophy of religion	218
Incarnation of Jesus Christ	232.1
Independent Fundamental Churches of America	289.95
see also Christian denominations	
Independent Fundamentalist and Evangelical churches	289.95
see also Christian denominations	
Independent Methodists	287.533
see also Methodist Church	
Indic religions	294
Islamic polemics	297.294
see Manual at 200.9 vs. 294, 299.5	
Indic religions and Islam	294
Indic view	294
Islamic view	297.284
Indulgences (Christian rite)	265.66
Inequality	
social theology	291.178 34
Christianity	261.834
Judaism	296.38
Inerrancy (Bible)	220.132
Infallibility	
Christian church	262.72
pope	262.131
Infancy of Jesus Christ	232.92
Infant baptism	234.161 2
public worship	265.12
theology	234.161 2
Initiation rites	
Christianity	234.161
public worship	265.1
theology	234.161
religion	291.38
Innate virtues (Christian doctrine)	234
Inquisition (Church history)	272.2
Insignia	
religious significance	291.37
Christianity	246.56
Inspiration	
Bible	220.13
Koran	297.122 1
Intercession of Jesus Christ	232.8
Interdenominational cooperation	280.042

Interfaith marriage		Islam and Indic religions	294
Judaism	296.444 3	Indic view	294
social theology	291.178 358 43	Islamic view	297.284
Christianity	261.835 843	Islam and Judaism	296.397
Interfaith relations	291.172	Islamic view	297.282
see also Interreligious relations		Jewish view	296.397
Intermediate state (Christian		Islam and Sikhism	294.617 2
doctrine)	236.4	Islamic view	297.284 6
International relations		Sikh view	294.617 2
ethics		Islamic education	297.77
religion	291.562 4	*see Manual at* 291.75 vs.	
Buddhism	294.356 24	200.71	
Christianity	241.624	Islamic ethics	297.5
Hinduism	294.548 624	Islamic fundamentalism	297.09
Judaism	296.362 4	*see Manual at* 320.55 vs.	
Islam	297.562 4	297.09, 322.1	
social theology	291.178 7	Islamic giving	297.54
Buddhism	294.337 87	Islamic law	
Christianity	261.87	religion	297.14
Hinduism	294.517 87	*see Manual at* 340.59 vs.	
Islam	297.272	297.14	
Judaism	296.382 7	Islamic legends	297.18
International Society for Krishna		Ismailis (Islamic sect)	297.822
Consciousness	294.551 2	Isrā'	297.633
Interpretation of tongues	234.13	Israel	
Interreligious marriage		Biblical geography and history	220.9
Judaism	296.444 3	Christian theology	231.76
social theology	291.178 358 43	Jewish theology	296.311 73
Christianity	261.835 843	Ithna Asharites (Islamic sect)	297.821
Interreligious relations	291.172		
Buddhism	294.337 2	**J**	
Interreligious relations (continued)			
Christianity	261.2	J document (Biblical criticism)	222.106 6
Hinduism	294.517 2	Jacob (Biblical patriarch)	222.110 92
Islam	297.28	Jacobite Church	281.63
Judaism	296.39	*see also* Eastern churches	
Introit	264.36	Jaina Agama	294.482
Irreligion		Jainism	294.4
religious attitude toward	291.172	Jains	
Christianity	261.21	biography	294.409 2
Isaac (Biblical patriarch)	222.110 92	James (Biblical book)	227.91
Isagogics		Jansenism	273.7
Bible	220.61	denominations	284.84
Isaiah (Biblical book)	224.1	Japanese religions	299.56
Islam	297	Jatakas	294.382 325
Islam and Buddhism	294.337 2	Jealousy	
Buddhist view	294.337 2	ethics	
Islamic view	297.284 3	religion	291.5
Islam and Christianity	261.27	*see also* Vices—religion	
Christian view	261.27	Jehovah's Witnesses	289.92
Islamic view	297.283	biography	289.920 92
Islam and Hinduism	294.517 2	*see also* Christian	
Hindu view	294.517 2	denominations	
Islamic view	297.284 5		

Jeremiah (Biblical book)	224.2
Jerusalem	
sacred place	
Christianity	263.042 569 442
Islam	297.355 694 42
Judaism	296.482
Jerusalem Bible	220.520 7
Jerusalem Talmud	296.124
Jesuits	255.53
church history	271.53
Jesus Christ	232
biography	232.901
Gospel text and criticism	226
see Manual at 230–280	
Islam	297.246 5
Jewish interpretations	232.906
rationalistic interpretations	232.9
see Manual at 232	
Jewish apocalypses	
pseudepigrapha	229.913
Jewish Bible	221
see Manual at 221	
Jewish-Christian dialogue	261.26
Christian theology	261.26
Jewish theology	296.396
Jewish Christians (Sects)	289.9
see also Christian denominations	
Jewish education	296.68
see Manual at 291.75 vs. 200.71	
Jewish Publication Society Bible	221.520 8
Jewish religious schools	296.680 83
Jews (Religious group)	
biography	296.092
specific denominations	296.8
role of leaders	296.61
Jihad	297.72
Jinn	297.217
Jnana yoga	294.543 6
Joachim, Saint	232.933
private prayers to	242.75
Job (Biblical book)	223.1
Joel (Biblical book)	224.7
John (Biblical books)	226.5
epistles	227.94
gospel	226.5
Revelation	228
John, the Baptist, Saint	232.94
Jonah (Biblical book)	224.92
Joseph (Son of Jacob)	222.110 92
Joseph, Saint	232.932
private prayers to	242.75
Joshua (Biblical book)	222.2
Judaism	296
Christian polemics	239.2
Islamic polemics	297.292
Judaism and Christianity	261.26
Christian view	261.26
Jewish view	296.396
Judaism and Islam	296.397
Islamic view	297.282
Jewish view	296.397
Judas's betrayal of Jesus Christ	232.961
Jude (Biblical book)	227.97
Judges (Biblical book)	222.32
Judgment Day	291.23
Christianity	236.9
Islam	297.23
Judith (Deuterocanonical book)	229.24
Jum'ah	297.36
Just war theory	
ethics	
religion	291.562 42
Christianity	241.624 2
see also War—ethics—religion	
Justice	
ethics	
religion	291.562 2
Buddhism	294.356 22
Christianity	241.622
Hinduism	294.548 622
Islam	297.562 2
Judaism	296.362 2
social theology	291.178
Christianity	261.8
Islam	297.27
Judaism	296.38
Justice of God	214
Christianity	231.8
comparative religion	291.211 8
Islam	297.211 8
Judaism	296.311 8
philosophy of religion	214
see also Theodicy	
Justification (Christian doctrine)	234.7
Juvenile delinquents	
pastoral care of	259.5

K

Kabbalah	296.16
see also Cabala	
Kadarites (Islamic sect)	297.835
Kalām (Islam)	297.2
Karaites	296.81

Karma	291.22
Buddhism	294.342 2
Hinduism	294.522
see Manual at 291: Common terms	
Karma yoga	294.543 6
Karo, Joseph ben Ephraim	
Jewish legal codes	296.182
Kashrut	296.73
Kelim	296.123 6
Keritot	296.123 5
Babylonian Talmud	296.125 5
Mishnah	296.123 5
Kethubim	223
Ketubbot	296.123 3
Babylonian Talmud	296.125 3
Mishnah	296.123 3
Palestinian Talmud	296.124 3
Ketuvim	223
Kharijites	297.83
Khuddakanikāya	294.382 32
Khuṭbah	297.37
Kiddushin	296.123 3
Babylonian Talmud	296.125 3
Mishnah	296.123 3
Palestinian Talmud	296.124 3
Kilayim	296.123 1
Mishnah	296.123 1
Palestinian Talmud	296.124 1
Kindness	
ethics	
religion	291.567 7
see also Love—ethics—religion	
King James version (Bible)	220.520 3
Kingdom of God	231.72
eschatology	236
Kings (Biblical books)	222.5
Kingship of Jesus Christ	232.8
Kinnim	296.123 5
Knighthood orders	
Christian religious orders	255.791
church history	271.791
Knights Hospitalers of St. John of Jerusalem	255.791 2
church history	271.791 2
Knights of Malta	255.791 2
church history	271.791 2
Knights Templars	255.791 3
church history	271.791 3
Knowledge of God	212.6
Christianity	231.042
comparative religion	291.211
philosophy of religion	212.6

Kodashim	296.123 5
Babylonian Talmud	296.125 5
Mishnah	296.123 5
Palestinian Talmud	296.124 5
Kohelet	223.8
Koran	297.122
Koran stories	297.122 2
Kosher observance	296.73
Kundalini yoga	
comparative religion	291.436
Hinduism	294.543 6
Kyrie	264.36

L

Labor	
ethics	
religion	291.564
Christianity	241.64
Islam	297.564
Judaism	296.364
religion	291.178 5
Christianity	261.85
guides to life	248.88
Judaism	296.383
Laboring classes	
social theology	291.178 345 62
Christianity	261.834 562
Lag b'Omer	296.439
liturgy	296.453 9
Laity (Church members)	262.15
biography	270.092
specific denominations	280
see Manual at 280	
church government	262.15
pastoral theology	253
Lamaism	294.392 3
Lamentations (Bible)	224.3
Last Judgment	
Christianity	236.9
Last Supper	232.957
Later Prophets (Biblical books)	224
Latin language	
Biblical texts	220.47
Latter-Day Saints	
biography	289.309 2
Latter-Day Saints Church	289.3
see also Mormon Church	
Lauds	264.15
see also Liturgy of the hours	
Law	
religious	291.84
see also Religious law	

Relative Index

Law (Theology)	
Christianity	241.2
Judaism	296.18
Law and gospel	241.2
Law of God	
Christianity	241.2
Lay brothers	
religious orders	255.093
church history	271.093
Lay ministry	253
ecclesiology	262.15
pastoral theology	253
Lay sisters	
religious orders	255.909 3
church history	271.909 3
Laying on of hands (Christian rite)	265.9
Laylat al-Barā'ah	297.36
Laylat al-Mi'rāj	297.36
Laylat al-Qadr	297.362
Laymen (Church members)	262.15
see also Laity (Church members)	
Lazarists	255.77
church history	271.77
Leadership	
Christian church	262.1
local church	253
Lectionaries (Public worship)	264.34
Anglican	264.030 34
texts	264.032
preaching	251.6
Roman Catholic	264.020 34
texts	264.029
Lecture method	
Christian religious education	268.632
Lent	263.92
devotional literature	242.34
sermons	252.62
Lesbianism	
social theology	291.178 357 663
Christianity	261.835 766 3
see also Homosexuality	
Lesbians	
religion	200.866 43
Christianity	270.086 643
pastoral theology	259.086 643
social theology	261.835 766 3
Judaism	296.086 643
social theology	291.178 357 663
Leviticus	222.13
Liberal Catholic Church	284.8
see also Old Catholic churches	
Liberal theology	230.046
Liberation theology	230.046 4
political aspects	261.7
Roman Catholic	230.2
socioeconomic aspects	261.8
Life	
medical ethics	
religion	291.564 24
Christianity	241.642 4
Judaism	296.364 24
respect for	
ethics	
religion	291.569 1
Buddhism	294.356 91
Christianity	241.691
Hinduism	294.548 691
Judaism	296.369 1
Islam	297.569 1
Life after death	
religion	291.23
Christianity	236.2
Islam	297.23
Judaism	296.33
philosophy of religion	218
Life sciences and religion	291.175
Christianity	261.55
philosophy of religion	215.7
Lighting	
religious significance	291.37
Christianity	246.6
see also Symbolism—religious significance	
Limbo	236.4
Lingayats	294.551 3
Litanies	264.13
Roman Catholic	264.027 4
Literary criticism	
sacred books	291.82
Bible	220.66
Talmud	296.120 66
Literary genres	
sacred books	291.82
Bible	220.66
Talmud	296.120 66
Literature and religion	291.175
Christianity	261.58
Little Church of France	284.8
see also Christian denominations	
Little Sisters of the Poor	255.95
church history	271.95
Liturgical dance	246.7
Liturgical objects	291.37
Christianity	247
Judaism	296.461

Liturgical renewal	264.001
Liturgical year	263.9
devotional literature	242.3
sermons	252.6
Liturgy	291.38
Christianity	264
see also Public worship	
Liturgy of the hours	264.15
Anglican	264.030 15
Roman Catholic	264.020 15
texts	264.024
Living Bible	220.520 83
Local Christian church	250
ecclesiology	262.2
specific denominations	280
see Manual at 260 vs. 251–254, 259	
Local religious organizations	291.65
Logos	232.2
Lollards	284.3
Lord's Prayer	226.96
private devotions	242.722
Lord's Supper	234.163
public worship	264.36
theology	234.163
Love	
ethics	
religion	291.567 7
Buddhism	294.356 77
Christianity	241.4
Hinduism	294.548 677
Islam	297.567 7
Judaism	296.367 7
God's love	212.7
Christianity	231.6
comparative religion	291.211 2
philosophy of religion	212.7
Love feasts	
Christian rite	265.9
Lower criticism	
Bible	220.404 6
Lubavitch Hasidism	296.833 22
Lucifer	
Christianity	235.47
Islam	297.216
Luke (Gospel)	226.4
Lust	
ethics	
religion	291.566
Christianity	241.3
see also Sexual relations—ethics—religion	

Lutheran church	284.1
church government	262.041
parishes	254.041
church law	262.984 1
doctrines	230.41
catechisms and creeds	238.41
general councils	262.541
guides to Christian life	248.484 1
missions	266.41
moral theology	241.044 1
public worship	264.041
religious associations	267.184 1
religious education	268.841
seminaries	230.073 41
theology	230.41
Lutheran Church in America	284.133
see also Lutheran church	
Lutheran Church—Missouri Synod	284.132 2
see also Lutheran church	
Lutheran Free Church	284.131 4
see also Lutheran church	
Lutheran sacred music	
public worship	
religion	264.041 02
Lutherans	
biography	284.109 2

M

Ma'aser Sheni (Tractate)	296.123 1
Mishnah	296.123 1
Palestinian Talmud	296.124 1
Ma'aserot (Tractate)	296.123 1
Mishnah	296.123 1
Palestinian Talmud	296.124 1
Maccabees (Biblical books)	229.7
Madhyamika Buddhism	294.392
Magi (Christian doctrines)	232.923
Magic	
religious practice	291.3
Magicians (Religious leaders)	200.92
biography	200.92
role and function	291.61
see Manual at 200.92 and 291–299	
Magisterium	262.8
Mahabharata	294.592 3
Mahasanghika Buddhism	294.391
Mahayana Buddhism	294.392
Mahdi	
Islamic theology	297.24
Mahomet, Prophet	297.63
Mahzorim	296.453

Relative Index

Maimonides, Moses	
Jewish legal writings	296.181
Major Prophets (Biblical books)	224
Makhshirin	296.123 6
Makka (Saudi Arabia)	
Islamic religion	297.352
Makkot	296.123 4
Babylonian Talmud	296.125 4
Mishnah	296.123 4
Palestinian Talmud	296.124 4
Malachi (Biblical book)	224.99
Malikites (Islamic sect)	297.813
Mandalas	291.37
Buddhism	294.343 7
Hinduism	294.537
Manicheism	299.932
Christian heresy	273.2
Mantras	291.37
Buddhism	294.343 7
Hinduism	294.537
Mar Thoma Church	281.5
see also Eastern churches	
Mariology (Christian doctrines)	232.91
Mark (Gospel)	226.3
Maronites	281.5
Maronites (Religious order)	255.18
church history	271.18
Marriage	
ethics	
religion	291.563
Buddhism	294.356 3
Christianity	241.63
Hinduism	294.548 63
Islam	297.563
Judaism	296.363
personal religion	291.441
Buddhism	294.344 41
Christianity	248.4
Hinduism	294.544 1
Islam	297.577
Judaism	296.74
religion	291.441
Christianity	248.4
Islam	297.577
Judaism	296.74
religious doctrine	291.22
Christianity	234.165
religious law	291.84
Christianity	262.9
Judaism	296.444
rites	291.38
Christianity	265.5
Judaism	296.444
liturgy	296.454 4
see also Public worship	
Marriage (continued)	
social theology	291.178 358 1
Christianity	261.835 81
Marriage counseling	
pastoral theology	291.61
Christianity	259.14
Judaism	296.61
Married persons	
Christian devotional literature	242.644
guides to religious life	291.441
Christianity	248.844
Islam	297.577
Judaism	296.74
see also Marriage—personal religion	
Martyrs	200.92
biography	200.92
Christian	272.092
see Manual at 230–280	
role and function	291.61
see Manual at 200.92 and 291–299	
Marxist-Christian dialogue	
Christian theology	261.21
Mary, Blessed Virgin, Saint	232.91
private prayers to	242.74
see Manual at 230–280	
Mass (Christian rite)	264.36
Anglican	264.030 36
texts	264.03
Roman Catholic	264.020 36
texts	264.023
Mass media	
religion	291.175
Christianity	261.52
evangelism	269.26
use by local church	253.78
administration	254.3
Judaism	296.37
Massacre of innocents	232.92
Materialism	
Christian polemics	239.7
Islamic polemics	297.298
Matins	264.15
Anglican	264.030 15
texts	264.033
see also Liturgy of the hours	
Matrimony	
sacrament	234.165
public worship	265.5
theology	234.165
see also Marriage	
Matthew (Gospel)	226.2

Maundy Thursday	263.925
devotional literature	242.35
sermons	252.625
Mawlid al-Nabī	297.36
Mazdaism	295
Mecca (Saudi Arabia)	
Islamic religion	297.352
Mechitarists	255.17
church history	271.17
Medals	
religious significance	291.37
see also Symbolism—	
religious significance	
Medical ethics	
religion	291.564 2
Buddhism	294.356 42
Christianity	241.642
Hinduism	294.548 642
Islam	297.564 2
Judaism	296.364 2
Medical missionaries	
Christian	266.009 2
Medical missions	
Christian	266
Medicine and religion	291.175
Christianity	261.561
Judaism	296.376
Medieval period	
church history	270.3
Medina (Saudi Arabia)	
Islamic religion	297.355 38
Meditation	
religion	291.435
Buddhism	294.344 35
Christianity	248.34
Hinduism	294.543 5
Islam	297.382
Sufi	297.438 2
Judaism	296.72
Meditations	
religion	291.432
Buddhism	294.344 32
Christianity	242
Hinduism	294.543 2
Islam	297.382 4
Sufi	297.438 24
Judaism	296.72
Megillah (Tractate)	296.123 2
Babylonian Talmud	296.125 2
Mishnah	296.123 2
Palestinian Talmud	296.124 2
Megillot (Bible)	221.044
Me'ilah	296.123 5
Babylonian Talmud	296.125 5
Mishnah	296.123 5
Melodic reading	
Koran	297.122 404 5
Men	
religion	200.81
Christianity	270.081
devotional literature	242.642
guides to Christian life	248.842
social theology	261.834 31
guides to religious life	291.440 81
social theology	291.178 343 1
Menaḥot	296.123 5
Babylonian Talmud	296.125 5
Mishnah	296.123 5
Mendicant religious orders	255.06
church history	271.06
Mennonite Church	289.7
church government	262.097
parishes	254.097
church law	262.989 7
doctrines	230.97
catechisms and creeds	238.97
general councils	262.597
guides to Christian life	248.489 7
missions	266.97
moral theology	241.049 7
public worship	264.097
religious associations	267.189 7
religious education	268.897
seminaries	230.073 97
theology	230.97
Mennonites	
biography	289.709 2
Mental health services	
pastoral theology	291.61
Christianity	259.42
social theology	291.178 322
Christianity	261.832 2
Mental illness	
Christian religious guidance	248.862
pastoral theology	291.61
Christianity	259.42
social theology	291.178 322
Christianity	261.832 2
Mentally ill persons	
guides to Christian life	248.862
Mercedarians	255.45
church history	271.45
Merit (Christian doctrine)	234
Messiahs	
Christianity	232.1
Judaism	296.336

Messiahs (continued)		Middle classes	
role and function	291.61	social theology	291.178 345 5
see Manual at 200.92 and 291–299		Christianity	261.834 55
		Middot	296.123 5
Messianic Judaism	289.9	Midrash	296.14
see also Christian denominations		Mikva'ot (Tractate)	296.123 6
		Mikveh	296.75
Messianic prophecies		Militarism	
Christianity	232.12	ethics	
Judaism	296.336	religion	291.562 42
Messianism	291.23	Christianity	241.624 2
Judaism	296.336	social theology	291.178 73
Methodist Church	287	Christianity	261.873
church government	262.07	see also War	
parishes	254.07	Military religious orders	255.791
church law	262.987	church history	271.791
doctrines	230.7	Millennium	
catechisms and creeds	238.7	Christianity	236.9
guides to Christian life	248.487	Minarets	297.351
missions	266.7	Minims (Religious order)	255.49
moral theology	241.047	church history	271.49
public worship	264.07	Ministerial authority	262.8
religious associations	267.187	Ministers (Christian clergy)	270.092
religious education	268.87	biography	270.092
seminaries	230.073 7	specific denominations	280
theology	230.7	see Manual at 230–280	
Methodist Church (U.S.)	287.631	ecclesiology	262.14
see also Methodist Church		pastoral theology	253
Methodist Episcopal Church	287.632	see also Clergy—Christian	
see also Methodist Church		Minor Clerks Regular	255.56
Methodist Episcopal Church, South	287.633	church history	271.56
		Minor Prophets (Bible)	224.9
see also Methodist Church		Minor tractates (Talmud)	296.123 7
Methodist New Connexion	287.53	Miracles	291.211 7
see also Methodist Church		Christianity	231.73
Methodist Protestant Church	287.7	of Jesus Christ	232.955
see also Methodist Church		Gospels	226.7
Methodist sacred music		of Mary	232.917
public worship		spiritual gift	234.13
religion	264.070 2	Judaism	296.311 6
Methodists		philosophy of religion	212
biography	287.092	Mi'rāj	297.633
Mevleviyeh	297.482	Mishnah	296.123
Mezuzot	296.461	Mishneh Torah	296.181 2
Micah (Biblical book)	224.93	Missals	264.36
Middle-aged persons		Anglican	264.030 36
guides to Christian life	248.84	texts	264.03
guides to Jewish life	296.708 44	Roman Catholic	264.020 36
guides to religious life	291.440 844	texts	264.023
social theology	291.178 342 44	Missionaries	291.720 92
Christianity	261.834 244	Christian	266.009 2
Middle Ages		occupational ethics	241.641
church history	270.3	see Manual at 230–280	
		occupational ethics	
		religion	291.564 1

Missionaries of Charity	255.97	Monotheism (continued)	
church history	271.97	Judaism	296.311
Missionary stories		philosophy of religion	211.34
Christianity	266	Monotheistic religions	291.14
Missions (Religion)	291.72	Moral Rearmament	267.16
Christianity	266	Moral renewal (Christianity)	248.25
Islam	297.74	Moral theology	291.5
Mithraism	299.15	Buddhism	294.35
Mitzvot		Christianity	241
Jewish ethics	296.36	*see Manual at* 241 vs. 261.8	
Jewish law	296.18	Hinduism	294.548
Modern art		Islam	297.5
religious significance	291.37	Sufi	297.45
Christianity	246.4	Judaism	296.36
Modernism		Morality	
church history	273.9	religion	291.5
Modesty		*see also* Moral theology	
moral theology	291.5	Moravian Church	284.6
see also Virtues—religion		*see also* Christian	
Moʻed (Order)	296.123 2	denominations	
Babylonian Talmud	296.125 2	Moravians (Religious group)	
Mishnah	296.123 2	biography	284.609 2
Palestinian Talmud	296.124 2	Mormon Church	289.3
Moʻed Katan	296.123 2	church government	262.093
Babylonian Talmud	296.125 2	parishes	254.093
Mishnah	296.123 2	church law	262.989 3
Palestinian Talmud	296.124 2	doctrines	230.93
Moḥammed, Prophet	297.63	catechisms and creeds	238.93
Molinism	273.7	general councils	262.593
persecution of	272.5	guides to Christian life	248.489 3
Monasteries	291.657	missions	266.93
Buddhism	294.365 7	moral theology	241.049 3
Christianity	255	public worship	264.093
church history	271	religious associations	267.189 3
religious significance of		religious education	268.893
buildings	246.97	seminaries	230.073 93
Monasticism	291.657	temples	246.958 93
Buddhism	294.365 7	theology	230.93
Christianity	255	Mormons	
church history	271	biography	289.309 2
personal religion	248.894	Morning prayer	264.15
Monks	291.657	Anglican	264.030 15
Buddhist	294.365 7	texts	264.033
Christian	255	Mortal sin	241.31
biography	271.009 2	Mosaic law (Bible)	222.1
see Manual at 230–280		Moses	
ecclesiology	262.24	Biblical leader	222.109 2
guides to Christian life	248.894 2	Islam	297.246
Monophysite churches	281.6	Mosques	297.351
see also Eastern churches		organization	297.65
Monotheism	211.34	Motazilites	297.834
Christianity	231	Mothers	
comparative religion	291.211	Christian devotional literature	242.643 1
Islam	297.211	guides to Christian life	248.843 1

Relative Index

Motion pictures	
ethics	
religion	291.565
Christianity	241.65
Mourning	
Christianity	
devotional literature	242.4
religious guidance	248.866
rites	265.85
devotional literature	291.432
Islam	
rites	297.385
Judaism	
rites	296.445
liturgy	296.454 5
religious guidance	291.442
rites	291.38
Muḥammad, Prophet	297.63
Murjiites (Islamic sect)	297.837
Mūsá	
Islam	297.246
Music	
ethics	
religion	291.565
Christianity	241.65
religion	291.37
Buddhism	294.343 7
Christianity	246.75
attitude toward secular music	261.578
Hinduism	294.537
Jainism	294.437
Judaism	296.462
public worship	291.38
Christianity	264.2
Judaism	296.462
see also Public worship	
Muslim ibn al-Ḥajjāj al-Qushayrī	
Hadith	297.124 3
Muslims	297.092
biography	297.092
specific sects	297.8
Sufis	297.409 2
see Manual at 297.092	
Mutazilites	297.834
Mystical body of Christ	262.77
Mystical Judaism	296.833
Mysticism	291.422
Buddhism	294.344 22
Christianity	248.22
Hinduism	294.542 2
Islam	297.4
see Manual at 297.4	
Judaism	296.712

Mythological interpretation	
Bible	220.68
Mythologists	291.130 92
Mythology	
African religions	299.62
Australian religion	299.921 5
Buddhism	294.333
Celtic religion	299.16
Chinese religions	299.51
Christianity	230
classical religion	292.13
Egyptian religion	299.31
Germanic religion	293.13
Greek religion	292.13
Hawaiian religion	299.924 2
Hinduism	294.513
Native American religions	299.72
North American	299.72
South American	299.82
Norse religion	293.13
Polynesian religion	299.924
religion	291.13
sources	291.8
Roman religion	292.13
Scandinavian religion	293.13
Semitic religions	299.2
Shintoism	299.561 13
see Manual at 398.2 vs. 291.13	

N

Nahum (Biblical book)	224.94
Names of God	
Islam	297.211 2
Judaism	296.311 2
Naming ceremonies	
Judaism	296.443
Naqshabandiyah	297.48
Nasā'ī, Aḥmad ibn Shu'ayb	
Hadith	297.124 5
Nashim	296.123 3
Babylonian Talmud	296.125 3
Mishnah	296.123 3
Palestinian Talmud	296.124 3
Nation of Islam	297.87
National Baptist Convention of America	286.134
see also Baptists	
National Baptist Convention of the United States of America	286.133
see also Baptists	

National conferences of bishops	262.12
National Council of the Churches of Christ in the United States of America	277.308 206
Nationalism	
social theology	291.177
Buddhism	294.337 7
Christianity	261.7
Hinduism	294.517 7
Islam	297.272
Judaism	296.382
Nativity of Jesus Christ	232.92
Natural law	
moral theology	
Christianity	241.2
Natural religion	210
Natural resources	
ethics	
religion	291.568
Buddhism	294.356 8
Christianity	241.68
Hinduism	294.548 68
Islam	297.568
Judaism	296.368
Natural theology	210
Nature	
Christian doctrine	231.7
religious worship	291.212
respect for	
ethics	
religion	291.569 1
Buddhism	294.356 91
Christianity	241.691
Hinduism	294.548 691
Islam	297.569 1
Judaism	296.369 1
Natures of Jesus Christ	232.8
Nazir	296.123 3
Babylonian Talmud	296.125 3
Mishnah	296.123 3
Palestinian Talmud	296.124 3
Nebiim	224
Nedarim	296.123 3
Babylonian Talmud	296.125 3
Mishnah	296.123 3
Palestinian Talmud	296.124 3
Nega'im	296.123 6
Negro Methodist churches	287.8
see also Methodist Church	
Nehemiah (Biblical book)	222.8
Neoplatonism	
Christian polemics	239.4
Nestorian churches	281.8
see also Eastern churches	

Nevi'im	224
Nevi'im aharonim	224
Nevi'im rishonim	222
New Age movement	299.93
Christian polemics	239.93
occultism	
Christian viewpoint	261.513
religion	299.93
see Manual at 299.93	
New Age religions	299.93
see Manual at 299.93	
New American Bible	220.520 5
New Century Bible	220.520 8
New English Bible	220.520 6
New International version (Bible)	220.520 81
New Jerusalem Bible	220.520 7
New Jerusalemites	
biography	289.409 2
New King James Bible	220.520 8
New religions	291.046
see Manual at 291: Denominations and sects	
New religious movements	291.046
see Manual at 291: Denominations and sects	
New Revised Standard version Bible	220.520 43
New Testament	225
New Testament pseudepigrapha	229.92
New Testament theology	230.041 5
New Thought	299.93
Christian	289.98
see also Christian denominations	
New Year	
Jewish	296.431 5
liturgy	296.453 15
Nezikin	296.123 4
Babylonian Talmud	296.125 4
Mishnah	296.123 4
Palestinian Talmud	296.124 4
Nicene Creed	238.142
Nichiren Shoshu	294.392 8
Niddah (Tractate)	296.123 6
Babylonian Talmud	296.125 6
Mishnah	296.123 6
Palestinian Talmud	296.124 6
Niddah practice	296.742
Night journey of Muḥammad	297.633
Ninth of Av	296.439
liturgy	296.453 9

Nirvana	
Buddhism	294.342 3
Hinduism	294.523
Noah (Biblical person)	
Bible stories	222.110 950 5
Non-Trinitarian concepts	
Christianity	
God	231.044
Jesus	232.9
Nonconformists (British churches)	280.4
see also Protestantism	
None (Divine office)	264.15
see also Liturgy of the hours	
Nontheistic religions	291.14
Nonviolence	
ethics	
religion	291.569 7
Buddhism	294.356 97
Christianity	241.697
Hinduism	294.548 697
Islam	297.569 7
Judaism	296.369 7
Norse religion	293
Northern Baptists	286.131
see also Baptists	
Novenas	264.7
Novitiate (Monastic life)	248.894 25
women	248.894 35
Nuclear warfare	
ethics	
religion	291.562 422
Christianity	241.624 22
social theology	291.178 732
Christianity	261.873 2
see also War	
Numbers (Biblical book)	222.14
Numerical interpretation	
Bible	220.68
Koran	297.122 68
Nuns	291.657
Buddhist	294.365 7
Christian	255.9
biography	271.900 2
see Manual at 230–280	
ecclesiology	262.24
guides to Christian life	248.894 3
Nursing orders (Christianity)	255.07
church history	271.07
women	255.907
church history	271.907

O

Obadiah (Biblical book)	224.91
Obedience (Christian doctrine)	234.6
Obituary sermons	
Christianity	252.9
Oblates	255.76
church history	271.76
women	255.97
church history	271.97
Obscenity	
ethics	
religion	291.566 7
Christianity	241.667
Occultism	
religious practice	291.3
see Manual at 133 vs. 200	
Occultism and religion	291.175
Christianity	261.513
polemics	239.93
Occupational ethics	
religion	291.564
Christianity	241.64
Islam	297.564
Judaism	296.364
see also Ethical problems—religion	
Odes of Solomon	229.912
Offenders	
pastoral care of	259.5
Offerings (Religion)	291.34
Christianity	248.6
Judaism	296.492
Offertory	264.36
Office hours (Religion)	264.15
Anglican	264.030 15
Roman Catholic	264.020 15
texts	264.024
Oholot	296.123 6
Old Catholic churches	284.8
church government	262.048
parishes	254.048
church law	262.984 8
doctrines	230.48
catechisms and creeds	238.48
guides to Christian life	248.484 8
missions	266.48
moral theology	241.044 8
public worship	264.048
religious education	268.848
theology	230.48
Old Catholics	
biography	284.8

Old School Baptists	286.4
see also Baptists	
Old Testament	221
see Manual at 221	
Old Testament Apocrypha	229
Old Testament pseudepigrapha	229.91
Old Testament theology	
Christianity	230.041 1
Older persons	
religion	200.846
Christianity	270.084 6
devotional literature	242.65
guides to life	248.85
pastoral care of	259.3
social theology	261.834 26
guides to life	291.440 846
Judaism	296.084 6
guides to life	296.708 46
social theology	291.178 342 6
Olivetans	255.13
church history	271.13
women	255.97
church history	271.97
Omens	
religion	291.32
Omnipotence of God	212.7
Christianity	231.4
comparative religion	291.211 2
Islam	297.211 2
Judaism	296.311 2
philosophy of religion	212.7
Omniscience of God	212.7
Christianity	231.4
comparative religion	291.211 2
Islam	297.211 2
Judaism	296.311 2
philosophy of religion	212.7
Oracles	
religion	291.32
Oral traditions (Religion)	291.83
Bible	220.663
Buddhism	294.383
Hinduism	294.593
Islam	297.1
Judaism	296.1
Ordinary of the mass	264.36
Ordination of clergy	291.61
Christianity	262.14
ecclesiology	262.14
sacrament	234.164
public worship	265.4
theology	234.164
Judaism	296.61
Ordination of women	291.610 82
Christianity	262.14
Judaism	296.610 82
Ordos	
Roman Catholic liturgy	264.021
Organizations	
religious	291.65
see also Religious organizations	
Oriental churches	281.5
see also Eastern churches	
Origin of life	
religion	291.24
Christianity	231.765
philosophy of religion	213
Origin of universe	
religion	291.24
Christianity	231.765
philosophy of religion	213
Original sin	233.14
Orlah	296.123 1
Mishnah	296.123 1
Palestinian Talmud	296.124 1
Orthodox Eastern Church	281.9
see also Eastern Orthodox Church	
Orthodox Judaism	296.832
Osee (Biblical book)	224.6

P

P document (Biblical criticism)	222.106 6
Pacifism	
ethics	
religion	291.562 42
Christianity	241.624 2
social theology	291.178 73
Buddhism	294.337 873
Christianity	261.873
Hinduism	294.517 873
Judaism	296.382 7
Paganism	292
Christian polemics	239.3
Palestine	
Biblical geography and history	220.9
Palestinian Talmud	296.124
Palm Sunday	263.925
devotional literature	242.35
sermons	252.625
Panentheism	211.2
Pantheism	211.2
Pantheistic religions	291.14
Papacy	262.13
Papal administration	262.136

Papal bulls and decrees	262.91
Papal infallibility	262.131
Papal schism, 1378–1417	282.090 23
Papal systems (Ecclesiology)	262.3
Parables in the Gospels	226.8
Paradise	291.23
Christianity	236.24
Islam	297.23
Parah	296.123 6
Paralipomena (Biblical books)	222.6
Parapsychology and religion	291.175
Christianity	261.513
see Manual at 133 vs. 200	
Parenting	
personal religion	291.441
Christianity	248.845
Judaism	296.74
Parents	
Christian devotional literature	242.645
guides to religious life	291.441
Christianity	248.845
Judaism	296.74
Parish missions	266.022
Parishes	250
administration	254
ecclesiology	262.22
see Manual at 260 vs. 251–254, 259	
Parseeism	295
Passion of Jesus Christ	232.96
Passion plays	
religious significance	246.723
Passionists	255.62
church history	271.62
Passiontide	263.92
devotional literature	242.34
sermons	252.62
Passover	296.437
liturgy	296.453 7
Passover Haggadah	296.453 71
Pastoral counseling	291.61
Christianity	253.5
Judaism	296.61
Pastoral Epistles	227.83
Pastoral psychology	291.61
Christianity	253.52
Pastoral theology	291.61
Christianity	253
Islam	297.61
Judaism	296.61
Pastors	270.092
biography	270.092
specific denominations	280
see Manual at 230–280	
Pastors (continued)	
ecclesiology	262.14
pastoral theology	253
see also Clergy—Christian	
Patience	
moral theology	291.5
see also Virtues—religion	
Patriarchate	262.13
Patriarchs	200.92
Biblical	222.110 922
biography	200.92
Christian	270.092
biography	270.092
specific denominations	280
see Manual at 230–280	
ecclesiology	262.13
see also Clergy—Christian	
Patristics (Christianity)	270
Pauline epistles	227
Peace	
ethics	
religion	291.562 42
Buddhism	294.356 242
Christianity	241.624 2
Hinduism	294.548 624 2
Islam	297.562 42
Judaism	296.362 42
social theology	291.178 73
Buddhism	294.337 873
Christianity	261.873
Hinduism	294.517 873
Islam	297.27
Judaism	296.382 7
Pe'ah	296.123 1
Mishnah	296.123 1
Palestinian Talmud	296.124 1
Pelagianism	273.5
Penance	291.34
Christianity	234.166
public worship	265.6
theology	234.166
Pentateuch	222.1
Pentecost	263.94
devotional literature	242.38
Jewish	296.438
liturgy	296.453 8
sermons	252.64
Pentecostal churches	289.94
see also Christian denominations	
Pentecostalism	270.82
independent denominations	289.94
Protestantism	280.4

Pentecostals	
biography	289.940 92
People of God (Church)	262.7
Persecutions (Christian church history)	272
Person of Jesus Christ	232.8
Personal religion	291.4
Buddhism	294.344
Christianity	240
Hinduism	294.54
Islam	297.57
Sufi	297.4
Judaism	296.7
Personifications (Religion)	291.214
Persons	
objects of worship	291.213
Pesach	296.437
liturgy	296.453 7
Pesaḥim	296.123 2
Babylonian Talmud	296.125 2
Mishnah	296.123 2
Palestinian Talmud	296.124 2
Peter (Biblical books)	227.92
Pews	247.1
Pharisees	296.812
Philemon (Biblical book)	227.86
Philippians (Biblical book)	227.6
Philippine Independent Church	284.8
see also Old Catholic churches	
Philosophy and religion	291.175
Christianity	261.51
Islam	297.261
Judaism	296.371
see Manual at 200 vs. 100	
Philosophy of religion	210
Phylacteries	296.461 2
Physics and religion	291.175
Christianity	261.55
philosophy of religion	215.3
Piarists	255.58
church history	271.58
Pidyon haben	296.442 3
liturgy	296.454 23
Pietism	273.7
Pilgrimage to Mecca	297.352
Pilgrimages	291.351
Christianity	263.041
Islam	297.35
Judaism	296.481
Pillars of Islam	297.31
Pious societies	
Christianity	267
Pirke Avot	296.123 47
Pitakas	294.382
Piyyutim	296.452
Plants in Bible	220.858
Plymouth Brethren	289.9
see also Christian denominations	
Poetic books (Old Testament)	223
pseudepigrapha	229.912
Polemics	
Christianity	239
comparative religion	291.2
Islam	297.29
Judaism	296.35
Political ethics	
religion	291.562
Buddhism	294.356 2
Christianity	241.62
Hinduism	294.548 62
Islam	297.562
Judaism	296.362
Politics and religion	
social theology	291.177
Buddhism	294.337 7
Christianity	261.7
Hinduism	294.517 7
Islam	297.272
see Manual at 297.26–297.27	
Judaism	296.382
see Manual at 322.1 vs. 296.382, 320.54095694	
see Manual at 322.1 vs. 261.7, 291.177	
Pollution	
social theology	291.178 362 8
Christianity	261.836 28
Polyglot Bibles	220.51
Polynesian religion	299.924
Polytheism	211.32
comparative religion	291.211
philosophy of religion	211.32
Polytheistic religions	291.14
Pontificale Romanum	264.025
Poor Clares	255.973
church history	271.973
Poor people	
social theology	291.178 325
Buddhism	294.337 832 5
Christianity	261.832 5
Hinduism	294.517 832 5
Islam	297.27
Judaism	296.38

Relative Index

Popes	282.092
biography	282.092
ecclesiology	262.13
Popular practices (Islam)	297.39
Population control	
social theology	291.178 366 6
Christianity	261.836 66
Pornography	
ethics	
religion	291.566 7
Christianity	241.667
Poverty	
religious practice	291.447
Buddhism	294.344 47
Christianity	248.47
Hinduism	294.544 7
social theology	291.178 325
Buddhism	294.337 832 5
Christianity	261.832 5
Hinduism	294.517 832 5
Islam	297.27
Judaism	296.38
Prayer	291.43
Buddhism	294.344 3
Christianity	248.32
Hinduism	294.543
Islam	297.382
Sufi	297.438 2
Judaism	296.45
public worship	291.38
Buddhism	294.343 8
Christianity	264.1
Hinduism	294.538
Islam	297.382
Sufi	297.438 2
Judaism	296.45
Prayer books	291.433
Buddhism	294.344 33
Christianity	242.8
public worship	264.13
Hinduism	294.543 3
Islam	297.382 4
Sufi	297.438 24
Judaism	296.45
Prayer desks	
church furniture	247.1
Prayer meetings	
Christianity	
public worship	264.7
Prayer of Manasseh (Bible)	229.6
Prayer shawls	296.461
Prayers (Private devotions)	291.433
Buddhism	294.344 33
Christianity	242
Hinduism	294.543 3
Islam	297.382 4
Sufi	297.438 24
Judaism	296.45
Prayers (Public worship)	291.38
Buddhism	294.343 8
Christianity	264.13
Hinduism	294.538
Islam	297.382 4
Sufi	297.438 24
Judaism	296.45
Pre-Islamic prophets	297.246
Preaching	291.61
Christianity	251
Islam	297.37
Judaism	296.47
Preaching orders (Christianity)	255.04
church history	271.04
Predestination	291.22
Christianity	234.9
Islam	297.227
Predictions	
religion	291.32
eschatological	291.23
Prehistoric religions	291.042
Prejudice	
ethics	
religion	291.567 5
Christianity	241.675
Judaism	296.367 5
see also Ethical problems—religion	
social theology	291.178 34
Christianity	261.834
Judaism	296.38
Premarital counseling	
Christian pastoral counseling	259.13
Premonstratensians	255.19
church history	271.19
Presbyterian Church	285
church government	262.05
parishes	254.05
church law	262.985
doctrines	230.5
catechism and creeds	238.5
general councils	262.55
guides to Christian life	248.485
missions	266.5
moral theology	241.045
public worship	264.05

Presbyterian Church (continued)	
religious associations	267.185
religious education	268.85
seminaries	230.073 5
theology	230.5
Presbyterian Church (U.S.A.)	285.137
see also Presbyterian Church	
Presbyterian Church in the United States	285.133
see also Presbyterian Church	
Presbyterian Church in the United States of America	285.132
see also Presbyterian Church	
Presbyterian Church of Wales	285.235
see also Presbyterian Church	
Presbyterian sacred music	
public worship	
religion	264.050 2
Presbyterians	
biography	285.092
Presbyteries	
Christian ecclesiology	262.4
Presentation of Jesus Christ	232.928
Presentation religious orders	255.977
church history	271.977
Pride	
moral theology	291.5
see also Vices—religion	
Priesthood	291.61
Christianity	262.1
pastoral theology	253
Jewish	296.495
Priesthood of believers	234
Priesthood of Jesus Christ	232.8
Priests	200.92
biography	200.92
Christian	270.092
biography	270.092
specific denominations	280
see Manual at 230–280	
ecclesiology	262.14
pastoral theology	253
see also Clergy—Christian	
Jewish	296.495
role and function	291.61
see Manual at 200.92 and 291–299	
Prime (Divine office)	264.15
see also Liturgy of the hours	
Primitive Baptists	286.4
see also Baptists	
Primitive Methodist Church	287.4
see also Methodist Church	
Primitive religions	291.042
Priories	
church history	271
religious significance of buildings	246.97
Prison chaplaincy	291.61
Christianity	259.5
Judaism	296.610 869 2
Pro-choice movement	
social theology	291.178 366 67
Christianity	261.836 667
Judaism	296.38
Pro-life movement	
social theology	291.178 366 67
Christianity	261.836 667
Judaism	296.38
Probation after death	236.4
Process theology	230.046
Processions	
religious rites	291.38
Christianity	265.9
Profanity	
ethics	
religion	291.569 5
Christianity	241.695
see also Ethical problems—religion	
Profession of faith	
Islam	297.34
Professional ethics	
religion	291.564
Christianity	241.64
Islam	297.564
Judaism	296.364
see also Ethical problems—religion	
Progressive National Baptist Convention	286.135
see also Baptists	
Promiscuity	
ethics	
religion	291.566
see also Sexual relations—ethics—religion	
Proofs of God's existence	212.1
Proper of the mass	264.36
Prophecies	
religion	291.32
Biblical	220.15
eschatological	291.23
Christianity	236
Islam	297.23
Judaism	296.33
Koranic	297.122 1

Prophecies
  religion (continued)
    messianic
      Christianity   232.12
      Judaism   296.336
Prophecy (Concept)   291.211 7
  Christianity   231.745
    spiritual gift   234.13
  in Bible   220.15
  Islam   297.211 5
  Judaism   296.311 55
Prophetic books (Old Testament)   224
Prophetic books
  (Pseudepigrapha)   229.913
Prophetic message
  Bible   220.15
Prophetic office of Jesus Christ   232.8
Prophets   200.92
  biography   200.92
  Islam   297.246
  role and function   291.61
  see Manual at 200.92 and
    291–299
Prophets (Biblical books)   224
Proselytizing
  Judaism   296.69
Protestant art
  religious significance   246.4
Protestant churches   280.4
  see also Protestantism
Protestant Methodists   287.53
  see also Methodist Church
Protestantism   280.4
  church law   262.980 4
  conversion to   248.244
  doctrines   230.044
  guides to Christian life   248.480 4
  missions   266
  moral theology   241.040 4
  public worship   264
  religious associations   267.180 4
  religious education   268.804
  seminaries   230.071 1
  theology   230.044
Protestants
  biography   280.409 2
Proverbs (Biblical book)   223.7
Providence of God   214.8
  Christianity   231.5
  comparative religion   291.211 7
  Judaism   296.311 4
  philosophy of religion   214.8

Prudence
  ethics
    religion   291.5
    see also Virtues—religion
Psalms   223.2
Psalters   264.15
  Anglican   264.030 15
    texts   264.038
  Roman Catholic   264.020 15
    texts   264.028
Pseudepigrapha   229.9
Pseudo gospels   229.8
Psychology and religion   291.175
  Christianity   261.515
  Judaism   296.371
Psychology of religion   200.19
Public life of Jesus Christ   232.95
Public relations
  local churches   254.4
Public worship   291.38
  Buddhism   294.343 8
  Christianity   264
  Hinduism   294.538
  Islam   297.38
  Judaism   296.45
  see also Worship
Punishment
  social theology   291.178 336
    Christianity   261.833 6
Puppetry
  Christian religious use   246.725
  religious education   268.67
Puranas   294.592 5
Pure Land Buddhism   294.392 6
Purgatory   291.23
  Christianity   236.5
Purim   296.436
  liturgy   296.453 6
Puritanism   285.9
  doctrines   230.59
  moral theology   241.045 9
  persecution of others   272.8
Puritans
  biography   285.909 2

Q

Q hypothesis (Gospels)   226.066
Qādirīyah (Islamic sect)   297.835
Qādirīyah (Sufi order)   297.48
Qiblah   297.382
Qirā'āt   297.122 404 5
Qohelet   223.8
Qoran   297.122

Quakers	289.6	Rebekah (Biblical matriarch)	222.110 92
biography	289.609 2	Recitation	
see also Society of Friends		Koran	297.122 404 5
Quietism	273.7	Reconciliation (Christian	
persecution of	272.5	doctrine)	234.5
Qumran community	296.815	Reconstructionist Judaism	296.834 4
Dead Sea Scrolls	296.155	liturgy	296.450 48
Quran	297.122	Recovery from addiction	
		devotional literature	291.432
R		Christianity	242.4
		pastoral theology	291.61
Rabbinical literature	296.1	Christianity	259.429
Rabbinical seminaries	296.071 1	religious guidance	291.442
Rabbis	296.092	Christianity	248.862 9
biography	296.092	social theology	291.178 322 9
specific denominations	296.8	Christianity	261.832 29
professional ethics	296.364 1	see Manual at 616.86 vs.	
role and function	296.61	158.1, 248.8629, 291.442,	
training	296.071 1	362.29	
Race relations		Recreation	
social theology	291.178 348	church work	253.7
Christianity	261.834 8	ethics	
Racism		religion	291.565
ethics		Christianity	241.65
religion	291.567 5	Judaism	296.365
Christianity	241.675	Redaction criticism	
Judaism	296.367 5	sacred books	291.82
see also Ethical		Bible	220.66
problems—religion		Talmud	296.120 66
social theology	291.178 348	Redemption	291.22
Christianity	261.834 8	Christian doctrine	234.3
Radha Soami Satsang	294	Christology	232.3
Radio		Islam	297.22
religion	291.175	Judaism	296.32
Christianity	261.52	Redemptorists	255.64
evangelism	269.26	church history	271.64
preaching	251.07	Reform Judaism	296.834 1
use by local church	253.78	liturgy	296.450 46
administration	254.3	Reformation	270.6
Radio evangelism	269.26	Reformed Christians	284.2
Raja yoga		American	285.7
Hinduism	294.543 6	biography	285.709 2
Ramadan	297.362	biography	284.209 2
Ramakrishna movement	294.555	European	284.2
Ramayana	294.592 2	biography	284.209 2
Rapture (Christian doctrine)	236.9	Reformed Church	284.2
Ras Tafari movement	299.676	church government	262.042
Rastafarians		parishes	254.042
biography	299.676 092	church law	262.984 2
Rationalism		doctrines	230.42
Christian polemics	239.7	catechisms and creeds	238.42
philosophy of religion	211.4	guides to Christian life	248.484 2
Reason (Theology)		missions	266.42
Christianity	231.042	moral theology	241.044 2
		public worship	264.042

Reformed Church (continued)	
religious associations	267.184 2
religious education	268.842
seminaries	230.073 42
theology	230.42
Reformed Church (American Reformed)	285.7
church government	262.057
parishes	254.057
church law	262.985 7
doctrines	230.57
catechisms and creeds	238.57
guides to Christian life	248.485 7
missions	266.57
moral theology	241.045 7
public worship	264.057
religious associations	267.185 7
religious education	268.857
seminaries	230.073 57
theology	230.57
Reformed Church in America	285.732
see also Reformed Church (American Reformed)	
Reformed Church in the United States	285.733
see also Reformed Church (American Reformed)	
Reformed Episcopal Church	283.3
see also Anglican Communion	
Reformed Hinduism	294.556
Reformed Presbyterian churches	285.136
see also Presbyterian Church	
Refugees	
social theology	291.178 328
Christianity	261.832 8
Regeneration (Christian doctrine)	234.4
Regular Baptists	286.1
see also Baptists	
Reincarnation	
religion	291.237
Buddhism	294.342 37
Hinduism	294.523 7
Relics	
Christianity	235.2
Relics of Passion of Jesus Christ	232.966
Religion	200
see Manual at 133 vs. 200; *also at* 200 vs. 100	
Religion and culture	291.17
Christianity	261
Islam	297.27
Judaism	296.38

Religion and politics	
social theology	291.177
see also Politics and religion—social theology	
Religion and secular disciplines	291.175
Buddhism	294.337 5
Christianity	261.5
see Manual at 261.5; *also at* 261.5 vs. 231–239	
Hinduism	294.517 5
Islam	297.26
see Manual at 297.26–297.27	
Judaism	296.37
philosophy of religion	215
Religion and state	
social theology	291.177
see also Politics and religion—social theology	
Religion historians	200.92
Religions	291
see Manual at 291	
Religious (Members of Christian orders)	255
biography	271.009 2
see Manual at 230–280	
church history	271
ecclesiology	262.24
guides to Christian life	248.894
Religious arts	
religious significance	291.37
see also Arts—religious significance	
Religious authority	291.65
Christianity	262.8
Judaism	296.67
Religious broadcasting	
Christianity	269.26
Religious buildings	
religious significance	291.35
Christianity	246.9
Judaism	296.46
Religious dance	
religious significance	291.37
Christianity	246.7
see also Arts—religious significance	
Religious dietary limitations	291.446
Hinduism	294.544 6
Islam	297.576
Judaism	296.73

Religious education	291.75
Buddhism	294.375
Christianity	268
see Manual at 268 vs. 230.071	
Hinduism	294.575
Islam	297.77
Judaism	296.68
see Manual at 291.75 vs. 200.71	
Religious experience	291.42
Buddhism	294.344 2
Christianity	248.2
Hinduism	294.542
Islam	297.57
Sufi	297.4
Judaism	296.71
Religious freedom	
social theology	291.177 2
Christianity	261.72
Judaism	296.382
see also Politics and religion—social theology	
Religious holidays	291.36
see also Holy days	
Religious language	210.14
Christianity	230.014
Religious law	291.84
Buddhism	294.384
Christianity	262.9
Hinduism	294.594
Islam	297.14
see Manual at 340.59 vs. 297.14	
Judaism	296.18
see Manual at 296.18 vs. 340.58	
Religious leaders	200.92
biography	200.92
Buddhist	294.309 2
biography	294.309 2
specific sects	294.39
role and function	294.361
Christian	270.092
biography	270.092
specific denominations	280
see Manual at 280	
see Manual at 230–280	
ecclesiology	262.1
occupational ethics	241.641
pastoral theology	253
personal religion	248.892
training	230.071 1

Religious leaders (continued)	
Hindu	294.509 2
biography	294.509 2
specific sects	294.55
role and function	294.561
Islamic	297.092
biography	297.092
specific sects	297.8
role and function	297.61
see Manual at 297.092	
Jewish	296.092
biography	296.092
specific denominations	296.8
professional ethics	296.364 1
role and function	296.61
training	296.071 1
occupational ethics	
religion	291.564 1
role and function	291.61
see Manual at 200.92 and 291–299	
Religious life	291.44
Buddhism	294.344 4
Christianity	248.4
Hinduism	294.544
Islam	297.57
Sufi	297.44
Judaism	296.7
see also Monasticism	
Religious medals	
religious significance	291.37
see also Symbolism—religious significance	
Religious mythology	291.13
see also Mythology—religion	
Religious observances	291.3
Christianity	263
Judaism	296.4
private	291.446
Christianity	248.46
Judaism	296.7
Religious orders	291.657
Buddhism	294.365 7
Christianity	255
church history	271
ecclesiology	262.24
organization	255
Religious organizations	291.65
Christianity	260
associations for religious work	267
denominations	280
local church	250
specific local churches	280

Religious organizations
  Christianity (continued)
    religious orders   255
    see Manual at 260 vs.
      251–254, 259
    congregations   291.65
  Islam   297.65
  Judaism   296.67
  see Manual at 322.1 vs. 261.7,
    291.177
Religious pageants
  religious significance   291.37
    Christianity   246.72
Religious plays
  religious significance   291.37
    Christianity   246.72
      religious education   268.67
Religious pluralism   291.172
  Buddhism   294.337 2
  Christianity   261.2
  Hinduism   294.517 2
  Islam   297.28
  Judaism   296.39
Religious rites   291.38
  see also Rites—religion
Religious services   291.38
  see also Rites—religion
Religious studies   200.71
  see Manual at 291.75 vs.
    200.71
Religious symbolism   291.37
  see also Symbolism—religious
    significance
Religious therapy
  religion   291.31
  see also Spiritual healing—
    religion
  see Manual at 615.852 vs.
    234.131, 291.31
Religious tolerance
  social theology   291.177 2
    Christianity   261.72
    Judaism   296.382
    see also Politics and
      religion—social
      theology
Reliquaries
  Christianity   247
Remarriage
  ethics
    religion   291.563
      Christianity   241.63
  Judaism   296.444

Remarriage (continued)
  social theology   291.178 358 4
    Christianity   261.835 84
Remonstrant churches   284.9
  see also Christian
    denominations
Remonstrants
  biography   284.9
Renaissance art
  religious significance   246.4
Reorganized Church of Jesus
    Christ of Latter Day Saints   289.333
  see also Mormon Church
Repentance   291.22
  Christianity   234.5
  Islam   297.22
  Judaism   296.32
Reproduction
  ethics
    religion   291.566
    Buddhism   294.356 6
    Christianity   241.66
    Hinduism   294.548 66
    Islam   297.566
    Judaism   296.366
Requiem mass   264.36
Reredoses   247.1
Responsa (Jewish law)   296.185
Responsive readings
  public worship   291.38
    Christianity   264.4
    Judaism   296.45
Resurrection   291.23
  Christianity   236.8
  Islam   297.23
  Judaism   296.33
Resurrection of Jesus Christ   232.5
  life   232.97
Retreats (Religion)
  Christianity   269.6
Return to Orthodox Judaism   296.715
Revelation (Biblical book)   228
Revelation of God   212.6
  Bible   220.13
  Christianity   231.74
  comparative religion   291.211 7
  Islam   297.211 5
    Koran   297.122 1
  Judaism   296.311 5
  philosophy of religion   212.6
Revised English Bible   220.520 6
Revised Standard version Bible   220.520 42
Revised versions of Bible   220.520 4
Revival meetings   269.24

Revolution			Rinzai	294.392 7
ethics			Rishonim	296.180 92
religion	291.562 1		Rites	
Christianity	241.621		religion	291.38
Judaism	296.362 1		African religions	299.64
social theology	291.177		Buddhism	294.343 8
Buddhism	294.337 7		Christianity	264
Christianity	261.7		Hinduism	294.538
Hinduism	294.517 7		Islam	297.38
Islam	297.272		Judaism	296.45
Judaism	296.382		Native American religions	299.74
Rheims-Douay Bible	220.520 2		Ritual bath	
Rhythmic arts			Judaism	296.75
religious significance	291.37		Ritual purity	
Christianity	246.7		Islam	297.38
see also Arts—religious			Judaism	
significance			family purity	296.742
Right and wrong			Ritual slaughter (Dietary laws)	291.446
religion	291.5		Islam	297.576
see also Ethics—religion			Judaism	296.73
Right to die			Rituale Romanum	264.025
ethics			Rituals	291.38
religion	291.569 7		Roman Catholic liturgy	264.025
Buddhism	294.356 97		see also Rites—religion	
Christianity	241.697		Rock (Music)	
Hinduism	294.548 697		attitude of Christianity toward	261.578
Islam	297.569 7		Roman Catholic Church	282
Judaism	296.369 7		canon law	262.9
medical ethics			church government	262.02
religion	291.564 24		parishes	254.02
Christianity	241.642 4		conversion to	248.242
Judaism	296.364 24		doctrines	230.2
Right to life			catechisms and creeds	238.2
ethics			general councils	262.52
religion	291.569 7		guides to Christian life	248.482
Christianity	241.697		Inquisition	272.2
Islam	297.569 7		liturgy	264.02
Judaism	296.369 7		missions	266.2
Right to life (Prenatal)			moral theology	241.042
ethics			papacy	262.13
religion	291.569 76		persecution under Queen	
Christianity	241.697 6		Elizabeth	272.7
Judaism	296.369 76		public worship	264.02
social theology	291.178 366 67		religious associations	267.182
Christianity	261.836 667		religious education	268.82
Judaism	296.38		religious orders	255
Right to life movement			church history	271
social theology	291.178 366 67		women	255.9
Christianity	261.836 667		church history	271.9
Judaism	296.38		seminaries	230.073 2
Righteousness (Christian			social teaching	261.808 822
doctrine)	234		theology	230.2
Rigveda	294.592 12		see Manual at 281.1–281.4	

Relative Index

Roman Catholic sacred music	
public worship	
religion	264.020 2
Roman Catholic schisms	284.8
see also Old Catholic churches	
Roman Catholics	282.092
Roman religion	292.07
Romanesque art	
religious significance	246.2
Romans (Biblical book)	227.1
Rood screens	247.1
Rosary	242.74
Rosh Hashanah	296.431 5
liturgy	296.453 15
Rosh Hashanah (Tractate)	296.123 2
Babylonian Talmud	296.125 2
Mishnah	296.123 2
Palestinian Talmud	296.124 2
Royal office of Jesus Christ	232.8
Rural churches	250.917 34
administration	254.24
pastoral theology	253.091 734
Russian Orthodox Church	281.947
see also Eastern Orthodox Church	
Ruth (Biblical book)	222.35

S

Sabbath	296.41
Christianity	263.1
Judaism	296.41
Sabbatianism	296.82
Sabbatical Year (Judaism)	296.439 1
Sabellianism	273.3
Sacramental furniture	247.1
Sacramentals	264.9
Sacramentaries	
Roman Catholic	264.020 36
texts	264.023
Sacraments	234.16
public worship	265
Anglican	264.030 8
texts	264.035
Roman Catholic	264.020 8
texts	264.025
theology	234.16
Sacred books	291.82
Buddhism	294.382
Christianity	220
Latter-Day Saints	289.32
Hinduism	294.592
Islam	297.122
Sacred books (continued)	
Judaism	296.1
Bible	221
see Manual at 221	
see Manual at 133 vs. 200	
Sacred Heart religious orders	255.93
church history	271.93
Sacred music	
public worship	291.38
see also Public worship	
religious significance	291.37
see also Music—religion	
Sacred places	291.35
Buddhist	294.343 5
Christian	263.042
Hindu	294.535
Islamic	297.35
Jain	294.435
Jewish	296.48
public worship	291.38
Sikh	294.635
Sacrifice of Jesus Christ	232.4
Sacrifices (Religion)	291.34
Judaism	296.492
Ṣadaqah	297.54
Sadducees	296.813
Ṣaḥābah	297.648
Saint Joseph religious orders	255.976
church history	271.976
Saints	200.92
biography	200.92
Christian	270.092
biography	270.092
specific denominations	280
see Manual at 230–280	
doctrines	235.2
Islam	297.092
Sufis	297.409 2
objects of worship	291.213
role and function	291.61
see Manual at 200.92 and 291–299	
Saints' days	263.98
devotional literature	242.37
sermons	252.67
Saivism	294.551 3
Ṣalāt	297.382 2
Salvation	291.22
Christianity	234
Islam	297.22
Judaism	296.32
see also Humans—religion	

Salvation Army	287.96	Screens	
see also Christian denominations		church furniture	247.1
Samaritan language		Scribes	
Biblical texts	220.45	Judaism	296.461 509 2
Samaritans (Judaism)	296.817	Scripture readings	
Samaveda	294.592 13	public worship	
Samhitas	294.592 1	Christianity	264.34
Samuel (Biblical books)	222.4	Scriptures (Religion)	291.82
Sanctification (Christian		see also Sacred books	
doctrine)	234.8	Second Coming of Christ	236.9
Sanctifying grace	234.1	Sects (Religion)	291.9
Sanctus	264.36	Buddhism	294.39
Sanhedrin	296.67	sources	294.385
Sanhedrin (Tractate)	296.123 4	Christianity	280
Babylonian Talmud	296.125 4	see also Christian	
Mishnah	296.123 4	denominations	
Palestinian Talmud	296.124 4	Hinduism	294.55
Sanskrit language		sources	294.595
Vedas	294.592 104 1	Islam	297.8
Santeria	299.674	Jainism	294.49
Santos		Judaism	296.8
religious significance	246.53	sources	296.15
Sarah (Biblical matriarch)	222.110 92	sources	291.85
Saravastivada Buddhism	294.391	see Manual at 291:	
Satan		Denominations and sects	
Christianity	235.47	Secular humanism	211.6
Islam	297.216	Christian polemics	239.7
Judaism	296.316	Secular institutes	
Satanism		Christianity	255.095
religion	299	church history	271.095
Satisfaction (Christian rite)	265.63	women	255.909 5
Saul, King of Israel		church history	271.909 5
Biblical leader	222.430 92	Secularism	211.6
Sauraism	294.551 7	Seder service	296.453 71
Sautrantika Buddhism	294.391	Sees	
Ṣawm	297.53	Christian ecclesiology	262.3
Ṣawm Ramaḍān	297.362	Self-control	
Scandinavian religion	293	moral theology	291.5
Schism between Eastern and		Christianity	241.4
Western Church	270.38	Judaism	296.369 9
Schisms		Seminaries	200.711
Christianity	262.8	Christianity	230.071 1
church history	273	Judaism	296.071 1
Science and religion	291.175	Semites	
Buddhism	294.337 5	religion	299.2
Christianity	261.55	Semitic languages	
Hinduism	294.517 5	Biblical texts	220.4
Islam	297.265	Semitic peoples	
Judaism	296.375	religion	299.2
philosophy of religion	215	Separation (Domestic relations)	
Scientists		ethics	
Islamic polemics	297.298	religion	291.563
Scientology	299.936	Christianity	241.63
		Judaism	296.363

Separation (Domestic relations) (continued)		Sexually abused children	
Judaism	296.444 4	social theology	291.178 327 2
social theology	291.178 358 9	Christianity	261.832 72
Christianity	261.835 89	Shabbat	296.41
Sephardic liturgy	296.450 42	Shabbat (Tractate)	296.123 2
Septuagint	221.48	Babylonian Talmud	296.125 2
Sequence	264.36	Mishnah	296.123 2
Sermon on the Mount	226.9	Palestinian Talmud	296.124 2
Christian moral theology	241.53	Shabuoth	296.438
Sermon outlines	251.02	liturgy	296.453 8
Sermon preparation	251.01	Shafiites (Islamic sect)	297.812
see also Preaching		Shahāda	297.34
Sermons	291.43	Shahādah	297.34
Christianity	252	Shaiṭān	297.216
Islam	297.37	Shaivism	294.551 3
Jewish	296.47	Shakers	289.8
Servites	255.47	biography	289.809 2
church history	271.47	see also Christian denominations	
Seven last words on cross	232.963 5	Shaktaism	294.551 4
Seveners (Islamic sect)	297.822	Shamanism	291.144
Seventh-Day Adventist Church	286.732	Shamans	200.92
see also Adventists		biography	200.92
Seventh-Day Baptists	286.3	role and function	291.61
see also Baptists		see Manual at 200.92 and 291–299	
Sex			
religious worship	291.212	Shanmukaism	294.551 6
theological anthropology	291.22	Sharia	
Christianity	233.5	religious law	297.14
Islam	297.22	see Manual at 340.59 vs. 297.14	
Judaism	296.32		
see also Humans—religion		Shavuot	296.438
Sexes		liturgy	296.453 8
social theology	291.178 343	Shehitah	296.73
Christianity	261.834 3	Shekalim	296.123 2
Sext	264.15	Mishnah	296.123 2
see also Liturgy of the hours		Palestinian Talmud	296.124 2
Sexual ethics		Shemittah	296.439 1
religion	291.566	Shevi'it	296.123 1
see also Sexual relations— ethics—religion		Mishnah	296.123 1
		Palestinian Talmud	296.124 1
Sexual relations		Shevu'ot	296.123 4
ethics		Babylonian Talmud	296.125 4
religion	291.566	Mishnah	296.123 4
Buddhism	294.356 6	Palestinian Talmud	296.124 4
Christianity	241.66	Shia Islam	297.82
Hinduism	294.548 66	doctrines	297.204 2
Islam	297.566	Hadith	297.124 8
Judaism	296.366	relations with Sunni Islam	297.804 2
laws of family purity	296.742	worship	297.302
social theology	291.178 357	Shin (Sect)	294.392 6
Christianity	261.835 7	Shintoism	299.561
		Shintoists	
		biography	299.561 092

Shivaism	294.551 3
Shrines	291.35
Buddhist	294.343 5
Christianity	263.042
Hindu	294.535
Islamic	297.35
Jain	294.435
Shinto	299.561 35
Sikh	294.635
Shroud of Turin	232.966
Shulḥan 'arukh	296.182
Sibyls	
religion	291.61
Sick persons	
devotional literature	291.432
Christianity	242.4
guides to religious life	291.440 877
Christianity	248.861
Judaism	296.708 77
pastoral care	291.61
Christianity	259.41
Judaism	296.610 877
religious rites	291.38
Christianity	265.82
social theology	291.178 321
Christianity	261.832 1
Siddurim	296.45
Sikhism	294.6
Islamic polemics	297.294
Sikhism and Islam	294.617 2
Islamic view	297.284 6
Sikh view	294.617 2
Sikhs	
biography	294.609 2
Simḥat Torah	296.433 9
liturgy	296.453 39
Sin	291.22
Buddhism	294.342 2
Christianity	241.3
original sin	233.14
Hinduism	294.522
Islam	297.22
Judaism	296.32
moral theology	291.5
Buddhism	294.35
Christianity	241.3
see Manual at 241.3–241.4 vs. 241.6	
Hinduism	294.548
Islam	297.5
Judaism	296.36
Single-parent family	
social theology	291.178 358 56
Christianity	261.835 856
Sirach (Bible)	229.4
Sisters (Women religious)	255.9
biography	271.900 2
see Manual at 230–280	
ecclesiology	262.24
guides to Christian life	248.894 3
Sisters of Bon Secours	255.94
church history	271.94
Sisters of Charity	255.91
church history	271.91
Sisters of Mercy	255.92
church history	271.92
Skepticism	
philosophy of religion	211.7
Sky	
religious worship	291.212
Sloth	
religion	291.5
see also Vices—religion	
Small groups	
pastoral work	253.7
Social classes	
social theology	291.178 345
Christianity	261.834 5
Social equality	
social theology	291.178 34
Christianity	261.834
Judaism	296.38
Social problems	
social theology	291.178 3
Buddhism	294.337 83
Christianity	261.83
see Manual at 241 vs. 261.8	
Hinduism	294.517 83
Islam	297.27
see Manual at 297.26–297.27	
Judaism	296.38
Social teaching of the Church	261
Social theology	291.17
Buddhism	294.337
Christianity	261
see Manual at 241 vs. 261.8	
Hinduism	294.517
Islam	297.27
see Manual at 297.26–297.27	
Judaism	296.38

Society of Friends	289.6
church government	262.096
parishes	254.096
church law	262.989 6
doctrines	230.96
catechisms and creeds	238.96
general councils	262.596
guides to Christian life	248.489 6
missions	266.96
moral theology	241.049 6
persecution of	272.8
public worship	264.096
religious associations	267.189 6
religious education	268.896
seminaries	230.073 96
theology	230.96
Society of Jesus	255.53
church history	271.53
Socinianism	289.1
Socioeconomic problems	
social theology	291.178
Buddhism	294.337 8
Christianity	261.8
see Manual at 241 vs. 261.8	
Hinduism	294.517 8
Islam	297.27
see Manual at 297.26–297.27	
Judaism	296.38
Sociology and religion	291.175
Christianity	261.5
Islam	297.27
Judaism	296.38
Sodalities	267
Soferim	296.461 509 2
Soferim (Talmudic)	296.120 092
Sōka Gakkai	294.392 8
Solomon, King of Israel	
Biblical leader	222.530 92
Somaschi	255.54
church history	271.54
Son of God (Christian doctrines)	231.2
Song of Solomon	223.9
Song of Songs	223.9
Song of the Three Children (Bible)	229.6
Sophonias (Biblical book)	224.96
Sorcerers (Religious leaders)	200.92
biography	200.92
role and function	291.61
see Manual at 200.92 and 291–299	
Sotah	296.123 3
Babylonian Talmud	296.125 3
Mishnah	296.123 3
Palestinian Talmud	296.124 3
Soteriology	291.22
Christianity	234
Islam	297.22
Judaism	296.32
see also Humans—religion	
Soto	294.392 7
Soul	
religion	291.22
Christianity	233.5
Islam	297.225
Judaism	296.32
philosophy of religion	218
see also Humans—religion	
Southern Baptist Convention	286.132
see also Baptists	
Sovereignty of God	212.7
Christianity	231.7
comparative religion	291.211 2
Islam	297.211 2
Judaism	296.311 2
philosophy of religion	212.7
Speaking in tongues	234.132
Spiritual beings	291.21
Christianity	235
Spiritual direction	291.61
Christianity	253.53
Spiritual exercises	291.43
Christianity	248.3
Spiritual gifts	
Christian doctrines	234.13
Spiritual healing	
religion	291.31
African religions	299.64
Christianity	234.131
miracles	231.73
miracles	291.211 7
Native American religions	299.74
see Manual at 615.852 vs. 234.131, 291.31	
Spiritual life	291.44
Buddhism	294.344 4
Christianity	248.4
Hinduism	294.544
Islam	297.57
Judaism	296.7
Spiritual renewal	291.3
Christianity	269
Islam	297.3
Spiritualism	
comparative religion	291.21

Spirituality	291.4
Buddhism	294.344
Christianity	248
Hinduism	294.54
Islam	297.57
Judaism	296.7
Sports	
ethics	
religion	291.565
see also Ethical problems—religion	
St. Thomas Christians	281.5
see also Eastern churches	
Stations of the Cross	232.96
Roman Catholic liturgy	264.027 4
Stewardship (Christian practice)	248.6
Stigmata	248.29
Substance abuse	
devotional literature	291.432
Christianity	242.4
pastoral theology	291.61
Christianity	259.429
religious guidance	291.442
Christianity	248.862 9
social theology	291.178 322 9
Christianity	261.832 29
see Manual at 616.86 vs. 158.1, 248.8629, 291.442, 362.29: Recovery from addiction	
Subud	299.933
Suburban churches	250.917 33
administration	254.23
pastoral theology	253.091 733
Suburban ministry	253.091 733
administration	254.23
Suffering	
consolatory devotions	291.432
Christinity	242.4
Judaism	296.72
religious guidance	291.442
Christianity	248.86
Judaism	296.7
theodicy	291.211 8
Christianity	231.8
comparative religion	291.211 8
Judaism	296.311 8
philosophy of religion	214
see also Theodicy	
theological anthropology	291.22
Christianity	233
comparative religion	291.22
Judaism	296.32
philosophy of religion	218
see also Humans—religion	
Suffrages (Liturgy)	264.13
Sufi orders	297.48
Sufis	297.409 2
Sufism	297.4
see Manual at 297.4	
Suicide	
ethics	
religion	291.569 7
Buddhism	294.356 97
Christianity	241.697
Hinduism	294.548 697
Islam	297.569 7
Judaism	296.369 7
pastoral care	291.61
Christianity	259.428
social theology	291.178 322 8
Christianity	261.832 28
Sukkah	296.123 2
Babylonian Talmud	296.125 2
Mishnah	296.123 2
Palestinian Talmud	296.124 2
Sukkot	296.433
liturgy	296.453 3
Sulpicians	255.75
church history	271.75
Sun	
religious worship	291.212
Sunday	
Christian observance	263.3
Sunday school	268
Jewish	296.680 83
Sunday school buildings	
administration	268.2
Sunni Islam	297.81
doctrines	297.204 1
relations with Shia Islam	297.804 2
worship	297.301
Supernatural beings	
religious	291.211
see also Gods and goddesses	
Suras (Koran)	297.122 9
Surrogate motherhood	
ethics	
religion	291.566
Christianity	241.66
Judaism	296.366
Susanna (Deuterocanonical book)	229.6
Sūtrapiṭaka	294.382 3
Suttapiṭaka	294.382 3
Suttee	
Hindu practice	294.538
Svetambara (Jainism)	294.492

Swearing	
ethics	
religion	291.569 5
Christianity	241.695
Swedenborgianism	289.4
see also Christian	
denominations	
Swedenborgians	
biography	289.409 2
Symbolism	
religious significance	291.37
Buddhism	294.343 7
Christianity	246.55
Hinduism	294.537
Islam	297.3
Judaism	296.46
Symbolism in the Bible	220.64
Symbolism in the Talmud	296.120 64
Synagogue dedication	296.446
liturgy	296.454 6
Synagogues	296.65
history of specific	
congregations	296.09
organization	296.65
religious symbolism of	
buildings	296.46
Synod of Bishops	262.136
Synod of Evangelical Lutheran	
Churches	284.132 3
see also Lutheran church	
Synods	
Christian ecclesiology	262.4
Synoptic Gospels	226
Synoptic problem (Gospels)	226.066
Syriac language	
Biblical texts	220.43
Syrian Orthodox Church	281.63
see also Eastern churches	
Syrians (Religious order)	255.18
church history	271.18
Syro-Malabar Christians	281.5
see also Eastern churches	

T

Ta'anit (Tractate)	296.123 2
Babylonian Talmud	296.125 2
Mishnah	296.123 2
Palestinian Talmud	296.124 2
Tabernacles	
Christian church furniture	247.1
Judaism	296.49

Tajwīd	297.122 404 5
Talismans	
Islamic popular practices	297.39
religious significance	291.37
see also Symbolism—	
religious significance	
Tallit	296.461
Talmud	296.12
Talmud Bavli	296.125
Talmud Yerushalmi	296.124
Talmudic literature	296.12
Tamid	296.123 5
Mishnah	296.123 5
Palestinian Talmud	296.124 5
Tanakh	221
see Manual at 221	
Tannaim	296.120 092
Tantras	
Buddhist	294.385
Hindu	294.595
Tantric Buddhism	294.392 5
Tantric Hinduism	294.551 4
Taoism	
religion	299.514
Taoists	
religion	299.514 092
Targums	221.42
Tawhid	297.211 3
Teachers	
religious educators	291.750 92
Christian	268.092
biography	268.092
see Manual at 230–280	
role and function	268.3
Jewish	296.680 92
biography	296.680 92
role and function	296.68
Teaching (Spiritual gift)	234.13
Teaching methods	
religious education	291.75
Christianity	268.6
Teaching office of the church	262.8
Teaching orders (Christianity)	255.03
church history	271.03
women	255.903
church history	271.903
Teachings of Jesus Christ	232.954
Technology and religion	291.175
Christianity	261.56
Islam	297.266
Judaism	296.376
philosophy of religion	215

Teenagers	
religion	200.835
see also Adolescents—	
religion	
Tefillin	296.461 2
Teleology	
philosophy of religion	210
Television	
ethics	
religion	291.565
Christianity	241.65
religion	291.175
Christianity	261.52
evangelism	269.26
preaching	251.07
use by local church	253.78
administration	254.3
Television evangelism	269.26
Temperance	
moral theology	291.568
Buddhism	294.356 8
Christianity	241.4
Hinduism	294.548 68
Islam	297.568
Judaism	296.368
Templars	255.791 3
church history	271.791 3
Temples	291.35
Buddhist	294.343 5
Hindu	294.535
Jain	294.435
Jewish temple in Jerusalem	296.491
Mormon	246.958 93
Shinto	299.561 35
Sikh	294.635
see also Synagogues	
Temporal power of pope	262.132
Temptation	
moral theology	291.5
Christianity	241.3
Temptation of Jesus Christ	232.95
Temurah	296.123 5
Babylonian Talmud	296.125 5
Mishnah	296.123 5
Ten Commandments	222.16
moral theology	
Christianity	241.52
Judaism	296.36
Tenth of Muḥarram	297.36
Terce	264.15
see also Liturgy of the hours	
Terminal care	
pastoral theology	291.61
Christianity	259.417 5
social theology	291.178 321 75
Christianity	261.832 175
Terumot	296.123 1
Mishnah	296.123 1
Palestinian Talmud	296.124 1
Test-tube babies	
ethics	
religion	291.566
Christianity	241.66
Judaism	296.366
Testaments	
pseudepigrapha	229.914
Teutonic Knights	255.791 4
church history	271.791 4
Tevul Yom	296.123 6
Textual criticism	
sacred books	291.82
Bible	220.404 6
Koran	297.122 4
Talmud	296.120 4
Theater	
religious significance	291.37
Christianity	246.72
religious education	268.67
see also Arts—religious	
significance	
Theatines	255.51
church history	271.51
Theism	211.3
Christianity	231
comparative religion	291.211
Islam	297.211
Judaism	296.311
philosophy of religion	211.3
Theistic religions	291.14
Theocracy	
religion	291.177 3
Christianity	261.73
Theodicy	291.211 8
Buddhism	294.342 118
Christianity	231.8
comparative religion	291.211 8
Hinduism	294.521 18
Islam	297.211 8
Judaism	296.311 8
philosophy of religion	214
Theologians	291.209 2
Christian	230.092
see Manual at 230–280; *also*	
at 230.04 vs. 230.092,	
230.1–230.9	

Relative Index

Theological anthropology	291.22
Christianity	233
philosophy of religion	218
see also Humans—religion	
Theological seminaries	
Christianity	230.071 1
Theology	291.2
Buddhism	294.342
Christianity	230
Hinduism	294.52
Islam	297.2
Sufi	297.41
Judaism	296.3
Theophanies	
Christianity	231.74
Theosophists	
biography	299.934 092
Theosophy	299.934
Theravada Buddhism	294.391
Thessalonians (Biblical books)	227.81
Third Order Regular of St. Francis	255.38
church history	271.38
women	255.973
church history	271.973
Third orders	
religious orders	255.094
church history	271.094
women	255.909 4
church history	271.909 4
Thirteen Articles of Faith (Judaism)	296.3
Three wise men (Christian doctrines)	232.923
Tibetan Buddhism	294.392 3
Tijānīyah	297.48
Times	
religious observance	291.36
Christianity	263
Islam	297.36
Judaism	296.43
Timothy (Biblical books)	227.83
Tipiṭaka	294.382
Tirmidhī, Muḥammad ibn 'Īsá	
Hadith	297.124 4
Tishah b'Av	296.439
liturgy	296.453 9
Tithes	
Christian practice	248.6
local church fund raising	254.8
Titus (Biblical book)	227.85
Tobacco	
ethics	
religion	291.568 7
see also Ethical problems—religion	
Tobias (Deuterocanonical book)	229.22
Tobit (Deuterocanonical book)	229.22
Today's English Bible	220.520 82
Tohorot (Order or tractate)	296.123 6
Babylonian Talmud	296.125 6
Mishnah	296.123 6
Palestinian Talmud	296.124 6
Toleration	
moral theology	291.5
Christianity	241.4
Judaism	296.369 9
social theology	291.177 2
Christianity	261.72
Judaism	296.382
see also Politics and religion—social theology	
Torah (Bible)	222.1
Torah scrolls	296.461 5
Tosefta	296.126 2
Totem poles	
religious significance	299.74
Totemism	291.211
Tradition (Theology)	
Christianity	231.042
Transcendence of God	212.7
Christianity	231.4
comparative religion	291.211 2
Islam	297.211 2
Judaism	296.311 2
philosophy of religion	212.7
Transfiguration of Jesus Christ	232.956
Trappists	255.125
church history	271.125
Trees	
religious worship	291.212
Trial of Jesus Christ	232.962
Tribulation (Christian doctrine)	236.9
Tribunals	
papal administration	262.136
Trinitarians (Religious order)	255.42
church history	271.42
Trinity	231.044
Trinity Sunday	263.94
devotional literature	242.38
sermons	252.64
Tripiṭaka	294.382

Twelve patriarchs pseudepigrapha	229.914
Twelve prophets (Bible)	224.9
Twelve step programs devotional literature	291.432
Christianity	242.4
pastoral theology	291.61
Christianity	259.429
religious guidance	291.442
Christianity	248.862 9
social theology	291.178 322 9
Christianity	261.832 29
see Manual at 616.86 vs. 158.1, 248.8629, 291.442, 362.29	
Twelvers (Islamic sect)	297.821
Tyndale Bible	220.520 1
Typology	
Biblical interpretation	220.64
Christian doctrines	232.1
Talmudic interpretation	296.120 64

U

Ukẓin	296.123 6
Ulama	
role and function	297.61
Ulema	
role and function	297.61
Umbanda	299.672
Unification Church	289.96
see also Christian denominations	
Unitarian and Universalist churches	289.1
church government	262.091
parishes	254.091
doctrines	230.91
guides to Christian life	248.489 1
missions	266.91
moral theology	241.049 1
public worship	264.091
religious associations	267.189 1
religious education	268.891
seminaries	230.073 91
theology	230.91
Unitarian churches	289.133
see also Unitarian and Universalist churches	
Unitarian Universalist Association	289.132
see also Unitarian and Universalist churches	
Unitarianism	289.1
Unitarians	
biography	289.109 2
United Brethren in Christ	289.9
see also Christian denominations	
United Church of Canada	287.92
see also Christian denominations	
United Church of Christ	285.834
see also Congregationalism	
United Church of Religious Science	299.93
United Conference of Methodist Churches	287.532
see also Methodist Church	
United Evangelical Lutheran Church	284.131 3
see also Lutheran church	
United Lutheran Church in America	284.133 5
see also Lutheran church	
United Methodist Church (Great Britain)	287.53
see also Methodist Church	
United Methodist Church (U.S.)	287.6
see also Methodist Church	
United Methodist Free Churches	287.53
see also Methodist Church	
United Pentecostal Church	289.94
see also Christian denominations	
United Presbyterian Church in the U.S.A.	285.131
see also Presbyterian Church	
United Presbyterian Church of North America	285.134
see also Presbyterian Church	
United Reformed Church in the United Kingdom	285.232
see also Presbyterian Church	
United Society of Believers in Christ's Second Appearing	289.8
see also Christian denominations	
Uniting Church in Australia	287.93
see also Christian denominations	
Unity	
Christian church	262.72
Unity of God	
Islam	297.211 3
Unity School of Christianity	289.97
see also Christian denominations	

Universal priesthood	234
Universalist churches	289.134
see also Unitarian and Universalist churches	
Universalists	
biography	289.109 2
Untouchables	
social theology	291.178 345 68
Hinduism	294.517 834 568
Unwed parenthood	
ethics	
religion	291.563
Christianity	241.63
social theology	291.178 358 56
Christianity	261.835 856
Upanishads	294.592 18
Urantia	299
Urban ministry	253.091 732
church administration	254.22
Ursulines	255.974
church history	271.974

V

Vaishnavism	294.551 2
Vaisnavism	294.551 2
Vedas	294.592 1
Vedic religion	294.509 013
Vegetarianism	
ethics	
religion	291.569 3
Buddhism	294.356 93
Christianity	241.693
Hinduism	294.548 693
Judaism	296.369 3
Venial sin	241.31
Vespers	264.15
Anglican	264.030 15
texts	264.034
see also Liturgy of the hours	
Viaticum	265.7
Vices	
religion	291.5
Buddhism	294.35
Christianity	241.3
see Manual at 241.3–241.4 vs. 241.6	
Hinduism	294.548
Islam	297.5
Judaism	296.369 8
Vijnana Buddhism	294.392
Vinayapiṭaka	294.382 2
Vincentians	255.77
church history	271.77
Violence	
ethics	
religion	291.569 7
Buddhism	294.356 97
Christianity	241.697
Hinduism	294.548 697
Islam	297.569 7
Judaism	296.369 7
Virgin birth of Jesus Christ	232.921
Virginity of Mary	232.913
Virtues	
religion	291.5
Buddhism	294.35
Christianity	241.4
see Manual at 241.3–241.4 vs. 241.6	
Hinduism	294.548
Islam	297.5
Judaism	296.369 9
Vishnuism	294.551 2
Visions	
religious experience	291.42
Christianity	248.29
Visitation Sisters	255.975
church history	271.975
Vocation (Ecclesiastical)	253.2
ecclesiology	262.1
guides to life	248.892
monastic and religious orders	255
men	255
guides to life	248.894 22
women	255.9
guides to life	248.894 32
Voice	
preaching	251.03
Voodooism	299.675
Votive offerings	291.37
Christianity	246.55
see also Symbolism—religious significance	
Vulgate Bible	220.47

W

Wahhabis (Islamic sect)	297.814
Wahhābīyah (Islamic sect)	297.814
Wakes	
Christian rites	265.85
Waldenses	
biography	284.4

Waldensian churches	284.4	Wisdom literature (Bible)	223
see also Christian denominations		Apocrypha	229.3
		Old Testament	223
Waldensianism	273.6	pseudepigrapha	229.912
denomination	284.4	Wisdom of God	212.7
see also Christian denominations		Christianity	231.6
		comparative religion	291.211 2
persecution of	272.3	Islam	297.211 2
War		Judaism	296.311 2
ethics		philosophy of religion	212.7
religion	291.562 42	Wisdom of Solomon (Bible)	229.3
Buddhism	294.356 242	Wise men (Christian doctrines)	232.923
Christianity	241.624 2	Witchcraft	
Hinduism	294.548 624 2	religious practice	291.33
Islam	297.562 42	African religions	299.64
Judaism	296.362 42	modern revivals	299
social theology	291.178 73	Native American religions	299.74
Buddhism	294.337 873	Witches (Occultists)	
Christianity	261.873	persecution by Church	272.8
Hinduism	294.517 873	Witches (Religious leaders)	200.92
Islam	297.27	biography	200.92
Judaism	296.382 7	modern revivals of old religions	299
Water			
religious worship	291.212	role and function	291.61
Way of the Cross	232.96	*see Manual at* 200.92 and 291–299	
Roman Catholic liturgy	264.027 4		
Wealth		Witness bearing	248.5
ethics		Wives	
religion	291.568	Christian devotional literature	242.643 5
Buddhism	294.356 8	guides to Christian life	248.843 5
Christianity	241.68	Wives of clergymen	
Hinduism	294.548 68	biography	270.092
Islam	297.568	specific denominations	280
Judaism	296.368	*see Manual at* 280	
Welsh Calvinistic Methodist Church	285.235	*see Manual at* 230–280	
		pastoral theology	253.22
see also Presbyterian Church		Wizardry	
Wesleyan Conference	287.53	religious practice	291.33
see also Methodist Church		Wizards (Religious leaders)	200.92
Wesleyan Methodist Church	287.1	biography	200.92
see also Methodist Church		role and function	291.61
Wesleyan Reform Union	287.534	*see Manual at* 200.92 and 291–299	
see also Methodist Church			
Wesleyan Reformers	287.53	Women	
see also Methodist Church		religion	200.82
Whitsunday	263.94	Christianity	270.082
devotional literature	242.38	devotional literature	242.643
sermons	252.64	guides to Christian life	248.843
Wisconsin Evangelical Lutheran Synod	284.134	social theology	261.834 4
		guides to life	291.440 82
see also Lutheran church		Islam	297.082
		guides to life	297.570 82

Women	
religion (continued)	
Judaism	296.082
guides to life	296.708 2
social theology	291.178 344
Women and religion	200.82
see also Women—religion	
Women clergy	200.92
biography	200.92
Christian	270.092
biography	270.092
specific denominations	280
see Manual at 230–280	
ecclesiology	262.1
ordination	262.14
pastoral theology	253.082
see also Clergy—Christian	
Judaism	296.092
see also Women rabbis	
ordination	291.610 82
role and function	291.610 82
see Manual at 200.92 and 291–299	
Women in the Bible	220.830 54
Women of the Bible	220.920 82
Women rabbis	296.092
biography	296.092
specific denominations	296.8
ordination	296.610 82
role and function	296.610 82
Word of God	
Bible	220.13
Jesus Christ	232.2
World Community of al-Islam in the West	297.87
World politics and religion	
social theology	291.177
Christianity	261.7
see also Politics and religion—social theology	
Worship	291.43
Buddhism	294.344 3
Christianity	248.3
Hinduism	294.543
Islam	297.3
Sufi	297.43
Judaism	296.45
see also Public worship	
Writings (Bible)	223
Wycliffe Bible	220.520 1
Wycliffites	284.3

Y

Yad ha-ḥazaḳah	296.181 2
Yadayim	296.123 6
Yajurveda	294.592 14
Yearly Conference of People Called Methodists	287.53
see also Methodist Church	
Yeshivot	296.071 1
Yevamot	296.123 3
Babylonian Talmud	296.125 3
Mishnah	296.123 3
Palestinian Talmud	296.124 3
Yezidis	
religion	299.159
YMCA (Association)	267.3
Yoga	
Buddhism	294.344 36
comparative religion	291.436
Hinduism	294.543 6
see Manual at 291: Common terms	
Yogacara Buddhism	294.392
Yom Kippur	296.432
liturgy	296.453 2
Yoma	296.123 2
Babylonian Talmud	296.125 2
Mishnah	296.123 2
Palestinian Talmud	296.124 2
Young adults	
religion	200.842
Christianity	270.084 2
devotional literature	242.64
guides to Christian life	248.84
pastoral care of	259.25
religious associations	267.6
religious education	268.434
social theology	261.834 242
social theology	291.178 342 42
Young Men's Christian Associations	267.3
Young people	
religion	200.83
Christianity	270.083
devotional literature	242.62
guides to Christian life	248.82
pastoral care of	259.2
religious education	268.432
social theology	261.834 23
guides to life	291.440 83
Judaism	296.083
guides to life	296.708 3
religious education	296.680 83
social theology	291.178 342 3

Young Women's Christian Associations	267.5
YWCA (Association)	267.5

Z

Zakat	297.54
Zavim	296.123 6
Zaydites (Islamic sect)	297.824
Zealots (Judaism)	296.81
Zechariah (Biblical book)	224.98
Zen Buddhism	294.392 7
Zephaniah (Biblical book)	224.96
Zera'im	296.123 1
Babylonian Talmud	296.125 1
Mishnah	296.123 1
Palestinian Talmud	296.124 1
Zevaḥim	296.123 5
Babylonian Talmud	296.125 5
Mishnah	296.123 5
Zohar	296.162
Zombiism	
African religions	299.64
Zoroastrianism	295
Zoroastrians	
biography	295.092

The 200 Religion Class, reprinted from the 21st edition of the Dewey Decimal Classification, was designed by Lisa Hanifan of Albany, New York. The book was composed in Times Roman and Helvetica by Inforonics, Inc. of Littleton, Massachusetts, and by Word Management Corporation of Albany, New York. The book was printed and bound by Hamilton Printing Company of Rensselaer, New York.